CONSTRUCTION, LAW AND THE ENVIRONMENT

Edited by

John Uff
Nash Professor of Engineering Law
King's College, London

Helen Garthwaite
Solicitor
Nabarro Nathanson

John Barber
Michael Brown Lecturer
King's College, London

Centre of Construction Law and Management
King's College London

WILEY
CHANCERY

A division of John Wiley & Sons Ltd
London, New York, Chichester, Brisbane, Toronto, Singapore

Published in the United Kingdom by
Chancery Law Publishing Ltd
Baffins Lane
Chichester PO19 1UD

Published in North America by
John Wiley & Sons Inc
7222 Commerce Center Drive
Colorado Springs CO 80919
USA

Typeset by
Dorwyn Ltd, Rowlands Castle, Hants

Printed in Great Britain by
Bookcraft (Bath) Ltd

ISBN 0471 95273 7

A copy of the CIP entry for this book is
available from the British Library

King's College, University of London
The Old Watch House, Strand
London WC2R 2LS

Tel 071 873 2446
Fax 071 872 0210

CONSTRUCTION, LAW AND THE ENVIRONMENT
Technical and Legal Issues

Proceedings of the Sixth Annual Construction Conference of the Centre of Construction Law and Management Sponsored by Nabarro Nathanson

Chaired by: David Bramson, Partner, Nabarro Nathanson

Organised by: Professor John Uff (Director), Pauline Gale (Manager), Helen Brownstone (Assistant) — Centre of Construction Law and Management

Michael Mendelblat, Partner, Helen Garthwaite — Nabarro Nathanson

Contents

Part 3
Liabilities, Remedies and Policy

Preface

For its Sixth Annual Conference, the Centre of Construction Law and Management took on the ambitious subject of the environment and its growing influence in the field of construction law. The subject is perhaps ideally suited to the multi-disciplinary approach of the Centre, spanning the full range of legal and technical areas which the Centre espouses. It is noteworthy that the speakers with a technical background were just as much at home with their subjects as were the legal contributors, and those with dual qualifications. This latter category included the Lord Mayor of London who opened the proceedings with some pertinent observations on the particular problems of the capital.

This Preface does not seek to summarise or encapsulate the many themes and strands of the papers delivered at the conference which are published in full in this volume and, in some cases, updated and augmented following the conference. There were, however, a number of recurrent issues which may serve as pointers to the subject and perhaps its future development. Notable among these was the evolution of environmental protection measures, where new statutes and regulations seemed to appear in a piecemeal fashion, from a variety of sources not obviously co-ordinated. While the detailed provisions could often be obscure an even greater problem was to discover what provisions were currently in force, and the possible dates for bringing into effect pending laws. Some of these matters have been the subject of wide press coverage, such as the Contaminated Land Register. But others have not and the problem of ascertaining and predicting what the law would be at a future date could be a worrying matter. This type of problem was by no means confined to the UK.

The conference was fortunate in being able to cover the European Community environment programme, including a number of future and pending proposals; and also the environmental framework in the two other major economies of the world, USA and Japan. These three groupings indeed form an interesting contrast with much in common but also with major differences. The attitude to freedom of information and public participation in the environment debate differed sharply between Japan and the West. It is also of some interest to trace the course of environment programmes abroad which have brought into force measures still at the stage of debate in Europe, such as the US Superfund.

In response to the challenges of the environment, major new technologies have evolved, particularly in the leading industrial countries. These must be the first line of environment protection, rather than the laws and regulations which, ultimately, can provide only legal sanctions. The problem of pollution and hazardous waste in its many forms is a very real one. Few of the delegates will forget the truly horrifying account of pollution in Eastern Europe, said to have the effect in one instance of significantly lowering the average life expectancy; and in another example to have caused major debilitating illness among children resulting in serious loss of education. One speaker suggested that implementation of proper environment controls in Eastern Europe would result in a major collapse of industry with mass unemployment, which could lead to migration on a scale hitherto unknown. These are frightening prospects which remind us that pollution is indeed a global problem which cannot be confined to those able to afford a clean environment.

In the West, the major environment problems might be seen as a combination of dealing with historical pollution while attempting to regulate current industrial practices on an optimal basis, as exemplified by the acronym BATNEEC (Best available techniques not entailing excessive cost). An even shorter expression of the problem is the question "Jobs or Environment?": how far can we afford to protect the environment? Without doubt a large part of the technical solution lies in new and developing environmental technologies, which ought at the same time to offer considerable potential for economic growth here and abroad.

How then are the principles of environment protection through the application of law to be developed? Clearly major policy issues arise. It is thought that in its application environment policy should be flexible rather than rigid and so capable of reacting to current thought and opinion. The common law would indeed be an ideal vehicle for this, were guiding principles to exist. In their absence, we must live by regulation. Perhaps in the long term, the solution lies in an environmental court capable of enforcing broad principles, but in real cases, rather than in secondary legislators drawing up abstract regulations to be applied irrespective of the circumstances. Beyond any doubt, this conference showed, through the quality of the contributions and the large audience, that environmental issues are very much alive and a key aspect of the construction and development process.

This conference was devised and organised jointly by the Centre of Construction Law and Management at King's College, London and Nabarro Nathanson, Solicitors, who also sponsored the conference. This joint approach reflects the policy of the Centre in seeking to reflect the current interests and concerns of the construction industry and the professions which serve it, and the policy of Nabarro Nathanson of giving support to academic ventures of relevance to industry and commerce. From Nabarro Nathanson's involvement in the construction and development process, we know of the ever increasing role which environmental issues play. We are sure that this conference has been of considerable importance in stimulating debate on such issues, and we commend to you the conference papers which follow.

David Bramson

List of Contributors

Conference Chairman: David Bramson, Partner, Nabarro Nathanson

Keynote Speaker: The Rt Hon The Lord Mayor of London, Sir Francis McWilliams

Participants

Peter Aeberli, MA(Edin.), BA(Oxon), Dip Arch, RIBA, ARIAS, SCI Arb

Peter Barber, MA, BCL (Oxon) Solicitor, Blake Lapthorne, Solicitors

John Barber, MA, LLB, CEng, MICE, FCIArb, Barrister, Michael Brown Lecturer at the Centre of Construction Law and Management

Helen Garthwaite, LLB, MSc, ACIArb, Solicitor, Nabarro Nathanson, Solicitors

Dr. Stephan Jefferis, MA, MEng, PhD, Golder Associates (UK) Limited

David Jones, Partner, Masons, Solicitors

Jack S. Kannry, PE, Counsel, Berman, Paley, Goldstein & Kannry

Michael Mendelblat, BA(Oxon), LLB (Cantab), Partner, Nabarro Nathanson, Solicitors

Philip Naughton QC, 3 Serjeants' Inn

Ingrid Persaud, LLB, LLM, Deputy Director of the Centre of European Law, King's College, London

Victoria Phillips, BA, LLM, Nabarro Nathanson, Solicitors

Michael Renger, MA(Cantab), Partner and Head of the Environmental Law Department, Nabarro Nathanson, Solicitors

Linda Spedding, LLB, LLM, PhD, Consultant to Masons, Solicitors

Professor John Uff, QC, PhD, FICE, FCIArb, Nash Professor of Engineering Law, King's College, London; Director, Centre of Construction Law and Management, King's College, London; Head of Keating Chambers in Outer Temple

Peter J. Young BSc, C.Chem, MRSC, MInst WM, MIWEM, Director, Aspinwall & Company

Keynote Address by the Rt Hon the Lord Mayor, Sir Francis McWilliams

Chairman, Director, Sheriff, Ladies and Gentlemen.

As a Lord Mayor, whose theme for the year is "The City and Industry in Partnership", and whose professional background is that of engineer, arbitrator and barrister, it gave me a great deal of pleasure to be asked to address you today at your 6th Annual Conference.

My only regret is that another engagement means that I must leave immediately after I have spoken. My going should not be treated as cowardice.

The subject of your conference, whereby you will be exploring the interface between environmental issues and construction, together with the links with legal and contractual matters are all highly topical issues throughout the world today. Environmental concern is an area of increasing importance in view of the ever increasing anxiety about the future of the world's ecosystem.

Recent experience in London has focused primarily on the regeneration of the former docklands area to the east of our capital city. Central government recognised the great difficulties, both social and economic, which need to be addressed when undertaking urban regeneration on this scale. The establishment of the London Docklands Development Corporation with wide ranging powers was clearly an essential pre-requisite for success.

What was essential in establishing that Corporation was that the organisation was given all the powers necessary to undertake such a massive task, whilst at the same time providing satisfactory safeguards and checks to ensure that the local populace were properly consulted at appropriate stages, and that they could acquire a sense of ownership as the plans progressed into reality.

Fundamental to the whole is a clear need to identify the necessary policies, strategies and long term funding to underpin the whole plan. In establishing the policies and strategies it is obviously of great importance that the local populace is consulted at that stage, in parallel with discussions with potential developers and other business and financial interests who will come together to undertake the necessary development work.

There is a clear need for the local populace to feel involved and to have their aspirations as to the future fulfilled. Whilst it may not be possible to have a totally consensus approach to each and every element within the whole plan, it is desirable that there should be some benefit to all parties if out and out opposition is to be avoided.

One of the more obvious failings of the London Docklands Development Corporation was its failure to establish an integrated transportation policy linked to proposed land uses. In this regard it would perhaps be fairer to say that the failure to establish such a policy lay with central government.

Over the last 10 years the progressive development within the docklands area east of the City of London has brought with it ever increasing traffic flows, culminating with the opening of the Limehouse Link earlier this year which alone has resulted in an increase of traffic at the Tower Hill junction of approximately 12%. A massive overall increase in traffic of some 30% is primarily due to the lack of an integrated transport policy and the almost total dependence of the docklands area on vehicular access rather than a balance with public transport.

The belated efforts to upgrade the Docklands Light Railway, and even now the uncertainty over the future of the Jubilee Line extension, fills one with dismay. If there had been clear thought applied at the outset, these vital public transport links could have been constructed and funded by government in partnership with the developers out of the benefits that have come from the regeneration of this area, and the increase in land values in particular.

One of the first matters that must be addressed in urban regeneration is the question of contaminated land and hazardous substances and how these will be tackled and disposed of, and by whom. It is fundamental that a full geological survey is undertaken in order to establish exactly what problems exist within the development site. Once you have identified these problems and any hazardous substances that exist, the difficulty that then arises is handling these substances, in terms of both their removal and subsequent disposal. There may even be problems with transporting certain particularly hazardous materials. This whole subject is currently a developer's nightmare.

There are many action groups that now exist who will watch every step that is taken very closely and will rightly expect those concerned to deal with these issues in a wholly professional and appropriate manner. Short term stop gap solutions are no longer accepted by the people of this country, and I would be surprised if this wasn't the case elsewhere within the developed world.

Dealing with contaminated land and hazardous substances is an expensive activity which could, of course, have a major impact on the overall development costs and the returns on investment anticipated by developers. Nevertheless, these are initial costs that must be properly identified and must be borne by those who seek to derive benefit in the future.

It is therefore important that whole life cost analyses are undertaken at the outset, because too often in the past developers have been accused of not undertaking the necessary initial investigations and thereby identifying all those additional early costs, only for the contaminated land issue to arise once development was started and the major environmental concerns commence at that time. It is very much harder for the developer to absorb what are potentially massive additional costs at that stage, at least readily!

A further reason that often arises with major urban regeneration programmes is that governments, anxious to procure early achievement programmes, relax the normal statutory procedures to facilitate the planning and implementation process. This has to be thought through very carefully whenever relaxation of statutory provisions is contemplated. The short term easy solution may well lead to medium and long term problems for organisations other than the initial developer and this causes massive resentment locally and with those organisations, generally the local authorities, who have to pick up the bill.

Even if all the necessary pre-planning stages have been properly undertaken, it is still absolutely essential that the whole construction programme is undertaken with the necessary supervision and control. The removal of hazardous substances I have previously mentioned. But the impact on individuals, both those working on construction sites and those living close to construction sites, can be quite marked. These problems relate to subjects which go under the general heading of health and safety and are generally covered by appropriate legislation.

Developers and their contractors must ensure that they take every possible measure to reduce the incidence of noise and dust, and possibly even vibration, to acceptable and pre-determined limits. These limits may be set by local environmental health officers, but they may also be the subject of consultation, discussion and agreement with the local populace. Similarly access routes for construction vehicles must be identified in advance and must be complied with at all times.

In my own Authority we recognise the need to control activities on site, and in particular in relation to the interface between building activities and highway users. Some 6 years ago the Corporation of London established a Considerate Contractors Scheme and this has operated very successfully with limited additional resource implications ever since.

The basic principles of this scheme require all builders to register with the Corporation and to undertake certain obligations whilst executing their works. These range from simply providing safe hoardings and scaffolding, which are generally decorated, but always well lit both at head level and at foot level, conspicuity being the key.

There must also be no wires, nails or other snags on which the clothing of passers-by could be caught. The footpath and highways immediately adjacent to all construction activity must be kept clean and free of dust and mud at all times. In general, works must be conducted having regard to the safety of both the people working on the site and anybody passing the site. This initiative has been welcomed in the City of London both by developers and the general public – efficiently organised sites are safe sites and are more economic to operate!

Failure to comply with the appropriate standards that have been agreed in connection with each construction activity can lead to lengthy legal action, frustration and cost, and there are really no winners in the end once problems have deteriorated that far. "Bridges" must be built at the beginning and they must not be dismantled until the very end. That leads me to my final point within this address, the question of tidying up and leaving the area in a proper condition on completion of all construction activity.

Many excellent projects of varying scale are spoilt, along with the reputations of the developers and the companies who carry out these works, simply because they do not tidy up the area disturbed by their activities on completion of the major works. It may well be that a separate contract is proposed to undertake this work, but should this be really necessary?

In my experience, it is overlooked on too many occasions and leads to alienation of the local populace just at the point in time when they should be welcoming the completion of any major new project and all the associated benefits, both social and economic, that this will bring. The tidying up of an area on completion of the works should be part of the original plans for the site and should not be compromised in any way or at any time by the developer or his contractors.

This has been a most satisfying occasion for me. Thank you for your patience, and I wish you all a fruitful and stimulating conference.

Table of Cases

Table of Legislation

Japan

United Kingdom

United States

Table of Statutory Instruments

Table of EC Legislation

Treaties

Directives

Regulations

Part 1

Public Law Aspects of Environmental Protection

1 Environmental protection: statutory provisions in the United Kingdom

Peter Aeberli

Introduction

There is a growing body of law in England and Wales that is more or less directly concerned with controlling human activity in order to prevent or minimise harm to the environment by pollution of air, water or land. This paper is an introduction to the central core of this growing body of environmental law. It does not cover more specialist areas of control such as those dealing with nuclear processes or genetically modified organisms.

The nature and sources of domestic environmental law

The bulk of domestic environmental law is statutory. Nevertheless the common law has a role in controlling polluting activities.

Common law controls over pollution

Common law actions in public and private nuisance, *Rylands* v *Fletcher*[1], trespass and negligence may provide remedies to those affected by pollution. Given the difficulty of establishing fault in relation to polluting activities the expansion of the strict liability torts might have proved useful, but this development was blocked by the House of Lords in *Cambridge Water Co.* v *Eastern Counties Leather Plc.*[2]

The principal difficulty with the common law as a means of pollution control is that, generally, it only recognises individual rights not environmental rights.

Exceptionally, activities that materially affect the reasonable comfort and convenience of a class of subjects may give rise to an action in public nuisance. Criminal sanctions can be imposed and injunctive relief can be sought by the Attorney General or, in certain circumstances, by local authorities.

1 (1868) L.R.3.H.L.330 (H.L.); affirming *sub nom. Fletcher* v *Rylands* (1866) L.R. 1 Exch.205.

2 *The Times* 10 December 1993.

Statutory controls over pollution

Historically, statutory protection for the environment has been piecemeal. The Environmental Protection Act 1990 indicates a move towards a more general system of environmental protection. Nevertheless the piecemeal approach remains dominant and there are numerous statutes containing measures for the protection of the environment.

Apart for this piecemeal approach to environmental legislation there are other difficulties with this area of law.

The widespread use of appointed day orders to bring into force provisions of statutes that have previously obtained the Royal Assent can provide a trap for the unwary. The Environmental Protection Act presents a particular difficulty in this respect as the timetable for its full implementation has been delayed.

Great reliance is placed on delegated legislation, not simply to flesh out particular statutory provisions but to enact what is, in effect, primary legislation. Thus, many environmental law statutes envisage the use of regulations to enact European Community environmental law directives into domestic law. Wide powers may be reserved to the Secretary of State to determine the processes and substances to be controlled by the legislation, to direct the nature and manner of controls over particular activities and to issue guidance notes indicating how controls should be exercised.

Regulatory bodies exercise considerable discretion in operating what are, apparently, mandatory controls and sanctions. Thus, pollution offences are generally expressed in terms of strict liability. Nevertheless regulatory bodies entrusted with enforcement are reluctant to bring prosecutions unless the conduct resulting in the offence is, in some way, wilful or reckless or the consequences are extremely serious. In fact this discretionary approach to prosecution has gained official recognition with the publication in 1989 of the National Rivers Authority's *Guidance Note on Enforcement and Prosecution*.

The basic structure of domestic environmental legislation

Despite the apparent diversity, much recent environmental legislation has certain principles in common. Action should be taken to prevent damage to the environment, any environmental damage that does occur should, preferably, be rectified at source and the polluter should pay. Furthermore there are similarities between the regulatory systems imposed under different statutes:

- Administrative responsibility is delegated to regulatory authorities, while the Secretary of State retains significant powers over the activities of that authority and those it regulates;

- control over potentially polluting activities is usually exercised through the use of conditional authorisations which can be varied or revoked in certain circumstances;
- regulatory authorities are entitled to levy fixed and periodic fees from those it regulates to recoup administrative costs;
- appeals lie from the authorisation decisions of regulatory authorities, generally to the Secretary of State;
- authorisations may be subject to an implied condition that the activity must be carried out using the best available techniques not entailing excessive cost ("batneec") or, occasionally, the best practicable means ("bpm"), to avoid pollution;
- regulatory authorities have wide investigatory powers, they can require polluters to clear up or abate pollution or can take action themselves and seek reimbursement from those responsible;
- criminal sanctions are imposed on those who carry out activities without the necessary authorisations or in contravention of authorisation conditions. Culpable employees or company directors can be prosecuted as well as their companies. Substantial, often unlimited, fines and, occasionally, imprisonment can be imposed; and
- persons affected by pollution are enabled to bring civil proceedings in order to obtain compensation from those responsible.

An overview of domestic environmental legislation

At present, domestic environmental legislation provides a small measure of integrated pollution control and more general, separate systems of control for water, air and land. There is also a range of miscellaneous pollution controls and, in some circumstances, planning authorities are required to consider the environmental implications of proposed developments.

Integrated pollution control

The Environmental Protection Act establishes a limited system of integrated pollution control over major industries in respect of emissions to air, water or land.

Industrial processes subject to integrated pollution control are those that have most potential for harmful pollution because of size, toxicity and impact on the environment as a whole. They are designated by the Secretary of State under the Environmental Protection (Prescribed Processes and Substances) Regulations 1991. Prescribed processes are listed either under Part A or Part B.

Part A processes are subject to integrated pollution control by Her Majesty's Inspectorate of Pollution ("HMIP"). Part B processes are subject to air pollution control by Local Authorities. Certain substances are also prescribed for emission to air, water or land and are subject to prohibition or control. These controls will not simply maintain the status quo but will be used to achieve a progressive improvement in quality standards and objectives.

The Part A list of prescribed processes includes major fuel and power, waste disposal, mineral, chemical, ferrous and non-ferrous metal, cement, asbestos, coatings, and timber facilities.

Such processes are regulated through a system of authorisation, supervision and enforcement procedures.

Authorisation procedures

Those wishing to carry out Part A prescribed processes must obtain authorisation from HMIP. Authorisation will not be given unless HMIP considers that the applicant will be able to carry on the process in accordance with any imposed conditions. There are transitional procedures for bringing existing processes into the new system between 1991 and 1996.

Authorisations are subject to an implied condition that the process must be carried out using the best available techniques not entailing excessive cost ("batneec") for preventing or, where impracticable, reducing to a minimum and rendering harmless the release of prescribed substances into the relevant environmental medium and for rendering harmless other substances that might cause harm if released into the environment. Harm means not simply harm to property or to the health of living organisms, but also offence to the senses.

The batneec condition covers both the design and construction of a process and its operating conditions. It is an ongoing obligation to review and update processes in the light of new pollution control techniques. Guidance notes on batneec for the various prescribed process are being issued by the Department of the Environment.

The implied batneec condition can be supplemented or overridden by express conditions requiring compliance with specific directions or regulations concerning environmental protection. Quality or emission standards emanating from the European Community, the Secretary of State or other legislation are implemented in this way.

Conditions cannot regulate emissions or deposits controlled under other statutory regimes. For instance conditions should not regulate the final disposal of controlled waste to land. HMIP must, however, notify the appropriate Waste Regulation Authority that the process involves the final disposal of waste to land.

HMIP must consult with and take account of the views of other regulatory bodies where discharge is envisaged into the medium for which they are responsible. For instance, it must impose any National Rivers Authority requirements on discharges to controlled waters.

HMIP must periodically review authorisations. In certain circumstances they can be varied or even revoked. Authorisations may be transferred to those taking over the authorised persons' undertaking.

Supervisory procedures

HMIP inspectors have wide powers over premises on which prescribed processes are conducted. These include powers of entry and inspection, to take and sample articles and substances and to require questions to be answered and records produced. These powers, particularly those concerning the answering of questions and the production of documents are subject to safeguards.

HMIP is required to maintain public registers containing specified information relating to its authorisations, notices and other decisions.

Enforcement procedures

Subject to transitional arrangements for bringing existing processes into the new authorisation system, it is an offence for anyone to operate a prescribed process without authorisation or in contravention of an authorisation or any conditions attached to it. Where a failure to comply with the implied batneec condition is alleged it is for the accused to prove that there was no better available technique not entailing excessive cost than that used.

HMIP can serve enforcement and prohibition notices on persons carrying on prescribed processes. Enforcement notices relate to contraventions of authorisation conditions. Prohibition notices are more general. They can be served, irrespective of whether or not there has been contravention of an authorisation condition if, in HMIP's opinion, the prescribed process involves a serious pollution risk. It is an offence to contravene an enforcement or prohibition notice.

Fines of up to £20,000 can be imposed in the Magistrates' Court and unlimited fines and/or two years' imprisonment on indictment. In certain circumstances the court can order remedial measures to be taken.

Remedial measures can also be taken directly by HMIP where harm has been caused as a result of certain offences. It can recover its reasonable costs from those responsible. In certain circumstances HMIP can seek injunctive relief in the High Court to stop a polluting activity.

Water pollution control

The Water Resources Act 1991 provides controls over the pollution of controlled waters. Controlled waters include all coastal, inland freshwater and ground water.

The controls are administered by the National Rivers Authority ("NRA") save as regards discharges to controlled waters from Part A prescribed processes. These are dealt with by HMIP under integrated pollution control, after consultation with the NRA.

Authorisation procedures

Those wishing to discharge matter into controlled waters should obtain a discharge consent from the NRA. Normally applications are publicised and when evaluating these, the NRA must consider representations made to it along with water quality criteria and discharge limits laid down by the Secretary of State giving effect, for instance, to European Community and other international water quality controls.

The NRA can attach conditions to a consent as it thinks fit. Conditions can relate to matters such as the manner and nature of the discharge and its pre-treatment to minimise pollution. The NRA has wide powers to prohibit discharges to controlled waters either absolutely or subject to conditions.

The NRA is obliged to review consents periodically and, in certain circumstances, it can modify or even revoke them.

The Secretary of State can also designate Water Protection Zones in order to prevent or control discharges of poisonous, noxious or polluting matter from specified activities into controlled waters. He can also designate Nitrate Sensitive Areas.

Special procedures apply to sewerage undertakers. They must obtain discharge consents from the NRA. In turn, they have powers to control discharges into their sewers under the Water Industries Act 1991. This Act permits occupiers of premises to discharge surface water and domestic sewage into sewers but provides that trade effluent can only be discharged into a sewer with the consent of a sewerage undertaker and on payment of an appropriate charge. Certain types of discharge, such as petroleum spirit and calcium carbides are prohibited.

Applications to discharge trade effluent should identify matters such as the composition, frequency and amount of the proposed discharge. In respect of certain types of discharge, "special category effluents", a sewerage undertaker must, unless it refuses consent, obtain the Secretary of State's determination whether the discharge should be prohibited or permitted subject to conditions. These functions are delegated to HMIP. Where the effluent is produced by a Part A prescribed process, it is not treated as a "special category effluent", instead authorisation must be obtained both from HMIP under integrated pollution control and from the sewerage undertaker

Special category effluents are listed in the Trade Effluent (Prescribed Processes and Substances) Regulations 1989 as amended ("the red list"). This gives effect to European Community obligations in respect of discharges of dangerous substances.

Sewerage undertakers must have regard to the need to allow trade effluent to be discharged into public sewers and to dispose of such discharges. Nevertheless they can, in appropriate circumstances, refuse consent or give consent subject to conditions similar to those that can be imposed by the NRA. They will be particularly concerned to ensure that, after treatment, discharge to controlled waters complies with the conditions imposed by the NRA. Sewerage undertakers can, in certain circumstances, vary existing discharge conditions.

Supervisory procedures

NRA inspectors have similar supervisory powers to those of HMIP inspectors. The NRA is required to maintain public registers of its activities.

Enforcement procedures

There is a range of offences of causing or knowingly permitting unauthorised discharges to water covering matters such as entry of poisonous, noxious or polluting matter or solid waste to controlled waters; entry of matter, other than trade or sewage effluent, to controlled waters from a drain or sewer in contravention of a prohibition; discharge of trade or sewage effluent to controlled waters; discharge of trade or sewage effluent in contravention of a prohibition from buildings or fixed plant to land or lakes or ponds which are not inland freshwaters; and entry of matter to inland waters which tends to impede their flow in a manner leading or likely to lead to substantial aggravation of pollution, or the consequences of pollution, from other causes.

For the purposes of these offences prohibitions may be notified by the NRA. They are also deemed to exist in respect of discharge limits or prohibitions affecting prescribed substances. Where there has been contravention of a prohibition, a discharge licence will not, generally, provide a defence.

Sewerage undertakers have additional defences where the contravention resulted from unauthorised discharges into their sewers.

Fines of up to £20,000 and/or three months imprisonment can be imposed in the Magistrates' Court and unlimited fines and/or two years' imprisonment on indictment. In certain circumstances, the NRA can carry out preventative or remedial works in respect of pollution of controlled waters. It can recover the reasonable cost of such works from those responsible. It may seek injunctive relief in the High Court to prevent pollution of controlled waters.

There is a range of offences relating to sewers including discharge of matter likely to injure a sewer or interfere with the free flow of its contents or their treatment; discharge of chemical and heated refuse or liquids which are dangerous or likely to cause injury to health; and discharge of petroleum spirit or calcium carbides.

An exemption from these offences is given to those who discharge trade effluent into a sewer in accordance with a sewerage undertaker's consent.

Fines can be imposed in the Magistrates' Court and unlimited fines and/or imprisonment on indictment.

Air pollution control

Under the Control of Pollution Act air pollution control over Part B prescribed processes and related emissions of prescribed substances is administered, generally, by the district or borough council for the area where the relevant process is conducted or, in respect of mobile plant, where the operator conducts the process or has its principal place of business. These authorities also administer the system of air pollution control provided by the Clean Air Act 1993.

Part B prescribed processes include certain medium and smaller scale combustion, waste incineration, ferrous and non-ferrous metal, mineral, cement, asbestos, glass, coatings, timber and rubber processes.

In general local authority administration of air pollution control is similar to that followed by HMIP in respect of integrated pollution control.

Authorisation procedures

Those wishing to carry out Part B prescribed processes must obtain authorisation from the relevant local authority. If the process involves discharges into controlled waters, separate authorisation must be obtained from the NRA. If the process involves the disposal of solid waste, this will be regulated under the land pollution regime. Transitional arrangements for bringing existing processes under the new controls are now, largely, complete.

Authorisations are subject to an implied condition that the process will be carried out using the best available techniques not entailing excessive cost ("batneec") for preventing or, where not practicable, reducing to a minimum and rendering harmless, releases into the air of substances prescribed for air and for rendering harmless other substances which might cause harm if released into air.

Express conditions can be imposed covering a similar range of air pollution matters to those covered by HMIP. Authorisations must be periodically reviewed and, in certain circumstances, can be varied or revoked. Authorisations may be transferred to those who propose to carry on the original authorised person's undertaking.

Supervisory procedures

Local authority inspectors have similar supervisory powers to those of HMIP inspectors. Local authorities are required to maintain public registers of their pollution control activities.

Enforcement procedures

It is an offence to operate a Part B process without authorisation or in contravention of an authorisation or its conditions. As with Part A processes, the accused must prove compliance with the implied batneec condition. Punishments are similar to those applicable to offences concerning Part A processes.

Local Authorities have similar powers to HMIP to issue enforcement and prohibition notices. In appropriate circumstances they can seek injunctive relief in the High Court.

The Clean Air Act

Further controls over emissions of dark smoke, dust and grit from chimneys and industrial and trade premises are provided in the Clean Air Act 1993. These controls only apply to processes that are outside Part I of the Control of Pollution Act.

It is, in general, a criminal offence to emit dark smoke from a chimney or from industrial or trade premises. In *Sheffield City Council* v *ADH Demolition Limited* (1984) L.G.R. 177 the later offence was held to have been committed by those responsible for a bonfire emitting dark smoke on a demolition site.

There are various statutory defences to these offences. In particular, with regard to smoke from industrial and trade premises, it is a defence to have taken all practical steps to prevent or minimise emissions. Regulations also give limited exemptions to certain types of activity, including burning of certain types of waste from demolition works and certain activities relating to road resurfacing works.

The Clean Air Act also imposes controls and prohibitions over the emission of dust and grit from furnaces and provides for the authorisation of certain categories of furnaces and chimneys.

The Act also allows for the designation of Smoke Control Areas and for further constraints on the emission of smoke in such areas.

Land pollution control

Land pollution is controlled primarily through regulation of waste management. Prior to the Environmental Protection Act control over the carriage and disposal of waste was provided by the Control of Pollution Act 1974 and the Control of Pollution (Amendment) Act 1989. The Environmental Protection Act introduces greater controls over waste management and separates the functions of waste regulation and waste disposal.

The transition to the new statutory regime is not yet complete and various provisions of the Environmental Protection Act, particularly those concerning waste management licensing and duties concerning closed landfill sites, are not yet in force.

The Environmental Protection Act regulates the management of controlled waste from creation to final deposit or re-processing. Controlled waste comprises household, industrial and commercial waste. This definition is further elaborated in the Act and in regulations. Waste includes scrap, effluent, unwanted surpluses from processes, broken or worn out items and spoiled or contaminated material. Industrial waste includes waste arising from construction, demolition or excavation. Materials may still be waste even though they have economic value or are put to some other use, for example infill. It appears that waste continues to be waste until its character is changed through re-processing.

The Control of Pollution Act gives the Secretary of State power to make regulations designating as "special waste" waste that is particularly difficult and dangerous to dispose of and to direct how such waste is to be kept, treated or disposed of. These provisions are not yet fully in force. At present special waste is regulated under the Control of Pollution Act. Regulations made under this Act designate as special waste materials such as asbestos, acids and alkalis where these occur in sufficient quantities in a substance to constitute a danger to life.

Different regulatory authorities are responsible for different aspects of the administration of waste control.

The principal licensing and enforcement authorities are Waste Regulation Authorities ("WRAs"). These are, generally, non-metropolitan county councils or, in metropolitan areas, district councils or specially constituted bodies.

WRAs are required to make waste disposal plans covering matters such as the amounts and methods of disposal of waste and the location of disposal sites. At present they are responsible for licensing waste disposal sites under the Control of Pollution Act and for registering waste carriers under the Control of Pollution (Amendment) Act. In due course they will be responsible for waste management licensing under the Environmental Protection Act and for the supervision of closed landfill sites.

Waste Disposal Authorities ("WDAs") are, generally, the same local authorities that are designated as WRAs. Their principal functions are to arrange for the disposal of waste collected in their area by waste collection authorities and to provide refuse amenity sites for the public. They have an involvement in waste recycling. They must carry out their functions through the use of waste disposal contractors.

Waste Collection Authorities ("WCAs") are, generally, district or borough councils. They are responsible for collecting most household waste in their areas and can, if requested and on payment of a reasonable charge, make arrangements for the collection of commercial and, subject to WDA consent, industrial waste from premises. They also have an involvement in waste recycling.

Authorisation procedures

Under the Control of Pollution (Amendment) Act persons carrying controlled waste must be registered with the appropriate WRA. The WRA can refuse an application where it considers it undesirable for the applicant to carry controlled waste. An applicant may be regarded as undesirable if he has been convicted of certain environmental offences. Registrations must be periodically reviewed. In certain circumstances they can be revoked.

Under the Control of Pollution Act waste disposal operators must be licensed by the appropriate WRA. If the proposed use constitutes "development" within the meaning of the planning legislation, planning permission is required. An established use certificate may not be sufficient.

Until planning permission is obtained a licence cannot be granted. If the facility has planning permission the WRA must not reject the application unless it is satisfied that this is necessary to prevent pollution of water or danger to public health. The NRA must be consulted, and investigations carried out into the effects of the operation on ground water, before a decision is reached.

The WRA can attach such conditions to a licence as it considers appropriate, provided these relate to the purposes of the legislation authorising the grant of licences. Controls over the duration of tipping and the materials to be tipped can be imposed and, arguably, requirements to maintain insurance and bonds during and after the cessation of activities.

Licences can be varied or revoked in certain circumstances. They can be transferred subject to objection by the WRA. They can be unilaterally surrendered by the holder.

When the relevant provisions of the Environmental Protection Act come into force, persons intending to treat, keep or dispose of controlled waste will have to obtain waste management licences from the appropriate WRA. Either a site licence or a mobile plant licence will be required, depending on the nature of the activity. Existing holders of waste disposal licences will be subject to the new waste management regime.

The matters to be considered by the WRA in deciding whether or not to grant a licence are similar to those addressed under the existing regime. In addition, detriment to local amenity can be taken into account and the WRA must consider whether the management of the activities will be in the hands of a technically competent person and whether the applicant is in a position to make adequate financial provision to discharge any obligations that may arise from the licence: for instance, aftercare conditions imposed in a planning permission.

The power to impose conditions is similar, but wider, than that applicable to waste disposal licences. In particular, a waste management licence can be subject to conditions that must be complied with after authorised activities have ceased.

Unilateral surrender of a site waste management licence will not be possible. Surrender will only be accepted by a WRA if it is satisfied that the condition of the land, due to its use for waste management, is such that it is unlikely to cause environmental pollution or harm to human health. Once a licence is surrendered former holders will not be liable to the WRA for measures it subsequently takes to deal with landfill gas or leachate on the site.

Licences can be varied, suspended or revoked by a WRA in certain circumstances. Those wishing to transfer licences will have to obtain approval from the WRA.

The placing of skips on highways and the manner in which these must be marked and secured is controlled under the Highways Act 1980. These provisions are operated by highway authorities.

Special waste

The Control of Pollution Act imposes additional controls on the movement of special waste through a consignment note system. This ensures that the WRA is notified of the movement of such waste and that records are kept of its movement and disposal. In certain circumstances the WRA can object to the proposed movement. Records must also be kept by those who deposit special waste to land.

Similar procedures will, in due course, be enacted under the Environmental Protection Act, with additional powers given to WRAs to recover the costs of operating the consignment note system from those involved in it.

Carriers of special waste are also subject to regulations concerning packaging and labelling made pursuant to the Health and Safety at Work Act 1974.

The duty of care

The Environmental Protection Act imposes a duty of care on any person, other than the occupier of domestic property in regard to his own waste, who imports, produces, carries, keeps, treats or disposes of controlled waste or, as a broker, has control of such waste. The duty is to take all reasonable measures to prevent anyone committing an offence under the Act relating to the management of the waste, to prevent its escape from his own or another's control and to secure that it is only transferred to an authorised person, or to a person for authorised transport purposes, and accompanied by proper documentation. Regulations describe the required documentation. Basically, it must be sufficient to enable others to avoid mismanagement of the waste.

The Department of the Environment has issued codes of practice and circulars explaining the nature of this duty. It is suggested that a producer of waste is not generally responsible for waste once it has left his premises but that he may have a duty to warn the WRA, or to terminate current arrangements, if he suspects that his waste is being unlawfully handled. Waste contracts should provide for termination in such circumstances.

Supervisory procedures

Inspectors can be appointed by WRAs, WDAs and WCAs. Their powers are similar to those of HMIP inspectors.

Under provisions of the Environmental Protection Act, yet to be brought into force, WRAs will be obliged to carry out periodic inspections of their areas to identify land that, because of its condition, may pollute the environment or harm human health due to noxious gases or liquids caused by deposits of controlled waste. In addition district and borough councils will be required to maintain and periodically update registers of land in their areas that may be contaminated.

Enforcement procedures

Under the Control of Pollution (Amendment) Act it is an offence for unregistered persons to transport waste in the course of a business or with a view to profit. Transport of waste within particular premises is exempted and regulations provide further exemptions. For instance, producers of controlled waste, other than building or demolition waste, are, generally, exempt. There are also various statutory defences to this offence.

On summary conviction fines not exceeding level 5 on the standard scale can be imposed. In certain circumstances vehicles involved in unlawful waste disposal can be confiscated.

Under the Control of Pollution Act it is an offence to cause or knowingly permit the deposit of controlled waste on land, unless that land is occupied by the holder of a waste disposal licence authorising that deposit and the deposit is made in accordance with the conditions of the licence. It is also an offence to use or cause or knowingly permit plant or equipment to be used to dispose of, or deal with, controlled waste in a prescribed manner unless the site of the plant or equipment is occupied by a licence holder. Prescribed processes include incinerating, pulverising, sorting or storing waste.

Regulations provide various exemptions to these offences. Exemptions include the keeping or disposal of household waste within the curtilage of that dwelling; the deposit of construction or tunnelling wastes on land where construction works are being carried out, for the purposes of those works, or its short term storage on that land; storage of waste on premises where it is produced; or short term deposit of small amounts of waste in a builder's skip on a highway. In general these exemptions do not apply to waste that is liable to give rise to environmental hazards. There is also a limited range of statutory defences to these offences.

Fines of up to £20,000 and/or six months' imprisonment can be imposed by the magistrates' court and, on indictment, unlimited fines and/or imprisonment up to two years or, in certain more serious cases, five years.

The WRAs and WCAs can require the occupiers of land on which controlled waste is unlawfully deposited to remove it or to deal with it in specified ways. In certain circumstances they can take such measures themselves and recover any costs necessarily incurred from those responsible for the deposit.

Under the Control of Pollution Act persons who unlawfully deposit or knowingly cause or permit deposit of waste which causes damage may be liable in civil proceedings for any damage caused, unless it was wholly due to the fault of the person who suffered it or was suffered by a person who voluntarily accepted the risk. Under the Environmental Protection Act it is an offence to treat, keep or dispose of controlled waste in a manner likely to cause pollution of the environment or harm to human health. It is also an offence to fail to comply with the statutory duty of care.

Once the waste management licensing scheme is enacted a range of offences relating to unlicensed management of waste and management of waste in contravention of waste management licence conditions will be introduced. As under the Control of Pollution Act, regulations will provide various exemptions to these offences and a limited range of statutory defences will be recognised.

The penalties for these offences are similar to those applicable to offences under the Control of Pollution Act. Offences involving special waste will be subject to the higher penalties but imprisonment cannot be imposed for breach of the duty of care. WRAs and WCAs will retain power to require the removal and treatment of unlicensed deposits of waste and to carry out such works themselves. The scope of statutory civil liability will also be widened once the relevant provisions of the Environmental Protection Act come into force.

Miscellaneous pollution controls

Local authorities are responsible for administering a variety of other pollution controls relating, in particular, to statutory nuisances and noise.

Supervision procedures

Provisions controlling statutory nuisances are now contained in the Environmental Protection Act. These controls are administered by district and borough councils. Statutory nuisances comprise premises, accumulations or deposits that are prejudicial to health or a nuisance, or emissions from, or effluvia arising on, premises that are prejudicial to health.

Local authorities are required to inspect their areas to detect statutory nuisances. If a statutory nuisance is identified, the local authority must serve an abatement notice, generally on the person responsible for the nuisance, requiring the abatement, prohibition or restriction of the nuisance and/or specifying steps to be taken for that purpose.

Persons aggrieved by a statutory nuisance can seek an order from the Magistrates' Court on similar terms to an abatement notice. Additional controls relating to noise are contained in the Control of Pollution Act and in the Environmental Protection Act. These controls are administered by district and borough councils.

Under the Control of Pollution Act local authorities can issue "Section 60 notices" in respect of noise from building sites, specifying required abatement measures. Alternatively, prior approval for proposed abatement measures can be obtained by seeking a "Section 61 consent". When exercising these controls local authorities must consider matters such as the best practicable means to minimise or prevent noise on the site. Appeals lie to the Magistrates' Court.

The Control of Pollution Act also contains provisions under which a local authority can designate noise abatement zones and impose noise emission levels on premises in that area. These procedures are complex and seldom used.

Under the Environmental Protection Act local authorities are required periodically to inspect their areas for noise nuisances. They can serve an abatement notice on those responsible, requiring the abatement, restriction or prohibition of the noise. Where a section 60 notice could have been served the requirements of a section 80 notice should not be more onerous. Persons aggrieved by noise nuisance may seek an order from the Magistrates' Court in similar terms to a noise abatement notice.

Enforcement procedures

It is an offence under the Environmental Protection Act to contravene or fail to comply with the requirements of a statutory nuisance abatement notice.

There are various statutory defences. In particular where the proceedings relate to industrial, trade or business premises, it is a defence to prove that the best practical means ("bpm") were used to prevent or counteract the effects of the nuisance. The legislation indicates how this test is to be applied.

Fines on summary conviction may be up to £20,000.

A local authority may also seek injunctive relief in the High Court to secure the abatement, prohibition or restriction of a statutory nuisance. Under the Control of Pollution Act it is an offence to contravene a section 60 notice or section 61 consent.

Under the Environmental Protection Act it is an offence to contravene a noise abatement notice. There are special defences available to those whose noisy activities are also controlled under the Control of Pollution Act.

Environmental protection under planning legislation

Historically, planning legislation had a limited role as a means of environmental protection. It was more concerned with the orderly management of change and with economic arguments than with environmental concerns.

The use of planning permission conditions to duplicate controls available under other legislation has been judicially disapproved and ministerial disapproval has been expressed of attempts to introduce environmental concerns unrelated to land use, such as air quality objectives, into local plans.

On the other hand the use of the planning system to control environmentally disruptive activities such as mineral works and waste disposal to land has long been accepted. Planning authorities are obliged to prepare mineral and waste disposal plans for their areas. Applications relating to such developments can be considered in the light of these plans.

More recently, there has been a greater recognition of the role of the planning system in environmental protection. Environmental information must now accompany applications for certain types of development; consultation is growing between planning authorities and environmental regulatory authorities and some encouragement has been given to the use of planning conditions for environmental protection.

Environmental assessments

The Town and Country Planning (Assessment of Environmental Effects) Regulations 1988 require those seeking planning permission for major developments to submit environmental statements along with their applications. Environmental assessment is compulsory for developments listed in Schedule 1 of the Regulations such as crude oil refineries, large power stations, integrated iron and steel and chemical works, major infrastructure projects and special waste treatment and disposal facilities.

Schedule 2 lists developments for which environmental assessment will be required where proposals are likely significantly to affect the environment, for instance, because of their size, nature or location. These include large scale agricultural facilities, mineral and other extraction industries, smaller power stations, bulk fuel storage, waste disposal, urban development, and medium scale manufacturing, industrial and infrastructure projects.

Local authorities can determine when environmental assessment is required with a particular application. In certain circumstances this decision should be made after consultation with HMIP and the NRA. The Department of the Environment has issued guidance notes to explain how the environmental assessment procedures should be used.

If environmental assessment is required, the timetable for the planning application process is extended and additional publicity requirements are imposed. In addition regulatory authorities concerned with environmental protection, such as HMIP and the NRA, must be notified of the application by the planning authority. These authorities may assist the applicant in preparing an environmental assessment.

The Regulations stipulate what information must and may be included in an environmental assessment. In particular information must be given to enable the main effects of the development to be identified and assessed, to describe the likely effects on the environment and to identify proposed measures to avoid significant adverse environmental effects. Information concerning the general characteristics of the development, its production processes, and the type and quantity of residues and emissions and their environmental effects may be included.

In considering an application to which environmental assessment applies the planning authority must consider representations made by the notified regulatory authorities and environmental issues.

Consultation procedures

In addition to consultation procedures relating to environmental assessments there are other procedures under which environmental regulatory authorities may be consulted. In particular a planning authority must consult the NRA over applications for oil storage or waste disposal facilities. Where ground water could be adversely affected the NRA is likely to oppose the application. Consultation is required with the Health and Safety Executive over developments that involve the manufacture or use of notifiable quantities of hazardous substances. WRAs must be consulted in regard to developments concerning landfill sites.

Where the application concerns the redevelopment of contaminated land or land adjacent to such land Planning Authorities can consider whether the development takes proper account of the contaminated land. If not, they can, in certain circumstances, refuse permission or grant it subject to conditions requiring investigation and remedial action.

Planning conditions and planning agreements

Generally, planning conditions and agreements should not be used to impose controls that are provided for under other regulatory regimes. But, more recently, Department of the Environment guidance has suggested that conditions may be imposed to protect the environment from appreciable risk of harm, but that onerous conditions should not be imposed where environmental problems are less certain to occur; adequate control being provided under other environmental legislation.

The imposition of after care conditions raises particular difficulties. Historically these have been imposed on permissions for landfill sites and mineral developments and they now have legislative recognition. Notice can be served by the planning authority requiring those in control of the relevant land to comply with such conditions. Failure to comply with such a notice is an offence subject on summary conviction to a level 3 fine.

Future directions

Most future initiatives concerning environmental law are likely to come from the European Community. The government is, however, actively considering the further integration of the various environmental regulatory authorities into a new Environmental Agency. The intention is to provide a "one-stop shop" for the administration of environmental controls. The planning system will not be affected. As for existing legislation, it will be some time before its full implications for industry are felt.

There is already some evidence that regulatory authorities are becoming more intolerant of industries that cause pollution. Government circulars emphasise the need for fines that reflect profits or savings made by the offender in committing an offence and Crown Court prosecutions are on the increase. In one serious case a fine of £1 million was imposed.

A further uncertainty concerns the use that regulatory authorities will make of their enhanced clean-up powers. Widespread use of these powers could impose significantly greater costs on industry than those imposed by criminal sanctions. Recent concern over the proposed contaminated land registers appears to have ignored the fact that it is these clean-up powers, not the maintenance of registers, that gives teeth to much environmental legislation.

In consequence purchasers of land will be increasingly concerned to ensure that they are not acquiring open-ended liabilities for clean-up costs. This may be reflected in an increased demand for environmental audits and vendor warranties or indemnities. These may, in certain circumstances, be appropriate but they should not become blanket requirements. A realistic assessment of the actual risks imposed by the legislation in the light of the past and present use of the land should be made.

Uncertainty also surrounds the effect of recent environmental legislation on the civil liability of polluters. The legislative tendency is to favour a limited strict liability regime when imposing civil liability for environmental harm. It is increasingly unlikely that this tendency will also infect the common law and lead to a re-emergence of the strict liability torts. In any event the courts will be left to resolve difficult issues of causation and damage assessment.

Finally, it should not be assumed that existing insurance arrangements will cover all the risks imposed by this growing body of environmental law. Public liability policies do not provide indemnity from criminal sanctions nor from claims resulting from deliberate acts or omissions. They may not cover clean-up costs imposed by regulatory authorities. Civil liability resulting from gradual pollution may also be excluded. If cover is required, special environmental liability policies may have to be obtained.

2 Building a greener Europe: EC environmental legislation and the construction industry

Ingrid Persaud

Summary

This paper is an attempt to assess the relevant EC environmental legislation for the construction industry and to give some indications as to the shape of future legislation.

The contention is that the EC's environmental programme prior to 1992 can be characterised as a piecemeal response to consumer sentiment. While 1992 marks a shift in the scope and nature of the EC's environmental policies, nevertheless, the programme continues to be responsive to public perception of the level of environmental protection required. Arguably the Community is moving from piecemeal legislation to more grandiose goals in its fifth environmental action programme[1] such as "sustainable development" and is seeking to give a more pro-active direction to Member States. Furthermore, it has the legal powers to make these plans a reality. However, these plans are currently being thwarted by a Europe-wide recession which has created competing goals of protection of employment and of the environment. This should not give rise to complacency in the construction industry. A change in economic fortunes and political will would mean that those aspects of EC environmental legislation which are presently without much bite, may in fact soon grow sharp teeth. The warning signs are there.

EC environmental legislation—form and substance

Community legislation in the field of environmental law, as in other spheres of Community activity, can take one of two binding forms—

The author would like to thank Avinash Persaud, Vice-President, JP Morgan and Michael Bowsher, Barrister, for their assistance with the preparation of this paper. All errors and omissions remain the author's responsibility.

1 "Towards Sustainability—An EC Programme of Policy and Action in Relation to the Environment and Sustainable Development", COM (92) Final, 27 March 1992.

regulations and directives.[2] A regulation, such as the eco-audit regulation,[3] is binding as to both form and substance and confers rights on individuals which are enforceable in domestic courts from the moment it comes into force. It is therefore said to have "direct effect" in creating enforceable rights both against the state and private individuals. Regulations do not require any implementing legislation.

Directives, such as the environmental assessment directive,[4] are binding as to the end result to be achieved but leave discretion to Member States as to the appropriate form and method necessary to achieve the stated objectives. In order to be binding at the domestic level directives require implementing legislation. In certain circumstances they may be enforced against the state or emanations of the state after the date for implementation has passed.[5] It may even be possible for an action in damages where the state has failed to implement a directive.[6] Additionally, there appears to be an obligation to interpret domestic law in the light of the wording and purpose of a directive even where that directive has not yet been implemented.[7] It is therefore important to be aware of proposed directives and to be prepared to act as if it were in place from the time they are agreed.[8]

By far the most popular form of legislation in the environmental field is the directive. Of the thirty-eight pieces of relevant legislation only one takes the form of a regulation.[9] This is of itself a significant fact. Directives as a legal instrument leave more discretion to states as to the content, form and interpretation of Community legislation. As such there is less chance of establishing a single market in environmental protection.

Whether the Community legislation takes the form of a regulation or a directive one thing is clear—in an instance where there is a conflict between Community law and domestic law, it is the Community law which will prevail. This is the principle of supremacy of Community law that is seminal to any appreciation of the effect of Community law at a national level.[10]

---

2 Art 189 of the Treaty of Rome.

3 see below.

4 see below.

5 *Marshall* v *Southampton Area Health Authority* [1986] ECR 723.

6 *Francovitch* v *Italian State* [1992] IRLR 84.

7 *Von Colson* v *Land Nordrhein-Westfalen* [1984] ECR 1891; and *Marleasing SA* v *La Comercial Internacional de Alimentacion SA* [1990] ECR I-4135.

8 The House of Lords has so far resisted such a wide interpretation of the effect of directives—*Webb* v *EMO Air Cargo (UK) Ltd.* [1993] 1 CMLR 259.

9 The Eco-audit regulation (see below).

10 *Van Gend en Loos* v *Nederlandse Administratie Der Belastingen* [1963] ECR 1.

Community decision-making and the enforcement of Community law

The Community bodies responsible for enacting Community legislation are principally the Council, Commission and the Parliament. For our purposes the Commission is the most important since it is the initiator of all legislation.[11] It is also entrusted with the task of enforcing all Community law—including of course environmental law. It is therefore this body which sets the environmental agenda and seeks to enforce it.

The Commission has set out its environmental agenda in the form of "action programmes". We are currently on the fifth action programme covering the period 1993–2000.[12] These action programmes are worth considering since they are an indication of the general framework within which the Community is likely to operate. It is suggested that the first four action programmes, despite the reiteration of lofty ideals, in fact produced nothing more than piecemeal measures confined to the traditional areas of environmental concern—air, water, land and waste, which we examine later.

To ensure that its agenda can be attained, the Commission has, by a process of gradual accretion, acquired more powers under the Treaty of Rome. By the Single European Act[13] environmental protection was made a Community goal in itself. Through the insertion of Article 130r (1) the Community has a mandate to "preserve, protect and improve the quality of the environment . . . contribute towards protecting human health . . . (and) to ensure a prudent and rational utilisation of natural resources."

Article 130r also gives legal backing to the principle that the polluter pays. Most uniquely though it states that "(e) environmental protection requirements shall be a component of the Community's other policies." This is the shot across the bow that we must all note. We have in place the legal mandate to allow quite extensive Community action relating to the environment in what might at first sight appear to be totally unrelated policies, such as the provision of services. At present there is no evidence that the Commission intends to make full use of its powers but the capacity to act is there.

By the SEA, Article 130t also allows Member States to maintain or introduce more stringent protective measures. Article 130r (4) further confirms the idea of subsidiarity,[14] that is, that Community action should only

---

11 Arts 155–163 of the Treaty of Rome.

12 See note 1.

13 The Single European Act amends the Treaty of Rome in particular by adding Title VII on the Environment, OJ 1987 L169/1.

14 This principle is also enshrined in Art 3b of the Treaty on European Union.

be taken at that level if a project by reason of its scale or effects, so requires. It is also worth noting that by virtue of Article 100a(3), also a product of the SEA, Commission proposals concerning the environment "will take as a base a high level of protection". This is also unique in terms of Community law since it gives a qualitative requirement to Commission proposals. The Treaty on European Union also proposes to make it easier to pass legislation concerning the environment by introducing qualified majority voting for proposals which use Article 130r as its legal basis.[15]

In addition to these specific measures dealing with the environment, the Commission also has at its disposal more general enforcement powers against Member States based on Article 169 of the Treaty of Rome.[16]

EC environmental policy—the products of the first four action programmes

We have earlier characterised the products of the first four environmental action programmes as piecemeal and within traditional areas of concern. The following is a selection of the most relevant Community legislation for the construction industry which illustrates this phenomenon.

General legislation

Environmental assessment directive[17]

This directive is an expression of the general principle that environmental law should be concerned with preventative action and therefore seeks to subject activities, such as construction projects, to an "environmental assessment" if they are likely to have significant effects on the environment. Accordingly, the Directive states that "the best environmental policy consists in preventing the creation of pollution or nuisances at source rather than subsequently trying to counteract their effects" coupled with "the need to take effects on the environment into account at the earliest possible stage in all technical planning and decision-making processes."

---

15 The importance of a choice of legal basis for environmental legislation is highlighted in the recent case of *Commission* v *Council*, C-155/91, 17 March 1993.

16 Art 169 states: "If the Commission considers that a Member State has failed to fulfil an obligation under this treaty, it shall deliver a reasoned opinion on the matter after giving the State concerned the opportunity to submit its observations. If the State concerned does not comply with the opinion within the period laid down by the Commission, the latter may bring the matter before the Court of Justice."

17 Directive on the assessment of the effects of certain public and private projects on the environment, 85/337/EEC (OJ 1985 L175).

Interestingly, this is not the directive that the Commission had hoped to push through to achieve these principles. Spurred on by the American experience, where, according to the National Environment Policy Act 1969, if a federal agency proposes a development it must produce an environmental impact statement before permission is granted, the Commission hoped to introduce a similar scheme covering all projects likely to have a significant environmental effect. During the space of three years (1977–80) it produced some twenty drafts. The directive in its final form is a much watered-down measure which does not apply to all development projects and certainly falls a long way behind the US model.

There are nine categories of projects for which an assessment is mandatory and twelve categories of project for which it may be required. Where the assessment is applicable it requires the developer to provide information on potential environmental effects which can then be used to inform the decision as to the granting or withholding of planning permission. Such has been the effect of this directive that it has been argued that it has led to "EC planning law", that is, local authorities and other competent bodies are using their powers quite extensively to ensure that the environmental impact on human beings, flora and fauna, air, soil etc. are taken into account.[18] This is what the public now demands of its elected officials. The Department of the Environment in the UK has indicated its dissatisfaction with the standard of assessments carried out thus far and has indicated that it will be issuing a guide as to how these assessments should be prepared and the appropriate criteria for evaluation.

While environmental assessments are premised on high ideals the reality is that this present format is a less than effective form of environmental protection since it contains no procedure for quality control.[19] It is also unclear as to how the requirements of the directive are meant to interact with the pre-existing decision-making process[20] thereby creating

---

18 See further Nigel Haigh, "The European Community and Land Use—An Incoming Tide", *Journal of Planning and Environment Law Occasional Papers*, No.16 at 58 and Michael Redman, "European Community Planning Law", *Journal of Planning Law* (1993).

19 See further, Edward Finch, "Environmental Assessment of Construction Projects", *Construction Management and Economics*, Vol 10, No.1, January 1992, at 5–18. In this article Finch argues that while we must accept that environmental assessments are necessarily subjective because of the marrying of environmental community goals with client needs, it is possible to construct a model steered by technical advice which can be adjusted to weigh environmental factors accordingly.

20 Indeed, the issue of the direct effect of the environmental assessment directive in British courts is itself controversial—see "Re Kincardine and Deeside District Council", *Journal of Environmental Law*, Vol. 4 No.2 (1992) at 289 and *Twyford Parish Council* v *Secretary of State for the Environment* [1992] 1 CMLR 276.

unnecessary complications for companies unsure of exactly which regulations they are meant to be complying with.

To make matters even more complex the UK did not pass any primary legislation to comply with this directive. Instead the new provisions were tacked on to existing town and country planning regulations[21] thereby creating uncertainty as to when an environmental assessment is necessary even though the project may need approval by some procedure other than planning procedure.

Environment Information Directive[22]

The public in 1993 demands to be informed about the level of environmental protection that decision makers are aiming for and this is achieved in part by the Environment Information Directive which provides for greater transparency of administrative action. Under this directive the public should be given free access to information held by public bodies on environmental matters. Information may only be refused on certain specific grounds, such as defence or sub judice. A refusal to grant information must be reviewable by a judicial or administrative body.

It is one thing to require access to information but the measure falls short in so far as it does not require the gathering of information. Therefore if a state does not have the information already stored your right of access becomes worthless.

Other relevant general environmental legislation

Other general environmental legislation of note for the construction industry includes the "Directive on vocational training for certain drivers of vehicles carrying dangerous goods by road" (Drivers Training Directive);[23] the "Directive on the prevention and reduction of environmental pollution by asbestos" (Asbestos Pollution Directive);[24] "Directive on the major accident hazards of certain industrial activities" (Major Accident Hazards Directive);[25] "Directive on combating air pollution from industrial plants"

---

21 The most important of these is the Town and Country Planning (Assessment of Environmental Effects) Regulations 1988 as amended by the Town and Country Planning (Assessment of Environmental Effects) (Amendment) Regulations 1990.

22 Directive on the freedom of access to information on the environment 90/313/EEC (OJ 1990 L158).

23 OJ 1989 L398.

24 OJ 1987 L85.

25 OJ 1982 L230 with amendments in OJ 1987 L85 and OJ 1988 L336.

(Emissions from Industrial Plants Directive);[26] "Directive on the limitation of emissions of certain pollutants into the air from large combustion plants" (Large Combustion Plants Directive);[27] "Directive on the reduction of air pollution from existing municipal waste incineration plants" (Existing Municipal Waste Incinerators Directive);[28] "Directive on the prevention of air pollution from new municipal waste incineration plants" (New Municipal Waste Incinerators Directive).[29]

Waste legislation

The Community has agreed a "Directive on waste" commonly refered to as the Waste Framework Directive[30] and a Directive on hazardous waste[31] both of which are of relevance to the construction industry. The Waste Framework Directive is premised on three notions: prevention of waste, recycling of waste, and safe disposal of waste which cannot be recycled. It covers almost all types of waste and introduces a system for waste management, disposal and control. Under the scheme Member States are required to comply with four different strands of the waste policy:

(1) encourage clean technology, prevention, reduction and recovery of waste,
(2) ensure waste disposal without environmental harm,
(3) establish a regime of authorisation and control for those engaged in producing, collecting and disposing of waste, and
(4) promote self-sufficiency in waste.

While these are clearly laudable aspirations the legislation lacks proper enforcement mechanisms or standards that could promote environmental protection within the goal of a single market. The Directive leaves it to individual Member States to establish how these objectives are to be achieved. It should have come into force in April 1993. For the UK it is clear that many of the requirements were already encompassed by the

26 OJ 1984 L188.

27 OJ 1988 L336 as amended by OJ 1993 C17.

28 OJ 1989 L203.

29 OJ 1989 L163.

30 OJ 1975 L194 as amended by OJ 1991 L78.

31 See OJ 1991 L377. A European Waste Catalogue is currently being drafted to apply to both these directives. It is expected that waste will be classified according to origin and the catalogue will specify the hazardous, potentially hazardous and the non-hazardous nature of each type of waste.

Environmental Protection Act 1990. However, the Department of the Environment has indicated that the Directive will require new legislation to cover the licensing regime for waste brokers. At the time of writing the draft Waste Management Licensing Regulations 1992 are not in force and there is no indication as to how soon we can expect them to come into operation. The UK is therefore in breach of its obligations under Community law and there is the risk that existing legislation will have to be interpreted as if the Directive had been fully implemented.

In terms of waste management the Commission has also proposed new directives that could impact on the construction industry. These include the proposed Directive on the landfill of waste[32] providing common rules on the landfill of waste; the proposed Directive on the incineration of hazardous waste[33] which sets out a permit system to operate incineration plants; proposed regulation on the supervision and control of shipments of waste within, into and out of the European Community[34] and finally the proposed directive on civil liability for damage caused by waste.[35] This proposed directive, also referred to as the Environment Liability Directive, would create a system of strict liability for the producer of the waste.

Noise legislation

The piecemeal nature of EC environmental legislation is nowhere more clear than in the area of noise. The Community sets out its policy in two framework directives. The Directive on the approximation of the laws of the Member States relating to the determination of the noise emission of construction plant and equipment (Noise Framework Directive No. 1)[36] which is an attempt at harmonisation of methodology for determining noise emitted from construction plant and equipment. The directive applies to machinery, appliances, plant and installations or components thereof used on civil engineering and building sites.

There is also the Directive on the approximation of the laws of the Member States relating to common provisions for construction plant and

32 OJ 1991 C190.

33 OJ 1992 C130.

34 OJ 1990 C289 as amended by OJ 1992 C115.

35 OJ 1989 C251 as amended by OJ 1991 C192. This directive is unlikely ever to become law. Indeed, the Commission's Green Paper on Remedying Environmental Damage COM(93)47 is the second attempt to discuss a regime for civil liability for environmental damage.

36 OJ 1979 L33 as amended by OJ 1981 L376 and adapted to technical progress by OJ 1985 L233.

equipment (Noise Framework Directive No. 2)[37] which promotes the introduction of common specifications for construction plant and equipment and common certification procedures.

These framework directives have given birth to what are called daughter directives which give the technical details for complying with the overriding objectives. These include Noise Directives relating to compressors[38], tower cranes[39], welding generators[40], power generators[41], concrete-breakers and picks[42], excavators, dozers and loaders.[43]

Water legislation

While there are no environmental measures pertaining to water aimed specifically at the construction industry again there are several general measures which are applicable. One of the most important measures is the Directive on urban waste water treatment[44] aimed at the reduction of pollution of coastal waters and freshwater by setting minimum standards for sewage treatment and discharge. There are also rules on the dumping of sewage sludge and a ban on dumping sludge at sea. Secondary treatment of sewage is regarded as the key safeguard against the dumping of insufficiently treated waste water. Communities are divided into "sensitive" and "less sensitive" areas all of which require the construction of sewage systems by 1998 for the sensitive areas with a little more leeway for the less sensitive. The financial implications of compliance are estimated by the Department of the Environment at £1 billion. Member States have until the end of 1993 to draw up implementation programmes but already the impact of this directive is changing government behaviour in that the government no longer require only primary treatment for estuary and coastal sewage discharges.

Other directives of note include the Directive relating to the quality of water intended for human consumption (Drinking Water Directive)[45] which lays down qualitative standards for all water for human consumption. It covers private and public water supplies as well as some bottled water but excludes mineral waters.

---

37 OJ 1984 L300 as amended by OJ 1988 L382.

38 OJ 1984 L300 as adapted to technical progress by OJ 1985 L233.

39 OJ 1984 L300 as amended by OJ 1987 L220.

40 OJ 1984 L300 as adapted to technical progress by OJ 1985 L233.

41 OJ 1984 L300 as adapted to technical progress by OJ 1985 L233.

42 OJ 1984 L300 as adapted to technical progress by OJ 1985 L233.

43 OJ 1986 L384 as adapted to technical progress by OJ 1989 L253.

44 OJ 1991 L135.

45 OJ 1980 L229.

The EC has also agreed the Directive on the quality of surface water abstracted for drinking (Surface Water for Drinking Directive)[46] which creates categories of surface water and outlines the treatment that must be applied to make it fit for drinking. As with many of these piecemeal measures the Directive imposes a general obligation on Member States to "ensure continuing improvement of the environment". This leaves it to each individual Member State to draw up a systematic plan for the improvement of surface water so there is no attempt to create Community-wide standards. There is also a long-standing proposed directive which would set up a Regulatory Committee to assist the Commission in revising the Surface Water for Drinking Directive[47] but there appears to be no political will to make this a reality.

In keeping with the piecemeal and evolutionary nature of EC environmental policy, the Directive on the methods of measuring frequencies of sampling and analysis of surface water used for drinking (Surface Water Sampling Methods Directive)[48] gives some guidelines but leaves it to Member States to decide on the method and frequency of sampling and analysis.

There are also Directives on the discharge of dangerous substances[49], on the discharge of mercury[50], hexachlorocyclohexane[51], cadmium[52] and "drins".[53]

The future

ECO-Auditing

The most recent addition to the plethora of EC environmental legislation is the controversial and little understood "environmental audit" (hereafter refered to as eco-audit) regulation.[54] The first obvious thing is that this measure is presented in the form of a regulation rather than the well used directive. This means that it is binding in its entirety as to both form and substance. It is also the first time that the Commission has proposed a

46 OJ 1975 L194.

47 OJ 1989 C13.

48 OJ 1979 L271, see also proposed Directive amending Directives relating to the abstraction of surface water for drinking and others, OJ 1989 C13.

49 OJ 1976 L129 and OJ 1986 L181 and proposed directive OJ 1990 C55.

50 OJ 1984 L74.

51 OJ 1984 L274.

52 OJ 1983 L291.

53 OJ 1988 L158.

54 OJ 1992 C76.

measure that is not based on existing legislation from a Member State and is therefore a departure from its previous passivity.

Whilst it is binding on Member States to provide the infrastructure for eco-auditing, the scheme itself will be a voluntary one. It is designed for certain industrial activities to provide:

> "... a management tool comprising a systematic, documented, periodic and objective evaluation of the performance of the organisation, management system and equipment designed to protect the environment with the aim of:
>
> (i) facilitating management control of the environmental practices;
> (ii) assessing compliance with company policies including observance of existing regulatory requirements."[55]

The objective of the eco-audit is therefore to "promote improvements in the environmental performance of industrial activities" in three ways:

> "(a) the establishment and implementation of environmental protection systems by companies;
> (b) the systematic, objective and periodic evaluation of the environmental performance of such systems;
> (c) the provision of information on environmental performance to the public."[56]

This should relate to matters such as emissions to air, land and water. It should also take into account legal constraints and public perceptions of the level of environmental protection required.

Should a company decide to take part in this voluntary endeavour the audit would follow certain defined stages. The first stage involves a definition, by the company, of its "environmental objectives", that is, "the detailed goals, in terms of environmental performance, which a company sets itself". The company must also have defined its "environmental policy", that is, "a statement of a company's overall aims and principles of action with respect to the environment".[57] All goals expressed must be capable of some form of measurement.

The second stage of an eco-audit is the setting up of an "environmental management" team with responsibility for "the aspects of the overall management function that determine and implement the environmental policy".[58]

Once the environmental objectives have been defined, and policy put in place with an environmental management team, the "sites" to which the scheme will apply must be selected. A "site" refers to "all land on which

55 This definition borrows heavily from that proposed by the ICC.
56 See Art 1 of the final version.
57 See Art 2(f) and 2(c).
58 See Art 2(d).

the industrial activities under the control of a company at a given location are carried out, including any connected or associated storage of raw material, by-products, intermediate products, end-products and waste material, and any equipment and infrastructure involved in the activities, whether or not fixed".[59] This definition has been recently expanded so that in the construction sector, for example, it would cover temporary work sites. The "company" in charge of the site is also widely defined to include "any organisation which has direct operational control over activities at a given site".[60]

It is for each company to decide which sites it wishes to bring within the scheme. This is therefore not a scheme about a company's general level of environmental consciousness but rather its chosen site-specific exposure.

Once the site has been selected the company must prepare an environmental review of it with a view to establishing an environmental protection system. The environmental statement of the site must then be prepared and submitted for validation by external, accredited auditors.[61] The auditor's evaluation will then be kept by a body deemed competent by the Member State and the information will be accessible to the public. Audits are to take place periodically at intervals of between one and three years. The UK has established a National Environmental Auditors Registration Board who will oversee the external assessors and decide matters of accreditation.

Those who take part in the scheme will be allowed to use the eco-logo—a circle of twelve stars with one of three prescribed forms of words inserted in the circle, at the site which is subject to eco-auditing.[62] A company can lose the use of the logo if it fails to submit a validated environmental statement within the deadline given in the previous statement, or, if the site fails to comply with either Community or national environmental standards. Where a company has been certified as complying with given national or international standards for environmental management it will be assumed that they are also in compliance with the requirements of an eco-audit and can therefore use the eco-logo. Such standards must, however, be certified by a nationally recognised body and the company concerned must meet the requirements of the environmental statements.[63]

59 See Art 2.

60 See Art 2.

61 See Art 7.

62 Annex 11 sets out the appropriate phrases: "All our production sites in the EEC participate in the Eco-audit scheme. All our production sites in [name of Community Member State] participate in the Eco-audit scheme. The following production sites of our company participate in the Eco-audit scheme."

63 For a comprehensive account of the workings of this scheme see Linda Spedding et al, *Eco Management and Eco-Auditing* (Chancery Law Publishing Ltd, 1993).

If one is concerned with ensuring proper environmental protection the voluntary nature of the scheme, as well as the fact that it is site-specific, makes the notion of eco-auditing as a method of making companies accountable for the environmental damage they may cause, not worth the recycled paper it is written on. The scheme does not introduce Community-wide standards and hence does not further the harmonisation process. Additionally since companies may choose the site(s) they wish to be part of the scheme it is possible to eliminate those less-green aspects of one's business from scrutiny.

The scheme will be reviewed in four years' time and it is expected that if the recession has lifted and the political will is there, the scheme may move from being a voluntary to a mandatory one. In this way, firms who participate now will have a competitive edge over their rivals. It is also a good public relations exercise to have an eco-logo displayed. That circle of stars could keep influential corporate customers and shareholders impressed. There are also financial incentives available to small and medium-sized firms to assist with the cost of this initiative.

If the Community were to move towards mandatory "green accounts" there are two styles of accounting presently followed. There is the "Anglo-American" model followed, for example, by Dow Europe which tabulates pollutants and lists the extent to which these are reduced over time. The "Teutonic" model instead seeks to capture the difference between what companies take in and what they produce, that is, a sort of "eco balance sheet".[64] The Community scheme gives no guidance as to which of these models it would prefer. In fact companies can decide just how little or how much information they want to put forward.

Conclusion

The fifth environmental action programme with its theme of sustainable development could herald a new direction for the construction industry. The measures so far have admittedly lacked proper enforcement and not promoted harmonisation. However, if the decision-makers believe that, with the predicted recovery in economic fortunes by 1994, industry is better able to bear the cost of, for example, mandatory eco-auditing, then it is likely that Community policy will evolve towards this goal.

Indeed, post-1992 marks a turning point in the EC as a whole with the Treaty on European Union and the setting of grand targets such as

64 For further discussion of these models see "A Green Account", *The Economist*, 4 September 1993, p.89.

monetary and political union—all of which is being held back by a deep recession and the attendant lack of political will. The grand plans remain in place so one must be aware that priorities could re-adjust themselves in the future. This would in the environmental field lead to a new generation of legislation that is less piecemeal but still responsive to consumer sentiment.

This is not to underestimate the contribution the construction sector makes to society. The activities of the construction sector are vital to society's socio-economic development in so far as it provides shelter, infrastructure and employment. This must be balanced against the fact that it is also an industry that can be responsible for major depletion of natural resources, degradation of fragile eco-zones, chemical pollution and the use of building materials harmful to human health. The challenge of sustainable development is about reconciling society's needs while minimising the harmful side-effects on human health and the biosphere. The Community appears poised to grasp this challenge.

3 The international perspective, including Japan

David Jones and Linda Spedding

Introduction

As improvements in communications make the world seem an increasingly smaller place, potential markets for commercial opportunity become ever more global. For any company whose activities extend beyond the UK and Europe into the international arena it is quite clear that it will be essential to consider various standards, regulations and requirements—both national and international—which are operative in the jurisdiction in which they intend to do business. Such considerations will be closely interlinked with less tangible concepts such as culture, work ethic and economic history, and as a company's horizons expand beyond the confines of the UK and Europe an appreciation of these broader concepts can be increasingly relevant to commercial decision-making.

Japan is particularly interesting when considering the international perspective in terms of this broader appreciation, as it is a significant example of a jurisdiction where economic development has been a priority to the degree that environmental issues have often been ignored in the quest for economic achievement. In order to grasp the impact of Japanese environmental laws on business, it is useful to realise that the Japanese legal system is fundamentally a civil law system, that is statute-based, rather than relying extensively on judge-made case law.

Given that public law, in contrast to private law, considers the principles and rules relating to the state (rather than individual parties), this discussion will cover the progress of environmental policy and legislation in Japan and their effect on construction actors and activities (rather than cases between parties) although it should be understood that Japan's attitude toward environmental protection was influenced by four highly publicised toxic tort cases in the late 1950s and early 1960s, shifting the focus from purely industrial concerns.

In addition brief comments will be made regarding the role of Japan in the development of global environmental policy and legislation, both in terms of its participation in international conventions (see Appendix I and II) and, more recently, its contribution to the Rio Summit and some developments thereafter.

Environmental policy

Although we are aware that similarities exist between environmental policies in different countries and regions of the world, it is true to say that each nation's policy has distinctive elements resulting from factors such as its legal structure, economic system and cultural context. It has been remarked that Japan's system of pollution control is a valuable example for other countries, but that Japan also has lessons to learn from other countries, especially with regard to nature conservation and public participation.

The structure and form of Japan's environmental policy-making has not changed greatly since 1971 when the Environment Agency (EA) was established. Although, therefore, very recently there have been efforts towards the greening of Japan through the initiative of a comprehensive environment bill, these have been blocked by the force of the lobbyists in other ministries and industries, and therefore the older regime still applies. As seen below, the EA is not the sole agency concerned with environmental matters: it does not have any overall control. For example the EA has no jurisdiction over aircraft noise, generation, storage and disposal of radioactive wastes, pollution control in specified factories, discharge of hazardous substances, special government financial measures for pollution control, settlement of pollution disputes or pollution crimes relating to human health. Furthermore, the EA only has an advisory role on the regulation of agricultural chemicals, waste disposal and sewerage and marine pollution, which are in the ambit of other agencies. Moreover the EA has no control over land use and development plans. In addition, although the Nature Conservation Act (1972) and the National Land Use Planning Act (1974) may be used to control development they are in general ineffective against the pressures favouring development. It is true to say that the EA's efforts to overcome jurisdictional rivalries and to promote an integrated environmental policy have been unsuccessful as a result of ministerial interference and vested interests. In fact the major ministries have even moved members to key positions in the EA: the recent death of the Environmental Bill (discussed below) illustrates (in this instance) the power of the construction ministry. Japan's National Environmental Policy has therefore been affected by the lack of a comprehensive environmental policy with a strong centralising force at the national level.

At the local level, while the local authorities have played a leading role in developing environmental policy their powers are restricted. In addition a difficult consensus has to be sorted out before environmental laws can be implemented, initially between the EA, the other ministries and the local government, the polluter and the regional administrators. The implementation of legislation and policy-making is therefore complicated and delayed.

Nevertheless, it can be said that Japan has instituted one of the world's most comprehensive environmental legislative systems, under-pinned by the Basic Law for Environmental Pollution Control (1967). Among the national environmental protection laws derived from the Basic Law are the Air Pollution Control Law, the Water Pollution Control Law, the Waste Disposal and Public Cleaning Law and the Industrial Health and Safety Law. Selected key national laws concerned with the control of specific types of pollution are:

Air pollution
- Road Transport and Motor Vehicle Law (1951)
- Gas Industry Law (1954)
- Road Traffic Law (1960)
- Electricity Power Industry Law (1964)
- Air Pollution Control Law (1968)

Water pollution
- Hazardous Substances Control Law (1950)
- Sewerage Law (1958)
- River Law (1964)
- Agricultural Soil Pollution Prevention Law (1970)
- Marine Pollution Control Law (1970)
- Water Pollution Control Law (1970)
- Seto Inland and Sea Environment Conservation Law (1973)
- Regulations for Waste Treatment and Disposal

Soil pollution
- Agricultural Soil Pollution Prevention Law (1970)

Noise and vibration
- Road Transport and Motor Vehicle Law (1951)
- Road Traffic Law (1960)
- Noise Regulation Law (1968)
- Vibration Regulation Law (1976)

Ground subsidence
- Industrial Water Law (1956)
- Law concerning the Pumping of Groundwater for Use in Buildings (1956)

Offensive odour
- Offensive Odour Control Law (1971).

It is important to know that Japan's national environmental laws emanate from the Basic Law for Environmental Pollution Control of 1967. The main feature of that Act is that it authorises the enactment of national environmental laws and authorises the prefectural and local government to implement and enforce those laws. Breaches of any of the national environmental laws lead to civil and criminal sanctions. As a result of the Basic Law the prefectural and local governments can enact stricter laws provided that they are consistent with the National Environmental Laws. This has happened in various areas, particularly the waste disposal area, where many of the prefectural governments have enacted stricter laws and standards. In this connection the Prefectural Governor has the power to enforce the legislation: such power may be delegated to a prefectural environmental agency. Sometimes the municipal governments in the larger cities are similarly actively involved: they may, for example, require a locally issued permit to enable the construction of a manufacturing plant having regard to the plant's pollution control. In general, a company must submit a report to the prefectural government describing the facility and planned activity in some detail prior to the installation, construction or modification of a plant, that is before commencing any environmentally sensitive operations. A company should also determine whether one of the national ministries, such as the Ministry of International Trade and Industry (MITI), or the municipality requires that such a report be submitted to it. The Prefectural Governor then reviews the report within a certain time limit (usually 60 days) in order to decide whether to reject, modify or approve the project. Where there are already serious pollution problems an EIA may be required which has to be submitted to the appropriate government body including the results of each study to determine the impact of the proposed plant on the surrounding environment. Again, in many large cities, such as Tokyo, specific arrangements exist in the form of an EIA Council which participates in the process and finally issues an opinion letter to the agency dealing with the approval or otherwise of the proposed activities.

As in other jurisdictions, in Japan, a plant, once operational, must not discharge pollutants in excess of national or prefectural standards. Reporting, monitoring and record retention requirements may be imposed on the plant, together with provisions relating to the release of hazardous substances. Where a plant fails to apply the relevant applicable environmental standards there may be an investigation and issuance of administrative guidance by the prefecture. The guidance may require corrective action to be taken; failure to follow the guidance may result in the issuance of an order, violation of which can result in civil or criminal penalties.

Although it is true to say that individuals or citizen groups do not appear to have the same extent of voice in Japan as in other places, they can report alleged polluters to the local government for an investigation. Another possibility is that the company may enter into a private agreement (noted further below) with individuals, groups or the local government which provides them with enforcement rights. As regards clean-up, the primary procedural means of obtaining this is by way of administrative guidance.

The Air Pollution Control Law (1968 as amended in 1970)

This Statute is concerned with ambient air quality standards in order to control emissions from plant, as well as mobile source controls. It established national emission standards for sulphur oxides, nitrogen oxides, carbon monoxide, particulate matter, photochemical oxidants and hydrocarbons. These limits may vary according to the area and type of facility.

Environmental pollution control programmes have been established by the Prefectural Governors specifying discharge limits and discharge reduction schedules for certain large facilities. Each regulated facility is given an annual discharge limit for a specific pollutant and newly constructed facilities are subject to even more stringent standards.

The owner of a plant is strictly liable for personal injuries caused by the emission of regulated air pollutants. However, this strict liability does not extend to property damage and circumstances of *force majeure*, together with any contribution from surrounding facilities, may be taken into account in assessing liability.

The Water Pollution Control Act (1970)

This Statute establishes water quality criteria for designated Public Water Areas and sets effluent standards for industries and businesses discharging certain pollutants to water. Public Water Areas include rivers, lakes, ports, harbours, coastal areas, public and irrigation waterways, and underground percolation of ground water.

The water quality criteria are intended to protect human health and the living environment. In 1978 the law was amended to require the total mass reduction of pollutants in certain areas so that large bodies of water affected by heavy population and industrialisation could be targeted such as Tokyo Bay, Ise Bay and the Inland Sea. Comparatively little attention, however, has been given to ground water pollution even though this is a major water source for Japan.

Prevention of Marine Pollution and Maritime Disaster Law

This generally prohibits the discharge of oils or oily mixtures, noxious liquid substances or waste from vessels at sea and specifies pollution control equipment for seagoing vessels. Discharge prohibitions also extend to offshore facilities. The Maritime Safety Agency enforces this law.

Waste Disposal and Public Cleaning Law (1970 as amended in 1976 and 1983)

This legislation deals with industrial and domestic solid and hazardous waste disposed in inland and coastal landfills, offshore reclamation sites and the ocean. The Ministry of Health and Welfare sets the standards for the collection, treatment, storage and disposal of solid and hazardous wastes, while the Ministry of Transport has jurisdiction over coastal reclamation and ocean dumping of waste and the EA has authority to identify substances as hazardous. The waste law extends to hazardous industrial waste and designated hazardous chemicals. The Statute requires a reduction in the amount of hazardous waste generated and the proper transportation and disposal of such waste. Generators must submit annual reports and must obtain the prefecture's permission prior to the disposal of hazardous industrial waste apart from the case of on-site disposal. The prefecture also grants permission to operate a hazardous waste treatment facility.

The Statute regulates the construction and maintenance of waste disposal facilities, the main types of waste disposal practices being inland landfills, coastal reclamation and ocean dumping. The law has been described as being less stringently regulated than, for example, the Resource Conservation and Recovery Act Programme in the US.

Chemical Substances Control Law

The manufacture, use or implementation of all chemicals is prohibited unless MITI and the Ministry of Health and Welfare have been notified. Analysis for bio-degradability, bio-accumulation and carcinogenicity must occur for all chemicals to be manufactured or imported and those that exhibit a slow rate of degradation, bio-accumulate or unknown carcinogenicity may be restricted.

Industrial Safety and Health Law (1972)

This Statute requires industrial designers, manufacturers and importers of machines or other equipment, importers of raw materials and building designers and constructors of buildings to comply with health and safety standards in order to minimise industrial accidents. The Ministry of Labour, as well as the Central Labour Standards Council administer this law. Employers must protect workers from exposure to hazardous substances by testing new chemical substances to determine if they are harmful and by monitoring air in the workplace to determine exposure levels.

Other environment related laws include the Nature Conservation Act (1972) which established an administrative framework for nature conservation and, the Pollution Related Health Damage Compensation Law (1973) which set up a system charging polluting facilities and automobile owners for the amount of pollution they generate and distributing funds to certified pollution victims (considered further later).

The enactment of the wide selection of environmental laws illustrates Japan's ability to adapt quickly once organised and motivated. Japan had one of the most complete statutory frameworks for environmental policy and some of the strictest environmental standards in the world by the mid 1970s. These laws emphasised compensation and dispute resolution and in many cases were enacted before their counterparts in the West. To understand how the law and policy evolved it is important to appreciate the division of governing powers within the Japanese system: the DIET (consisting of a House of Representatives and a House of Councillors) has the legislative powers; the Prime Minister (who is elected by the House of Representatives) has the executive power; the Supreme Court of Japan has the judicial power. In addition Japan's 47 prefectures are headed by elected governors and the municipal governments by elected mayors.

As in many parts of the world, in Japan one of the major difficulties relating to effective environmental protection has been the number of ministries involved and the lack of co-ordination among them. It is useful therefore just to run through the relevant agencies that are concerned. These are:

(1) The national government acting through agencies and ministries and the Prime Minister's Office: generally these establish environmental policy and objectives such as the establishment of air quality standards. Three main bodies regulate environmental policy: the EA, the Environmental Pollution Control Committee and the Pollution Adjusting Committee. Other ministries such as the Ministry of Health and Welfare and MITI are also involved in environmental legislation and regulating certain industries;
(2) the prefectural governments who (as seen) may set more stringent pollution standards than those in the national laws; and

(3) Municipal governments in larger cities, such as Tokyo, Osaka and Kobe which promulgate and enforce environmental laws.

The environmental ordinances of local governments are a key feature in Japan's environment policy. For example the Tokyo Metropolitan Government was ahead in enacting such ordinances, with regulations for the Control of Industrial Pollution (1949) Noise (1954), Smoke and Soot (1955) and Environmental Pollution (1969). The latter ordinance aimed to prevent and eliminate all pollution that could disrupt the quality of life of Tokyo citizens and was unique in its emphasis of environmental issues over the need for economic growth. Osaka also enacted a Pollution Prevention Ordinance in 1964 and initiated the preparation of Regional Environmental Management Plans in 1973. Indeed regional requirements are often noteworthy for their more rigid environmental standards.

Having said this, Japanese environmental policy-making has not dealt with or has misinterpreted several factors considered in other jurisdictions.

(1) Japan's environment laws still stress remedial pollution abatement measures rather than preventive measures, such as EIAs (discussed below).
(2) Public participation in policy making is very restricted and is usually limited to letters of complaint, opinion surveys and public hearings. When hearings do occur they tend to be strictly regulated explanatory sessions rather than forums for meaningful participation. In spite of continuous efforts by citizens and lawyers to introduce freedom of information legislation like that of the USA, the Government is unlikely to expand public participation because it considers that the administration can be entrusted to control pollution problems. Since most citizens have been ready to accept this view, their acceptance has generally undermined environmental protest groups.
(3) The policy appears unaware of ecological issues, with probable grave implications for nature conservation. The Basic Law defines pollution as air, water and soil pollution, noise, vibration, land subsidence and offensive odours while omitting radioactivity. It highlights known pollution causes which affect human health and the living environment without considering eco-system degradation unless it affects human health. (Although some local authorities have adopted a wider definition, such as that of the Tokyo Metropolitan Government which defines pollution as "any infringement on the environment" and applies to yet unknown forms of pollution.)
(4) Whereas, as seen below, Japan has raised its level of international activity since UNCED Japan has, historically, failed adequately to

> consider global environmental issues and has been reluctant to control environmentally destructive activities of Japanese companies overseas. Environmental laws have not been interpreted to apply outside Japan and administrative guidance has not covered external environmental issues. (It should be noted that Japan, in its National Report to UNCED 1992, has sought to raise its awareness of international environmental obligations, as well as the domestic environmental requirements).

The ways in which environmental policy is implemented in Japan include:

- Administrative guidance;
- compensation system;
- environmental monitoring;
- environmental standards;
- nature conservation;
- pollution control agreements; and
- regional pollution control programmes.

Methods of enforcement

The four main methods of enforcement of environmental legislation are detailed below.

Administrative guidance

Following Japanese history and tradition, in practice Japanese environmental agencies enforce the environmental laws primarily through administrative guidance. This is an informal, non-authoritative process whereby the Government aims to enlist industry's voluntary co-operation. It involves discussions and consultations and may take the form of non-written directions, requests, warnings, suggestions or encouragement. A Government agency may well issue a number of administrative guidances before any formal enforcement action is taken. The reason, of course, is that Japanese bureaucracy has possessed greater power than, for instance, American bureaucracy because the orders of Government officials were considered to be almost equivalent to the rule of law; judicial review of these orders was carefully circumscribed. In addition Japanese culture has placed considerable emphasis on governmental decision-making through consensus. It should also be noted that Japanese industry tends to comply with administrative guidance because the Government has extensive discretionary authority over the issue of environmental permits (referred to above) required for the operation of a plant. As a result any violator may find it difficult to obtain the future co-operation of the Government. Historically, therefore, because of the shared basic objective of Government and industry relating to post-war economic rehabilitation, there is relatively little formal administrative or judicial environmental enforcement in Japan. The growing emphasis on environmental protection and awareness has, however, meant an increase in the formal enforcement mechanism although the basic administrative guidance concept remains deeply rooted in Japanese bureaucracy.

Private agreements

These are often used to achieve environmental controls whether between individuals or citizen groups and companies. They result from private party negotiations or from the initiation of civil litigation; Government agencies generally do not rely on these agreements.

Criminal enforcement

Many of Japan's individual pollution control statutes provide for criminal enforcement and the umbrella law—the Law for the Punishment of Crimes Relating to Environmental Pollution—makes endangering as well as harming the environment a criminal offence, establishes a presumption of causation and provides for punishment of both the individual and the corporation. However, such provisions are rarely used in Japan. Here again the main reason is a strong tendency to rely on negotiation and administrative guidance and to avoid direct coercive measures. In addition criminal enforcement requires referral of the matter to prosecutorial agencies with a corresponding loss of control by the bureaucracy. In general the agencies regard the guidance as much more effective than lengthy criminal trials.

The Pollution Dispute Settlement Act

This Act, which was passed in 1970 in an effort to codify environmental mediation and dispute resolution procedures, is primarily aimed at the resolution of complaints by citizens against pollution sources. Relief can include the abatement of pollution and compensation. One of the major objectives of this law is to balance the bargaining powers of the parties. Every prefecture has a councillor who acts as an advisor to obtain information and expert assistance and to make an independent assessment of the facts. These councillors have been effective in assisting citizens to obtain relief.

The alliance between Government and industry

One of the crucial points which comes out of the examination of Japanese environmental protection is the alliance between Government and industry. To illustrate both the national and international ramifications of such an alliance one can look at Japan's "new approach" to CFCs – the decision to phase out ozone depleting chemicals by the end of 1995 (the international comment occurs below). MITI hurried to set the deadline earlier to bring Japan into line with Europe and the USA because both the regulators and the regulated appeared to be whole-heartedly in favour of this target. In the car industry Honda Motor was the latest large corporation to set the 1995 deadline following Nissan's deadline of the end of 1994. Meanwhile Toyota announced the official deadline of the end of 1995. Further, in electronics, Nippon Electric Corporation (NEC) which has claimed to have been the first Japanese company to set up an environmental control division in August 1970, intends to be on schedule to eliminate all CFCs in production processes by March 1995; its competitors generally have announced the year's end even prior to the Government's new approach.

MITI has encouraged companies to exchange information on environmental protection measures. The head of NEC's environmental engineering subsidiary has said that informal contacts have already taken place between Toshiba, NEC and Fujitsu on environmental matters and governmental approval has been given to such contacts taking place. In addition the Government has assisted second and third tiers of the Japanese economy and small firms, in view of the recession. The initiative of interest free loans for investments that reduce consumption of ozone damaging chemicals has ensured that industry has not argued against deadlines. The power industry provides another example of cross industry collaboration: nine electricity generators have set up a group to prepare policies on carbon dioxide emissions. (Further comments on corporate initiative occurs below in the discussion on recent developments.)

Prognosis regarding Japan's environmental policy

Whereas the EA was created to ensure an integrated environmental policy as yet this policy has been concerned with the protection of human life and health and with the abatement of damage caused by environmental pollution, causing it to rely excessively on technological aspects of pollution control. In addition Japan has been seen to want to export this approach to developing nations, supporting the idea that only money and technology are needed to solve global environmental problems. In order to achieve sustainable development, however, a fundamental change in values is required.

Unfortunately, however, no consensus exists about the nature of an environmentally sound economy nor has there been any real blueprint for an alternative approach to decision making. Moreover there has been no authentic political leadership on environmental issues and political activity is seldom tuned into the public interest. Indeed the ruling party has equated public interest with economic growth. Although recommendations had been made from 1972 concerning the need for anticipative and preventive policies the EA report of 1981 noted that very little progress had in fact been made. Although there have been some improvements regarding pollution research and monitoring and concerning the intervention of local governments and in expanding participation, the essential problem remained that neither the EA nor local government had the power to forbid environmentally structured projects from being built in relatively clean areas nor their further concentration into already polluted areas.

Within the Government itself, there has been a problem in the sheer number of bodies involved in planning and paying for activities to improve the environment. For instance, a study by a Government audit agency found that 17 state supported bodies were organising environmental research, many with overlapping programmes. Government policy on hazardous substances is complicated by the involvement of three Government agencies: MITI, the Ministry of Health and Welfare and the EA.

At the international level Japan's failure to ratify the Basel Convention on Toxic Waste Shipments is a case in point to show the struggle between the different agencies. The three Ministries still argue over whose responsibility it would be to enforce the law. The creation of a single powerful environment ministry would solve some of these problems. However MITI, which carries huge political clout as the architect of Japan's economic miracle, is still fighting this suggestion.

Insofar as Japan's environmental policy only defines pollution in terms of human health its scope and effectiveness has not been fully realised, and a real consensus at the national level has not occurred. The history of the development of EIA, as well as discussion of recent environmental issues (below) in Japan illustrate the problems and opportunities that the process of improving environmental policy faces.

Environmental impact assessment

A discussion of EIAs is clearly relevant to the construction industry. It has already been commented that cultural issues are significant in the development of environmental protection; this comment is very well illustrated in the instance of environmental impact assessment. In the traditional Japanese view environmental preservation is not "right" in the same sense as western societies view it. Therefore an essentially western concept like EIA which emphasises protecting the natural environment from human destruction could not have been imported into Japan without some adaptation. As a result the "Japanised" EIA has become a much weaker version in comparison with that of the West. If one is to consider the goal of EIAs to be that of preventing environmental damage according to some schools of thought an ideal EIA system would:

(1) apply to all projects anticipated as having a significant environmental impact and address all such significant impacts;
(2) compare alternatives to the proposed project, management techniques and mitigation measures;
(3) include wide public participation and stringent administrative review procedures;
(4) include monitoring and feedback procedures;
(5) have a timetable which provides information for decision-making;
(6) be enforceable; and
(7) end in a clear statement which conveys the importance of the likely impacts and the specific characteristics to non-experts as well as experts.

Such an ideal system may be reflected upon when considering Japan's system. As is clear from the discussion below relating to a comprehensive Green Bill initiative, EIA in Japan does not have a legal basis partly because of the Japanese preference for administrative guidance and non-interventionism, bearing in mind the close relationship between industry and the government. Whereas there have been recent efforts to make EIAs compulsory, the close link between industry and government has ensured that such an initiative has failed and therefore the list of projects subject to the EIA remains severely limited. When comparing the projects with those covered under the EC directive and environmental assessment it should be noted that the following types of development which are considered to have a significant environmental impact under European law are not subject to Japan's national EIA procedures:

- crude oil refineries;
- installations for extracting and processing asbestos;
- installations for storing and disposing of radioactive waste;
- integrated chemical installations;
- integrated works for the initial smelting of cast iron and steel;
- thermal and nuclear power stations;
- trading ports.

Furthermore, whereas the European directive lists eighty types of development which may have significant environmental effect and should be assessed if the Member State considers their characteristics are required, only eight of these are covered by Japan's national guidelines.

It should be noted, however, that Japan's local authority EIAs do tend to be more comprehensive than the national system (and therefore take longer) and apply to:

- recreation facilities;
- waste treatment facilities;
- ports and harbours;
- factories;
- distribution centres;
- redevelopment projects; and
- power plants.

Nevertheless there is not any real examination of environmental consequences of policy options. Since assessment occurs at the project stage of the planning process any alternatives would have long been discarded despite the introduction by local authorities of a system of environmental management based on the concept of carrying capacity which integrates the EIA and environmental monitoring. Another form of assessment would include a two-tier arrangement in terms of major resource projects to include aims, demand forecast, safety and environmental protection in the first stage and the repercussions of individual projects in the second stage.

Insofar as Japan has shown a greater concern with human health impact and pollution control than with the natural environment the national guidelines do not cover accidents, radioactivity, impediment to television and sunshine reception, cultural heritage, the maintenance of mixed natural/man-made scenery or long-term and cumulative effects of pollution. Although socio-economic factors are touched upon, their in-depth assessment is not thought necessary as they are sensitive issues closely related to costs, benefits and distribution. It has been argued that socio-economic impact assessments might give local residents too much control over the way forward for projects and that since the role of an EIA is to look at negative aspects of development—while the economic effects are usually regarded as positive in Japan—an assessment would not be required.

Since there is no requirement to look at alternatives the developer has no incentive to consider less environmentally damaging developments or management methods, or the possibility of not developing. Moreover the approach of major Japanese construction companies is to solve environmental problems by adding enough pollution control measures rather than to consider any alternative developments. Again this indicates Japan's views of the roles of economic development and environmental policy: development is considered necessary and environmental policy merely counteracts its negative effect.

It should be said that the EIA system is improved by its higher degree of technical sophistication because Japan has very advanced systems of data collection, analysis and simulation. In addition environmental monitoring is well established. On the other hand, the level of public participation illustrates how Japan still does not see this as necessary in terms of a more environmentally and socially conscious decision-making, in strong contrast to the West. Both the role of public participation (to provide information to decision makers rather than helping to set policy) and the mode of public participation (inspection and comment often occurring after the decision-making process) have narrowed the potential of the EIA. A further weakness of the EIA system as it stands is that public hearings are often so formal and given at such short notice that any opponents cannot prepare for them adequately in terms of large national projects. Although local authorities generally have more open decision-making, more public involvement, and more accountability, the EIA does not seem to have affected the development of any of the projects under its scrutiny. Indeed since local governments rely to a large extent on national funding and often there is a close link between industry and the national Government, the projects are often judged by ministries which are intrinsically in favour of economic development and therefore of the project. Indeed review by the EA (which is the only agency concerned purely with environmental protection) is only at the request of the concerned ministry and only after the final Environmental Impact Statement has been completed and made public; as the EA's advice is usually not in the best interest of the concerned ministry, it is unlikely to ask for such a review. In addition, the EA is sensitive to its negative image among the ministries and tries to accommodate them.

Whereas in the US the Freedom of Information Act has played a key role in opening up the decision-making process, Japan has no equivalent although some local authorities have produced their own version. Indeed in Japan EIA has not altered the balance of power in this process and is often seen merely as a form of project justification.

Finally, Japan's EIA procedures are often unnecessarily complex, non-uniform and duplicative, varying purely on the basis of geographical location without real co-ordination. For the developer and government, the system ensures that environmental factors are considered in the decision-making process without undue delay and cost. The imposition of strict time scales with a "go-ahead" default gives the developer much power and eases administrative responsibilities. In contrast the US system with its minimum time scales and "stop" default leads to frequent and costly delays in project implementation, uncertainty about approval of the projects and more administrative work. Environmental groups would obviously prefer a system like that of the US whose process of scoping and timing enable a more comprehensive analysis of a project's environmental impact negotiation and administrative guidance. Legally speaking mandatory EIA systems also offer more citizen control and guidelines. In addition, although the principle of EIA in Japan is fairly well established the practice is far from satisfactory insofar as it is often used as a tool to justify development and overcome local opposition. As most impact studies tend to conclude that the project's environmental impact will be small the consideration of long term environmentally detrimental effect seems to be a side issue.

A bill for a new law that would have mandated environmental impact reports prior to starting major construction projects was abandoned at the end of March of this year (see Appendix III). The Bill had been re-submitted to the Diet in March by the EA. However, evidently the EA signed an official Government memo through the persuasion of dissenting Government ministries and agencies promising that the bill would not be put before the Diet any time in the near future. The original submission of the bill, which provides for a new environmental standard law, was in 1981. The EA had intended that the bill would serve as the basis of Japan's environmental policies. Although the Agency was apparently keen to legalise environmental assessment within the context of its comprehensive Green Bill evidently the demands of other Government bodies and influential industry lobbyists forced it to concede. In particular the Construction, International Trade and Industry and other ministries and agencies opposed mandatory environmental assessments and even opposed the bill as re-submitted which in fact stopped short of a legal requirement. The ministries and agencies have argued that the step might trigger a barrage of law suits aimed at stopping construction projects and make large projects extremely difficult. Although the EA has made a verbal pledge not to introduce such legislation in the near future the Deputy Director General of the EA had denied at a news conference hearing of such an accord.

Recent trends

General awareness

A growing environmental awareness has led varying grass root projects from a debate over a proposed national green tax to proposals for making the country more eco-friendly in terms of the use of recycled paper (for such items as toilet tissue) to writing the comprehensive environmental legislation. The Government had planned to lay a new green foundation under the nation's economy, key elements being the institution of a system of deposits on product containers, imposing a green tax, as well as the requirement of the EIAs. Container deposits would be added on to the prices of various products and refunds on the return of empty containers made in a manner similar to the systems already in existence for bottles and cans in US and parts of Europe. However, the idea to regulate carbon dioxide emissions by imposing a levy on fossil fuels (the consumption of which generates most of Japan's carbon dioxide emissions), was opposed by industrial leaders and MITI. Whereas the EA was convinced that no harmful economic effects would occur with careful planning, industry and MITI remained convinced that the tax would affect Japan's international competitiveness. This again has demonstrated the battle between MITI and the environmental policy making. The Ministry has in fact supported the raising of the existing energy tax and use of the revenue to develop energy saving technology. While the EA officials were able to argue that a green tax would actually improve corporate investment in anti-pollution measures and that the pollution control technology would raise product quality and create new markets—just as it has done in the US and European markets—the industrial leaders and MITI did not accept the tax proposal. Although the Ministry of Finance did cautiously support the green tax concept it preferred to use revenues for general rather than green purposes largely because of the poor state of the economy and the possibility of igniting a debate about totally overhauling the national tax system.

Whereas environmentally unfriendly principles of mass production and consumerism have been flourishing in Japan, it is to be noted that more and more municipal governments and citizens are demonstrating an increased awareness which the Government and industrialists should well take note of. To give a few examples:

(1) Shoppers in Tachikawa in suburban Tokyo can pick Tachikawa original brand toilet paper made from the city's re-cycled milk cartons. The local government has stocked schools and municipal offices with the tissue since 1991, the manufacture of which is contracted out to local paper makers.

(2) In March of this year a strong anti-dam movement emerged to demonstrate concern at the threat to the Nagara Rivers' ecosystem. This again exposed the ties between the bureaucrats, the politicians and the construction companies in Japan. Engineering experts agreed

with the Construction Ministry's assessment that the dam at Nagashima was required for flood control purposes while the outcry has demonstrated an increase in environmental awareness in the country. It has been suggested that possibly the cost of Japan's phenomenal economic progress has been too high and that people are realising now what it exacted in environmental and social terms.

(3) In April of this year the Neguro Ward in Tokyo opened a Re-cycle Plaza where re-cycled goods are sold and broken furniture is mended.

(4) In Nagoya the local government covers the costs of re-cycling for shopping areas that collect waste and try to do away with surplus packaging.

(5) Simultaneously Tokyo, Chiba Prefecture, Hokkaido and other regions are moving on with ambitious plans to use heat generated in urban areas as an energy source to operate air conditioning systems.

(6) Kanagowa Prefecture is trying to harness energy from sunlight and rainwater.

(7) Local governments fairly often try to use electric vehicles and methanol powered autos for official transportation.

(8) Six prefectures including Tokyo and Osaka will start loaning less polluting cars to local businesses this year with the support of the EA.

(9) Authorities in Wakayama, south of Osaka, and in Kitano in Fukuoka Prefecture are toughening the penalties for litterbugs.

(10) Other municipal bodies have been looking overseas for co-operation with their green efforts.

(11) Last August the city of Kitakyushu commenced an "International Environment Co-operation Centre" and a "Maintenance Co-operation Centre" to foster anti-pollution technologies developed jointly with local companies and to take on trainees from developing countries. This city, an industrial town, was commended at the Rio Earth Summit for its commitment to combating its serious pollution problems.

(12) This summer the Government acknowledged the expanding national role of non-government organisations in environmental conservation by setting up a funding system for those involved in green efforts. Whereas independent civic organisations are less involved in environmental protection in Japan than in the US and Europe an increasing number of Japanese businesses are donating part of their revenues to such groups. In June the Government held the symposium at the request of NGOs that attended the Earth Summit to examine the extent of progress made on projects agreed at the summit.

(13) Analysts have warned that it is increasingly necessary for Japanese politicians at least to appear "green" as voters have grown increasingly worried about environmental issues. According to a Prime Minister's Office Survey released on May 31 1992 91.7% of the 3,754 citizens polled in February of that year expressed concern about the present or future state of the global environment. "The survey shows a high degree of concern in the environment" an EA official said "however, when it comes to action, the situation is less than satisfactory".

(14) It should also be noted that the development of next generation transport systems and environmentally friendly technologies have been proposed as opportunities in the recovery in Japan's economy. In order to cope with global environmental issues development and transfer of technology are considered essential. The UNEP Governing Council approved a Japanese proposal that an international environmental technology centre of UNEP should be established in Japan in May 1991. This centre was intended to focus on environmentally sustainable management of big cities and fresh water lakes/ reservoir basins. It would provide training and consulting services and establish a database, using appropriate technologies from all over the world.

(15) Very recently, there has also been disappointment over the EA's rejection of a proposal to conduct priority monitoring of three Japanese wetlands that may be endangered. Despite the suggestion of the Ramsar Bureau (which administers the International Ramsar Treaty on Wetlands and Water Fowl Protection) the Japanese Government decided not to place the wetlands on the Montreux record, a list of Ramsar sites where ecological changes merit priority monitoring and therefore nothing could be done. The EA has said that no marked environmental damage has been observed.

Corporate awareness

Companies are starting to monitor their own efforts at protecting the environment largely through pressure from international initiatives. They have been setting up internal bodies to check on their own protection efforts in industries such as electrical machinery, electrical power, construction and textiles by responding to the global environment charter established by the Federation of Economic Organisations (Keidanran) in 1991 and the work of the Rio Summit 1992.

Corporate environmental activities differ from company to company but they include updating the end of the use of CFC gases as noted above, accelerating the re-cycling of used paper and plastics and enforcement of afforestation projects. As regards forests, Japan had promoted the idea of an "international charter for the world's forests" at the first session of the UNEP preparatory committee in August 1990. This would be a non-binding instrument including basic principles and initiatives to be taken for the conservation and sustainable development of forests. The essential philosophy behind a non-binding instrument is to adopt a practical step by step approach so as to avoid prolonged negotiations which might hinder the timely action. Regarding tropical forests, evidently Japan has been increasing its assistance to the ITTO (located in Yokohama Japan) whose main task is to promote sustainable trade in tropical timber and to develop and conserve tropical forests in order to maintain their eco-systems. As noted above, Japan has shown a commitment to promote mobilisation of financial resources to assist developing countries in tackling environmental problems. The Japanese delegation of UNEP has expressed the view that the financial and institutional aspects should be integral parts of the conventions to be adopted (see Appendix I and II).

As has been discussed, recycling initiatives have become very important in Japan and a law concerning the promotion of utilisation of recycled resources was approved by the Diet and promulgated on April 26 1991. An amendment to the law concerning waste disposal was approved and promulgated on October 5 1991. This new statute requires citizens and certain industrial operators to comply with the programmes and measures initiated or taken by the State and municipalities for the reduction and recycling of waste materials. Industrial operators are required to present a prior assessment of the feasibility of recycling or proper disposal of waste products.

As seen earlier, corporate targets are usually provided in concrete numerical terms. As noted, Toshiba has worked out an action programme intended to abolish totally CFCs in the fiscal 1993 and a 30% reduction of industrial waste emissions from the fiscal 1990 level. The company will expand the annual internal monitoring already being carried out by its environment control centre at each plant to cover office buildings and research facilities within its annual internal monitoring. It will rate them in regard to about 100 items and site facilities that score high points. The company is encouraging all employees to do their part in the environmental campaign. Sharp Corporation will introduce fully fledged monitoring in the fiscal year 1994. Tokyo Gas Company intends to introduce a monitoring system in this fiscal year.

All of these initiatives are based on internal inspections rather than external agency monitoring on the basis that details can be better checked and to avoid the leak of industrial secrets. Bearing in mind the need for objective conclusions, there is some concern, however, that third party inspection, which is common in the US and the EC, has not been adopted. There is a desire that an independent organisation should be set up by the private sector in Japan. Meanwhile Tokyo Electric Power Company has adopted a two-way approach to this: it has scheduled to set up an advisory council consisting of 20 outsiders to check the monitoring done by an internal environmental committee.

Environmental auditing is quite new in the local market although some local and foreign firms have begun to use audits to assess and minimise future liabilities. Certain pre-purchase audits have occurred on sites. National standards for air and water pollution are not the final word because each prefecture and municipality has the right to use their own stricter limits for effluent and emission discharges. Companies intending to establish new industrial facilities must negotiate an environmental agreement with the prefecture or municipal government. In addition the new recycling laws introduced in 1991 place a greater burden on business to minimise waste within the production process and produce recyclable products.

Although many major Japanese trading houses and manufacturing companies have established environment management divisions or R&D sections these are largely seen as a public relations or business development tool.

Liability for environmental damage : recent case law

Although, generally speaking, case law has not been highlighted in this paper, it is relevant when considering liability for environmental damage. Under Japanese law this is based on the civil code and certain laws regarding pollution, which determine civil, criminal and administrative liability. The many cases of environmental damage to persons and property have resulted in Japanese judges interpreting the laws in favour of the injured parties. As a result the laws concerning air and water pollution discussed earlier have been amended so that the polluter is liable for any damage even in cases where it is not his fault. As regards bodily harm the principle of strict liability applies while in other cases the fault of the polluter has to be proven. In order to improve the injured party's position Japanese law has developed two theories, that of tolerance limits and of the probability theory. The first theory means that certain nuisances must be tolerated by people and if these are exceeded the injured party may take legal action, the limits being determined according to the nature of the damage. Such limits may be bodily harm, damage to property or nervous shock. The second theory means that the injured party only has to show the possibility of the existence of the causal link between the wrongful act and the damage itself.

Where the polluters are not identifiable there is a compensation fund which gives immediate assistance to all parties who have suffered bodily injury. Under the Japanese law of October 5 1973 (amended in 1988) on compensation for bodily injury resulting from pollution, any injured party suffering damage to health caused by water or air pollution receives compensation, after examination by a board, without having to identify the person responsible or prove any fault. The fund is constituted from levies on pollutant emissions and from a proportion of the tax on motor vehicles. Compensation is automatic, however, only in major risk areas and for specifically listed illnesses. (It should be emphasised that whereas concern for public health rates high in Japan the natural environment has suffered although the 1988 amendment did focus more on the prevention of pollution by the establishment of a pollution prevention fund).

As stated, mention should be made here of the relevant Japanese case law as an important second tier to Japanese legislation. In particular, a recent decision—on March 29 1991—in the Osaka District Court, the *Nishi-Yodogawa Air Pollution* case. Nishi-Yodogawa has been designated one of the worst atmospherically polluted areas in Japan and a suit was filed by 117 residents against 10 corporations operating in the area, the State of Japan and the Public Highway Authority, claiming a total of 2.8 billion Yen as compensation, and requesting an injunction regarding omissions of certain chemical substances into the atmosphere. The 117 residents were patients and their heirs designated under the Law on Pollution Related Health Damage Compensation. This case involved extremely difficult causation problems, including the relationship between the local air pollution and emissions from the defendants' corporations' factories on the one hand and Emissions from the vehicle traffic on the highways controlled by the defendants' state and the public authority on the other, as well as between ambient pollution (sulphur oxide, particulate matter and nitrogen oxide) and the plaintiffs' impaired health. While the court did not accept the plaintiffs' assertions that the factories had been the major cause of the pollution, nevertheless it was held that the corporations were liable as joint tortfeasors. Thus the court accepted a portion of the plaintiffs' claim for compensation while dismissing the request for an injunction. (This case is subject to appeal in the Osaka High Court).

Closing remarks

It should be recalled that the regulatory national pollution standards are only guidelines—the actual regulations that local and foreign factories must follow are set by the prefecture or municipal authorities in a pollution control agreement with the company involved. These are generally stricter for new plants and usually go beyond the national guidelines. Local authorities base their standards on national figures together with whatever is necessary to maintain what they judge to be an acceptable level of pollution for their particular area.

As elsewhere, benefits from tougher regulations have been offset by steadily increasing pollution levels. For example, while the 1970 Water Pollution Control Law has been amended several times, waste water loads from urban areas have also increased and the infrastructure cannot cope, despite the trend toward drafting new laws and regulations to deal with pollution issues. Here again, MITI and the Ministry of Health and Welfare seem to vie with the EA in terms of the legislation. Nevertheless, overall business will be forced to become less wasteful in its use of resources which will probably increase costs in the short term, but should result in long term savings. It should also be noted that, given the current renewed concern for the environment arising from global and local pollution problems, the outlook for the Japanese environmental goods and services market may well rise significantly: Crédit Suisse estimates that it will rise to yen 10.15 trillion by the year 2000—an annual average growth rate of 5.2%. A final point is that while the majority of future investment will be in industrial waste management, municipal refuse collection and disposal and sewage collection and treatment, foreign pollution control firms will have difficulty in obtaining a market there. Japan prides itself on its own technological development and its waste management market is controlled by the central and municipal governments who are generally more comfortable doing business with Japanese firms.

Addendum

In preparing my paper for the Sixth Annual Construction Conference, I am greatly indebted to the enormous help I received from Dr Linda Spedding, an International Law Consultant to Masons, together with assistance from our Hong Kong Office and in particular their Japanese-speaking solicitors.

In collating my material I was struck by three themes which not only highlighted certain aspects of the Japanese approach to environmental management but also reflected the variety of attitudes which exist through the international community. I raise the following three points with a view to encouraging debate beyond the Conference about the existence of different approaches to environmental law:

- compliance versus enforcement;
- the preventative approach versus "end of pipe" solutions; and
- a strong environmental agency versus "administrative guidance".

Compliance versus enforcement

There seem to be two fundamental approaches which can be adopted in relation to the application of environmental legislation—that which relies upon compliance, and that which assumes the necessity of enforcement. As is apparent from Jack Kannry's paper, the USA adopts a fairly tough enforcement approach to the environment through use of a strong Environmental Protection Agency. Meanwhile Europe tends to adopt a mixture of the two approaches, as is evidenced by the UK which has fairly tough enforcement agencies such as the National Rivers Authority and to a lesser extent, Her Majesty's Inspectorate of Pollution, yet in the area of health and safety the compliance approach tends to be favoured by the Health & Safety Executive. In addition, there are a number of voluntary schemes encouraging compliance, in particular, the Responsible Care Programme initiated by the Chemical Industries Association. The Dutch Government has recently developed an initiative which relies heavily on the compliance approach, and encourages industry to buy into improved environmental performance by negotiating discharge permits in return for long-term commitment to overall emission reductions. In its Fifth Action Programme the European Commission stresses the importance of shared responsibility in relation to sustainable development; if sustainable development is to be achieved, all sectors of society must be committed to that end, which tends to favour voluntary compliance rather than external enforcement.

As a nation, Japan relies heavily on the compliance approach to environmental law. Since World War II, development of its economy has been a key goal, and although the 1960s and 1970s saw a number of toxic tort problems which resulted in a lot of fairly stringent legislation not dissimilar to UK legislation of the time—the Control of Pollution Act 1974 and the Health and Safety at Work Act 1974—it is only recently that the environment has become a major political issue. Since 1967 an Environmental Pollution Control Act has been in force and in 1971 Japan created an Environmental Agency. However, the Environmental Agency is not the sole agency concerned with environmental matters and it has no overall control. While local authorities have played a leading role in development of environmental policy at a local level, their powers too are restricted. A difficult consensus has to be sorted out before environmental laws can be implemented, initially between the Environmental Agency, the other ministries and local government and then between the polluter and the regional administrator. In practice, Japanese environmental agencies seek to enforce environmental law primarily through administrative guidance in accordance with Japanese history and tradition. This is an informal, non-authoritative process whereby the Government seeks to induce industry's voluntary co-operation. It involves discussions and consultations and may take the form of non-written directions, requests, warnings, suggestions or encouragement. Government agencies may well issue a number of administrative "guidances" before any formal enforcement action is taken. The reason for this stems from the fact that historically, Japanese bureaucracy generally possesses greater power than, for instance, that of America; orders from Government officials are considered to be virtually equivalent to the rule of law, and judicial review of these orders is carefully circumscribed. Furthermore, Japanese culture places considerable emphasis on governmental decision-making through consensus.

It should also be noted that Japanese industry tends to comply with administrative guidance because the Government has extensive discretionary authority over the issue of environmental authorisations required for the the operation of a plant. As a result, any violating organisation will find it difficult to obtain the future co-operation of the Government. Thus there has tended to be relatively little formal administrative or judicial enforcement in Japan because of the shared objective between the Government and industry relating to post-war economic rehabilitation. The growing world emphasis on environmental protection has, however, meant an increase in formal enforcement mechanisms although the basic concept of administrative guidance remains deeply rooted in Japanese bureaucracy.

The preventative approach versus "end of pipe" solutions

One of the most significant factors in this debate is the changing attitude towards increased openness in the decision-making process in relation to the environment. In America there is already a considerable body of law relating to freedom of access to information, and Europe is fast following along similar lines. The EC's Fifth Environmental Action Programme stipulates that the general public should be viewed as a resource not as a nuisance, and in the United Kingdom we have seen the recent introduction of the Environmental Information Regulations which are intended to implement the Freedom of Access to Information Directive.

However, as has been discussed, Japan has a rather fragmented system of regulatory control which tends to mean that opportunities for public participation are limited. Furthermore, industry and government alike each have a long history of rating achievement of economic goals as a priority, which tends to discourage allocation of resources to improving public awareness of commercial activities. Japan has no equivalent of the US Freedom of Information Act, although regionally some local authorities have sought to produce their own version. In the UK, planning and development is perhaps the area which provides the greatest opportunity for public participation during the decision-making process, particularly where Environmental Impact Assessments are involved. However, Japan's planning process involves the imposition of strict timescales, with a "go ahead" default which gives the developer considerable power and eases administrative responsibilities. This is to be contrasted with the US system with its minimum timescales and "stop" default which often lead to frequent and costly delays in project implementation, uncertainty about approval of the project and additional administrative burdens.

The area of environmental impact assessment provides an example of the way in which Japan has tended to prefer "end-of-pipe" solutions to adoption of a more preventative approach. In contrast, Europe is committed to this latter approach, as demonstrated by the new Directive on Environmental Impact Assessment. In Japan there is no such legal requirement, although environmental impact assessments for a very limited range of projects are the subject of administrative guidance. Generally speaking, development in Japan is considered necessary and environmental policy merely aims to counteract any negative effect it might have. Since there is no requirement to look at alternatives, the developer has no incentive to consider less environmentally-damaging developments or management methods, or even the possibility of not developing a particular site at all. Moreover, the approach of major

Japanese construction companies to dealing with environmental problems tends to revolve around "bolting on" pollution control measures rather than considering any other alternative development. This enables industry to push ahead with the knowledge that should an environmental difficulty arise, a technical solution must be found. This approach is felt to be preferable to becoming immersed in bureaucracy with the risk that a development will be further delayed because of detailed environmental considerations and consultations.

The third area to consider in the context of this section is the influence of law in management systems. Europe is moving towards the implementation of management systems by way of a legal requirement as a means of enforcing a more preventative approach. A potential difficulty with regulatory law is the enormous cost of enforcement in the event of non-compliance. To prevent the problem at the outset (thereby reducing the enforcement cost) good management systems are being encouraged. On a voluntary basis Europe has already witnessed a number of different standards which have been produced with the aim of ensuring good management practices, such as BS5750, BS7750, and the ISO9000 series. However, management obligations are now beginning to be imposed by law. An example is the EC Construction Sites Directive, which is to be implemented in the UK by the 1992 Construction (Design and Management) Regulations. To a certain extent, one can see a similar approach applied in respect of public procurement and the management of tendering procedures. There is also the new voluntary scheme introduced by the EC's Eco Audit and Eco Management Regulation which the Commission has indicated may become compulsory in five years' time if there is not sufficient industry interest in the Scheme.

Japan has no legal requirements in respect of management systems. Its economic goals are, for the most part, founded within the culture of total quality management (TQM), which has become an essential part of the philosophy of Japanese industry and therefore a legal requirement to support this philosophy is not required. However, what is interesting is the fact that the environment is rarely seen to have a part to play within the TQM culture because it does not have prominence as a "stakeholder" in Japanese organisations, as is increasingly the case elsewhere in the business world. As TQM principles are based on "what the customer wants", Japan seems unlikely to change in this regard until its customers begin to demand that the environment is viewed as a priority stakeholder in all industrial activities. Seeing the relatively low level of public participation and limited access to information in the Japanese environmental arena, changes in this area are not like to occur overnight.

A strong environmental agency versus "administrative guidance"

As evidenced again by Jack Kannry's paper, it is apparent that America has a very strong environmental agency. Europe is now in the process of establishing a European Environmental Agency and the UK is anticipating the merger of HMIP and NRA to form one environmental agency by 1995. How powerful these agencies will be in reality remains to be seen, but current indications suggest that they will take their role very seriously and will seek to become more powerful in their enforcement of environmental laws. Cynics might suggest that funding of the UK agency will be determined by the degree to which it is deemed to be a "success", which may well be judged in terms of the number of successful prosecutions it achieves in a given financial year. Certainly the US EPA is very "result-oriented" in order to ensure continuing Government support for its operations.

Inevitably agencies under pressure to get results in order to keep going will become increasingly aggressive and enforcement-oriented. This is in sharp contrast with Japan where the various agencies with environmental responsibilities tend to be fairly weak in comparison to the Government and the variety of industrial lobby groups, such as that of the construction industry. "Administrative guidance" is about the use of negotiation and compromise to achieve compliance, which is very different from the distancing effect achieved by environmental agencies in other parts of the world who tend to be unwilling to give industry advice on compliance, particularly where they recognise a breach of regulations has occurred.

Conclusion

There must be an increasing risk that with so much regulatory law emanating from Brussels one may place too much of a legal stranglehold around industry and create too many administrative barriers to allow Member States to trade and to develop effectively. Signs of the resulting frustration which is developing are beginning to manifest themselves: the UK Government's drive towards deregulation, and its attitude to Europe's inability to sign the Uruguay round of the GATT talks because of one Member State's difficulty, in particular, over its farming lobby are both examples of this mounting pressure. Japan, however, with its "administrative guidance" approach, has not become immersed in regulatory law. It pushes ahead with development and seeks, when required, "bolt-on" solutions to environmental problems. Although many pressure groups are critical of Japan, their approach does have the benefit of speed. At a time when many people believe that the planet has a very short fuse in terms of global energy use, limited natural resources and population explosion, Japan's approach may have more to recommend it than perhaps many of its critics believe. From Europe's point of view, the desire to legislate as a means of environmental control, however well-intended and commendable, may be viewed as the slippery slope to total immersion in bureaucracy, rather than a means of pioneering solutions to the many environmental problems facing us today.

Appendix I

Key International Conventions on the Environment

	Organ	*Made*	*In Effect*		*Amended*
Intervention Convention, Brussels		1969	1975		
Conference on the Human Environment, Stockholm	UN		1972		
London Dumping Convention			*1972*		*1979*
Cultural and Heritage Convention, Paris			1972		
Oslo Convention			1972	1975	
CITES, Washington				1973	
MARPOL, London				1973	1978
Paris Convention			1974	1978	
Geneva Convention	UNECE			1979	1983
Bonn Convention				1979	
Environmental Program Session, Nairobi	UN			1982	
UNCLOS, Montego Bay	UN			1982	
Protocol on Oil Spills in the Caribbean, Cartagena			1983	1988	
Vienna Convention	UN		1985		
Helsinki Protocol	UNECE			1985	
Montreal Protocol	*UN*		*1987*	*1989*	*1990*
Sofia Protocol	UNECE			1988	
Lome IV Convention, Togo			1989	1991	
International Convention on Salvage				1989	
Basel Convention	UN			1989	
Bergen Conference	UN			1990	
Amendments to the Montreal Protocol	*UN*		*1990*	*1992*	
Convention on E.I.A., Espoo, Finland	UN		1991		
Convention on the North East Atlantic		1992	1992		

Those to which Japan is a signatory or which concern Japan are indicated in italic type.

Appendix II

Specific conventions and international instruments affecting Japan

London Dumping Convention

Convention on the Prevention of Marine Pollution by Dumping of Waste 1972, amended 1979.

The amendments are addressed chiefly to the industrialised West and Japan.

The Convention convened with representatives from: Western industrialised nations, Eastern Bloc, and developing nations, as well as non-governmental organisations (NGOs), governmental organisations and UN organisation observers. The convention is based on the notion that the ability of the sea to accept and absorb waste is limited and furthermore the right of a sovereign nation to exploit its resources is limited by the need not to damage the resources of other nations in the process. The signatories pledge as a group to use the best practicable means possible to prevent pollution, according to each nation's scientific, technical and economic capabilities.

The Convention defines dumping as the deliberate discharge of waste, and not the incidental waste generated and discharged by the normal operation of seagoing vessels. The wastes generated by the exploitation of off-shore minerals is not addressed in this convention. Parties are required to establish a system of permits for dumping, including appropriate authorities to issue both general and "special" dumping permits. General permits govern reoccurring or cyclic dumpings, "special" permits govern extraordinary occurrences and exemptions for prohibited dumpings. No permits are required for emergency dumping that saves human lives or protects vessels, but such incidences must be reported. Special permits may only be issued after the impact has been well researched, and affected states consulted. National authorities must keep records of all permits, monitor dumpings, and report their findings. All parties are responsible for vessels flying their flags, as well as those in their territorial waters.

Sanctions and enforcement

Signatories must use all appropriate measures to prevent and punish contravention in their jurisdictions, and co-operate for enforcement on the high seas. Parties are encouraged to engage in regional, bilateral and multilateral agreements to facilitate the Convention. An international codification of signals to be used by vessels engaged in dumping is to be enacted.

Classification of materials

Annex I describes materials that shall only be dumped with a special permit, including organo-halogens, mercury, cadmium, persistent plastics, hydrocarbons, high level radioactive materials, biological or chemical warfare agents, or any other material making sea foods inedible or endangering human health. Annex II describes materials that should be dumped only with special care, including arsenic, lead, copper, zinc, organo-silicons, cyanides, fluorides, pesticides, scrap metals, and low level radioactive materials. No permit for the dumping of any of the above materials may be authorised without a precise scientific study of the character of the material, including its toxicity, bio-accumulation, etc., as well as the characteristics of the dumping site, including the characteristics of the waters and the methods to be used in the dumping.

1979 amendments by the ad hoc committee on incineration at sea

These amendments are addressed chiefly to the industrialised West and Japan, and include all current and any possible future methods of incineration. The organisation must be given notice of any special incineration permit issued. The permit must include such information as the issuing authority, period of validity, origin of waste, industrial process giving rise to the waste, area of incineration, and expected frequencies. Incinerated wastes that are incidental to the normal operation of vessels are excluded from the convention. Parties are required to research alternatives to incineration before issuing a permit. The appropriate authority must monitor, record, and report all discharge from incineration. Destruction must exceed 99.9% of wastes incinerated. Pilot test burns must precede issuance, with a "black box" in place to ensure that the incineration does not exceed organisation standards for carbon monoxide, carbon dioxide or visible smoke. Only wastes whose exhaust will be rapidly rendered harmless or present only as trace contaminants may be authorised permits. Permits will be allowed for certain wastes only after extensive consultation with other parties, and the materials are found to be non biodegradable, not persistent, and leave no acute or chronic toxic affects or bioaccumulation, especially in food species or humans. Finally, all alternative methods of disposal of the waste must be itemised. Chile, Portugal, and the former USSR all opt out of the dispute settlement procedures.

Montreal Protocol on substances that deplete the ozone layer

Made: 16 September 1987. In force: 1 January 1989

The protocol establishes graduated decreasing levels of emissions, based on 1986 consumption, for various substances to be listed in subsequent amendments. It also established a timetable after which such substances may not be traded to non-members, from which such substances may not be imported from non-members, and a ban on imports of products manufactured with, but not containing, the enumerated substances. Signatories are obliged to control the emissions of CFCs, *inter alia* in aerosols, by any means at their disposal, including controls on production or use, to the maximum extent practicable. The protocol encourages members to urge non-members to become signatories. Under certain circumstances, and with notice to the Secretariat, members who under-produce their quota may transfer the difference to other members. Parties are discouraged from the export of CFC technology except that used in containment, recovery, recycling or destruction. The special situation of developing nations is noted. It sets forth the method of adjustment of allowable levels and the method for the calculation of levels. It calls for increasing public awareness and establishes a procedure for dealing with non-compliance.

Approved by the EC by Council Decision, 14 October 1988.

[See 1990 Amendments and Vienna Convention, 1985].

Amendment to the Montreal Protocol

(Japan is a signatory to this amendment).

Made: London, June 1990. In force: 1 January 1992

The amendments adjust the definition of controlled substances, to include isomers and, in relation to production, shortens the time by which the emission of these substances are to be phased out. It sets levels of various substances such as fully-halogenated CFCs, carbon tetrachloride and methyl chloroform. The annexes to the amendment contain the complete list of controlled substances covered by the amendment and by the Montreal Protocol and the Vienna Convention.

Japan approved the London amendments on 26 March 1991 by amending their own national law concerning protection of the ozone layer. Their Control of Certain Substances (Law No. 53 of 1988), implemented the Montreal Protocol initially; the amendments to the Protocol on 5

September 1991 were implemented in Japanese national legislation by way of Law No. 8 of 1991. In accordance with the stipulations of the amended Protocol, the Ministry of International Trade and Industry (MITI) is setting production limits for the five Japanese manufacturers of CFCs. A number of major corporations have set a specific year by which they will phase out the use of CFCs.

[See also Vienna Convention.]

Approved by the EC by Council Decision, 1991.

Vienna Convention for the protection of the ozone layer

22 March 1985

The Convention is based on the notion that a state has a sovereign right to exploit its resources with a responsibility not to cause damage outside the limits of its national jurisdiction. The Member States agree to conduct research and exchange information regarding the ozone layer and to adopt the necessary legislative and administrative measures to limit activities with adverse effects, with special attention given to alternative substances and technologies, as well as the socio-economic ramifications. Member States are to co-operate in establishing standards for implementing the convention and in creating protocols to the convention. Signatories are encouraged to take into account the special needs of developing countries, and to promote direct and indirect transfer of technology and knowledge to them via competent international bodies. The convention establishes a Secretariat to conduct meetings, issue reports, carry out the functions of the convention, and to act in co-ordination with other international bodies.

[See also Montreal Protocol, 1987, and its amendments, 1990.]

Approved by the EC by Council Decision, 14 October 1988

EC Member States must give their approval by 31 October 1988

Other International Treaties to which Japan is a signatory

The Russian Federation previously the Soviet Union

Japan concluded an agreement on 18 April 1991, with the then Soviet Union, concerning co-operation in the field of environmental protection. The two countries have made co-operative efforts since 1973 under the agreement on co-operation in the field of science and technology. Both governments agreed to establish a joint commission for overseeing programmes carried out under the agreement which encompass exchange of experts and joint research initiatives. This agreement, in common with other treaties and agreements concluded by the Soviet Union, is to be succeeded by the Russian Federation. It is envisaged that agreements of this kind will be made with China and other countries of East Asia in future thereby establishing a network of environmental co-operation.

Protocol on environmental protection to the Antarctic Treaty

Made October 1991.

Japan signed this treaty on 4 October 1991. The Japanese delegation played an active role in mediating between the conflicting positions of a group of states supporting the possibility of mineral resource activity and the other opposing group who were trying to place a total and indefinite ban on such activities. The compromise reached provides that under Art 7, any activity relating to mineral resources, other than scientific research, shall be prohibited. But Art 25 provides for possible relaxation of this prohibition and indeed of the treaty as a whole, by holding a possible review conference for the purpose of modifying the amendment of the Protocol after fifty years from the date of its entry into force. The Japanese Government and public have welcomed the adoption of this instrument for the protection of the Antarctic area.

Appendix III

Note on the History of the Environmental Green Law

September 1992

Two advisory councils to the EA proposed a new tougher law to achieve sustainable environmental protection, with new taxes and surcharges to share costs widely and impartially. The draft proposed compulsory EIAs prior to new construction projects. The earlier bill submitted to the Diet in 1981 had been killed by heavy opposition from industry. The Central Council for Environmental Pollution Control and the Nature Conservation Council were the two advisory councils involved.

December 1992

The actual draft hints at the introduction of a new environmental tax and mandatory assessments, the draft being tentatively entitled "Environmental Standards Law". It specifically proposed that planners of major development projects be required to detail what effects their projects would have on the environment and to make provisions for protecting the environment. Even projects not involving construction would be prompted voluntarily to file environmental assessments, detailing the proposed use of products and methods to be used in waste disposal.

The draft continued that the Government "take necessary and appropriate measures to levy economic costs" on entities that emit polluting substances into the atmosphere. The statement hinted at the future introduction of an environment tax.

January 1993

Copies of the draft were circulated to other ministries and agencies.

March 1993

Re-submitted to the DIET by the EA.

June 1993

The Environment Bill was reportedly put down by opponents as toothless and lacking in clarity. Whereas it was considered to be an opportunity to set out Japan's environmental constitution the lack of binding EIA requirements and of guarantees that citizens and NGOs would have a voice in projects affecting the environment was a major cause for concern. The bill was described as a "masterpiece of bureaucratic literature", more the product of the powerful Ministries of Construction and International Trade and Industry than of the Environment Agency.

In any event the EA was unsuccessful in getting the legislation through the Diet ("Parliament") because of the Diet's dissolution and the bill was immediately killed.

The aborted legislation should have been an omnibus law for existing environment-related laws: now the Agency has to prepare a new bill.

Part 2

Impact on Construction Activities

4 Waste: its disposal and use*

Peter Barber and Andrew Jackson

Introduction

The law governing waste management is currently in a state of flux, caught principally between old and new statutory regimes. Whilst the Environmental Protection Act 1990 has been on the statute book for three years, its implementation, particularly in relation to its waste management provisions, has been piecemeal. A substantial part of the Act providing a new statutory regime for the licensing of waste management is not yet in force. Those involved in the construction process and confronting waste disposal issues must therefore consider a range of old, new and prospective provisions.

A number of issues arise:

(1) Whether the handling of waste (including its use) in the construction process requires either a waste disposal licence or (in the future under the Environmental Protection Act) a waste management licence;
(2) The effect of the "Duty of Care" on the management of waste imposed under the Environmental Protection Act;
(3) The control of the transport of waste to and from a site under the Control of Pollution (Amendment) Act 1989;
(4) The control of waste that is "special" waste; and
(5) Civil liability for damage caused by waste.

The requirement for a waste disposal or waste management licence

At the time of this paper, the statutory regulation of waste management and waste disposal in the UK is by a mixture of the Control of Pollution Act 1974 and the Environmental Protection Act 1990 and regulations made under these Acts. Though these Acts do not specifically implement it, regard must also be had to the EC Waste Framework Directive. Both UK statutory regimes centre on a requirement for a licence where waste is deposited or treated in a particular manner, with the Environmental Protection Act imposing an additional control by way of a duty of care on the handling of waste.

* This paper was prepared by the authors according to the law as at 23 September 1993. The reader is therefore referred to the changes brought about by the Waste Management Licensing Regulations 1994 and the accompanying Waste Management Papers and Circular.

Under both UK statutory regimes, a number of important exemptions limit the effect of the statutory control, in particular on the use of waste material in the construction process. The exemptions are not such, however, that the statutory provisions can be ignored.

The Control of Pollution Act 1974

In terms of waste disposal the central provision of the Control of Pollution Act 1974 is section 3(1). By that section it is a criminal offence to:

(a) deposit "controlled waste" on any land or knowingly permit controlled waste to be deposited on any land; or
(b) use any plant or equipment or knowingly permit any plant or equipment to be used, for the purpose of disposing of controlled waste or of dealing in a prescribed manner with controlled waste

unless the land in question is occupied by the holder of a waste disposal licence authorising the deposit and the deposit is made in accordance with any conditions specified in the licence.

Liability on summary conviction is to imprisonment for a term not exceeding six months or a fine not exceeding £5000 or both. Liability on conviction on indictment is to imprisonment for a term not exceeding two years or a fine or both. The penalties are increased[1] where the waste in question is "poisonous noxious or polluting" and its presence on the land is likely to give rise to an "environmental hazard".[2]

It is a defence[3] for a person charged with an offence under the section to show:

"(a) that he
  (i) took care to inform himself, from persons who were in a position to provide the information, as to whether the deposit or use to which the charge relates would be in contravention of; [s3(1)]
  (ii) did not know and had no reason to suppose that the information given to him was false or misleading and that the deposit or use might be in contravention of that sub-section;

---

1 S3(3)(a), (b) and (c).

2 By s4(5) of the Act the presence of waste on land gives rise to an environmental hazard if "the waste has been deposited in such a manner or in such a quantity (whether that quantity by itself or cumulatively with other deposits of the same or different substances) as to subject persons or animals to a material risk of death, injury or impairment of health or as to threaten the pollution (whether on the surface or underground) of any water supply". By subsection (6) the degree of risk is to be assessed with particular regard to the measures taken for minimising the risk to the likelihood of the waste or any container in which it is deposited being tampered with by children or others.

3 S3(4).

(b) that he acted under instructions from his employer and neither knew nor had reason to suppose that the deposit or use was in contravention of the sub-section;

(c) in the case of an offence of making, causing or permitting a deposit or use otherwise than in accordance with conditions specified in a disposal licence that he took all such steps as were reasonably open to him to ensure that the conditions were complied with;

(d) that the acts specified in the charge were done in an emergency in order to avoid danger to the public and that, as soon as reasonably practicable, after they were done, particulars of them were furnished to the disposal authority in whose area the acts were done."

Three particular issues arise which are of importance for the construction process:

- what constitutes waste and controlled waste for the purposes of section 3(1);
- what constitutes a deposit or the use of plant or equipment for dealing with controlled waste in a prescribed manner; and
- subject to the specific exceptions, whether a waste disposal licence is required for the management and use of waste on a construction site.

The meaning of waste

The definitions of "waste" and "controlled waste" are fundamental to both the Control of Pollution and Environmental Protection Acts. For the purposes of the Control of Pollution Act "waste" is defined as:[4]

"(a) any substance which constitutes a scrap material or an effluent or other unwanted surplus substance arising from the application of any process; and

(b) any substance or article which requires to be disposed of as being broken, worn out, contaminated or otherwise spoiled."

Despite its apparent simplicity this definition has been considered judicially on a number of occasions. The important issue has been whether the definition of "unwanted" should be considered from the point of view of the producer or whether the possibility of future use of the material in question by someone else can alter its character.

A number of the cases have involved construction contexts particularly in relation to material received on site for use in the construction process. In *Long* v *Brooke*,[5] the facts were that Wimpey Limited had wished to dispose of large quantities of subsoil and clay diggings excavated from a

4 S30(1); note that a substance which is an explosive within the meaning of the Explosives Act 1875, is specifically excluded from the definition.

5 [1980] Crim LR 109.

site. Nearby, the owner of a disused quarry wished to cover the regraded slopes of his quarry with soil before grassing them over. He was approached by Wimpey who on two occasions tipped their excavated material on to his land for the privilege of which they paid him the sum of £2.50 per load. The value per load equated to the cost of the bulldozer used to spread the material. There was no profit from the tipping.

The quarry owner was convicted in the Magistrates' Court of knowingly permitting the deposit of controlled waste on land which he occupied without being the holder of a waste disposal licence authorising the deposit, contrary, as above, to section 3 of the Control of Pollution Act.

The quarry owner had argued that the excavated material was not waste as it had some value to him for use on his land. On appeal the Crown Court dismissed this argument stating that although one man's waste may constitute another man's valuable material, on its true construction the Act defines waste from the point of view of the person discarding the material. To be waste, therefore, it need not be useless, merely unwanted.

That ruling was specifically approved in *Berridge Incinerators Limited* v *Nottinghamshire County Council*.[6] There P J Crawford QC sitting as Deputy High Court Judge held:

> "It is, of course, a truism that one man's waste is another man's raw material. The fact that a price is paid by the collector of material to its originator is, no doubt, relevant; but I do not regard it as crucial. If I have an old fireplace to dispose of to a passing rag and bone man, its character as waste is not affected by whether or not I can persuade the latter to pay me 50 pence for it. In my judgment, the correct approach is to regard the material from the point of view of the person who produces it. Is it something which is produced as a product, or even as a by-product of his business, or is it something to be disposed of as useless? I notice that this was the approach adopted by His Honour Judge Chapman QC in the Crown Court (*Long* v *Brooke* [1980] Crim LR 109) and I respectfully agree with it".[7]

The principle was applied more recently by Pill J in *Kent County Council* v *Queenborough Rolling Mills Limited*.[8] In that case material had been removed from the site of a former porcelain factory and regraded into four

6 1987, unreported but quoted with approval at para 2.7 Annex 2 DoE Circular 13/88 "The Control of Pollution Act 1974, the Collection and Disposal of Waste Regulations" and subsequently at paragraph 15 of Circular 14/92 "The Environmental Protection Act 1990"—Parts II and IV: The Controlled Waste Regulations. Note that it was made clear in *R* v *Rotherham MBC ex p Rankin* [1990] JPL 503 at 506 that the context of the Berridge Incinerator Decision was actually planning control.

7 Though, because he uses the term "useless" the judge's rhetorical question is not actually an accurate reflection of the principle he is attempting to follow.

8 *The Times* 9 February 1990.

grades. A particular grade was offered to the respondent company as ballast for infill and was deposited on their land. The company having been acquitted by the Magistrates Court of an offence under section 3 of the Control of Pollution Act, the County Council appealed.

Pill J held that the issue was whether the deposited material was "controlled waste" within the meaning of the Act:

> "In my judgment the purpose to which the material was put is irrelevant in the present situation. The nature of the material must first be considered at the time of its removal from the Stelrad site. The material had earlier been discarded and had lain on the site for many years. When removed from the site it was waste within the meaning of that word in section 30. It bore the same quality when it was deposited at Coal Washer Wharf. The usefulness, if it be so, of the deposit as fill on the receiving site did not change the character of the material. Neither did the fact that the material was separated from other material before deposit deprive it of its identity as waste. Different considerations might apply if the material is recycled or reconstituted before the deposit complained of. The material being waste material, it was not seriously disputed that it was or included industrial waste and, therefore, controlled waste under section 3 of the Act".

The judgment confirmed the approach taken in earlier cases suggesting that any material received on a construction site which is not "new" is likely to be considered waste, as is the material produced on site to be taken away even though it may be useful to someone else.

An interesting remark from Pill J in the *Queenborough* case, however, was that the considerations would have been different if the waste had been "recycled or reconstituted". That remark raises a number of questions, not least why the Judge did not consider in the particular case that regrading equated to a reconstitution of the material. It might be best not to place too great a reliance on his remarks, one view being that waste remains waste even when subject to recycling.[9]

This is also inconsistent with the European Court judgement in *Vessoso and Zanetti* (ECJ joined Cases C-206/88 and C-207/88). The Court had been asked to rule on the meaning of waste in the Waste Framework Directive, [10] which requires harmonisation of national laws on waste disposal. The issues were whether the concept of waste covered things which are capable of economic re-use, whether the definition of waste within the directive[11] presupposes the establishment of an intention to abandon on the part of the holder and whether national legislation which defined waste as excluding substances and objects capable of economic re-utilisation

9 See generally the commentary on the case [1990] LMELR 28.

10 Directive 75/442 as now amended by Directive 91/156.

11 By Article 1 "any substance or object in the categories set out in Annex 1 [to the Directive] which the holder discards or intends or is required to discard."

would be compatible with the directive. The Court ruled in the positive to the first question and in the negative to the second and third. It is unlikely, therefore, that the comments of Pill J in *Queensborough* could be pursued, although it may be questioned whether there are not situations where a recycling process applied to waste fundamentally alters its character.

A decision which does not sit easily with that in *Long* v *Brooke* and the subsequent decisions is that in *Charles Neil Ashcroft* v *Michael McErlain Limited*[12] which is unreported but quoted by Schliemann J in *R* v *Rotherham MBC*.[13] The case again concerned the meaning of controlled waste under the Control of Pollution Act.

There the material in question was soil which had been excavated from a field in order to reduce its level so that a road could be constructed. The excavated soil had then been taken by cart to a paddock to raise the level of the paddock. The court held first of all that excavated soil is capable of being waste. In the particular case, however, the Justices had been perfectly correct in finding that it was not.

It is difficult, of course, to see the distinction between those facts and the facts in *Long* v *Brooke*, unless it is in the close proximity of the land required for the road and the land comprising the paddock. Otherwise, the use to which the excavated material was to be put appears to have determined that it was not "waste".

A similar decision was reached (although in the context of planning control rather than the Control of Pollution Act) in *Northavon District Council* v *Secretary of State for the Environment*.[14] There the issue was whether planning permission was required for the removal of eighteen inches of top soil from an area of a farm and its replacement with compacted non-toxic filling material such as builder's rubble. The local planning authority determined that planning permission was required for the operation, this being the deposit of refuse or waste material and consequently a material change in the use of the land. The court agreed with the Inspector who on appeal had found that it was not. The Inspector had ruled that the proposal was designed primarily to improve the agricultural quality of the land. It did not therefore amount to the deposit of refuse or waste materials. The Secretary of State had agreed with his Inspector.

The case can be distinguished, of course, from the line taken in *Long* v *Brooke* in that the issue was not strictly the meaning of waste within the meaning of the Act. The issue before the court was strictly the nature of the use for planning purposes.

---

12 (1985).

13 See note 6.

14 [1980] 40 P and CR 332.

Despite these decisions the starting point in deciding whether material received or produced on site is waste is clearly to consider the material from the point of view of the producer. Then if, on the above principles, it is waste then it is also "controlled waste" within the meaning of the Control of Pollution Act and therefore potentially subject to control?

Controlled waste

For the purposes of the Control of Pollution Act "controlled waste" is defined in section 30(1) as "household, industrial and commercial waste or any such waste". For present purposes, the important category is "industrial waste". By the same section, "industrial waste" consists of:

> "waste from any factory within the meaning of the Factories Act 1961 and any premises occupied by a body corporate established by or under any enactment for the purpose of carrying on under national ownership any industry or part of an industry or any undertaking, excluding waste from any mine or quarry"

On the face of it construction waste would not seem to fit within that description at all (by section 175 of the Factories Act 1961 a construction site would not be within the definition of a factory). However, in relation to construction waste the Secretary of State has used the power given to him under section 30(4) of the Control of Pollution Act to provide that waste of a prescribed description is to be treated as industrial waste. Thus, under the Collection and Disposal of Waste Regulations 1988[15] Schedule 3, the following types of waste (as far as is relevant for present purposes) are to be treated as industrial waste:

> " 5. Waste from dredging operations;
> 6. Waste arising from works of construction or demolition, including waste arising from work preparatory thereto;
> 7. Waste arising from tunnelling or from any other excavation;
> 12. Waste removed from land on which it has previously been deposited and any soil with which such waste has been in contact;
> 14. Poisonous or noxious waste arising from (*inter alia*) mixing or selling paints;
> 17. Waste oil or waste solvent other than from a private dwelling or residential home;
> 18. Waste which is a scrap metal within the meaning of section 9 of the Scrap Metal Dealers Act 1964 other than that from a private dwelling or residential home."

15 SI 1988/819.

Clearly, this means that if what is produced on a construction site is "waste", then it will almost certainly be controlled waste in any event. By contrast, for used material received on site, something of its history will need to be known to determine whether it is controlled waste. What is of interest is that construction waste (given the volumes produced) was not specified in its own right as a particular category of waste. It may perhaps be questioned whether the Secretary of State acted strictly within his powers in prescribing that construction related waste be treated as "industrial waste" when that description (at least according to its statutory definition) does not apply to it.

If material does constitute controlled waste then, as noted above and subject to the exceptions made in respect of the construction process, a waste disposal licence will be required if that waste is either deposited on land or knowingly permitted to be deposited or any plant or equipment is used or knowingly permitted to be used for the purpose of disposing of the waste or of dealing with it in a prescribed manner.

The deposit of waste

As with the definition of "waste" the meaning of "deposit" has been uncertain. In the main the uncertainty has been whether deposition includes the temporary storage or deposit of waste or whether the Act was intended to control only final disposal.

For a time, the leading decision was that in *Leigh Land Reclamation* v *Walsall.*[16] There the meaning of "deposit" was considered in the context of a prosecution for the deposit of waste in breach of conditions on a waste disposal licence. The facts were that the appellants operated a landfill site in the Midlands subject to a waste disposal licence containing a condition permitting the deposit of non-liquid waste only. The company and its site clerk were accused and found guilty of the deposit, in breach of the conditions of the licence, of carboys of liquid waste, a drum of waste oil and a drum of contaminated water.

On appeal by way of case stated both argued that, on the facts, the waste they were accused of depositing illegally had not reached the working face of the landfill site and had not therefore reached its final resting place. As a consequence there had been no deposit within the meaning of the Act.

Bingham LJ[17] agreed with those arguments and found that the provisions of the Act and the conditions in the licence were aimed at the

16 [1992] 1 Env. L.R.16.

17 Waterhouse J agreeing.

"mode of final disposal". In the Judge's view, waste was to be regarded as deposited for the purposes of the Act when:

> "It is dumped on the site with no realistic prospect of further examination or inspection to reject goods of which deposit is not allowed under the licence."

Although there were arguments that it applied only to "deposits" on licensed and not unlicensed sites[18] the decision in *Leigh Land* was for a time a thorn in the flesh of waste regulation authorities as defendants argued that the waste they had been accused of depositing without a licence had not reached its final resting place and had not strictly, therefore, been the subject of a deposit within the meaning of the Act.[19]

The matter has now been considered afresh by the Divisional Court in two cases: *R* v *Metropolitan Stipendiary Magistrates ex p London Waste Regulation Authority and others* and *Berkshire County Council* v *Scott*.[20] In both cases the question was whether section 3(1) of the Control of Pollution Act could apply to acts in relation to waste which was not in its final resting place.

The cases concerned waste being dealt with at a waste transfer station. The court disagreed with the decision reached in *Leigh Land*. It could depart from that decision (this also being a Divisional Court matter) if convinced that the decision was wrong. The court took a purposive view[21] and concluded that section 3(1) of the Control of Pollution Act was *not* concerned only with final deposits or disposals of waste. To hold otherwise would involve eroding the efficacy of the Act which was concerned with protecting against damage as much from waste transfer stations as from sites where waste is finally disposed of. The decision in *Leigh Land* had been to the contrary and so the court was driven to conclude that it was wrongly decided.

Whilst this means there are now two conflicting Divisional Court decisions on the meaning of "deposit" it is likely that the decision in the more recent case will be followed.

The importance of the case in the construction context is clearly that, if what is being received or is created and stored on site is waste, then

---

18 See Laurence "When does a deposit of controlled waste occur?" UKELA Journal, Winter, at 84.

19 In Circular 13/88, the view of the Department of the Environment was that "deposit" included both permanent and temporary deposit within the ordinary meaning of the word. On the other hand, in regulation 14 of the Control of Pollution (Special Waste) Regulations 1980 "deposit" seems to be seen as denoting final resting place, an argument made by counsel for the appellants in *Leigh Land*.

20 *The Times* 14 January 1993 [1993] 3 All ER 113.

21 As indeed had Bingham L J in *Leigh Land*.

questions need to be asked as to whether it is in fact "deposited" such that the site requires a waste disposal licence. If, for example an existing building is demolished, the material produced will be controlled waste. If that material is then stored on site for any period before removal then, apart from any statutory exceptions, there could be an argument that a deposit of that waste has occurred and that a waste disposal licence is required. The position is even more clear with materials brought on site for use in construction. If these constitute controlled waste then their temporary storage and perhaps, in the case of material used for infill or landscaping, even their final use will constitute a deposit and again, strictly speaking, would require a licence.

As previously noted, however, the Act was not intended to cover all these situations. Thus, the Collection and Disposal of Waste Regulations 1988 provide for exemptions from the requirement for a licence. The exceptions were originally provided for in the Control of Pollution (Licensing of Waste Disposal) Regulations 1976. Department of the Environment Circular 76/76, in commenting on the Regulations, indicated that the exemptions were aimed at ensuring that a licence is not required where waste produced during the "course of building and certain civil engineering work" is made use of in other construction work without causing an environmental hazard (para 12). The specific example given is the use of builder's rubble as foundation material.

By Regulation 9 and Schedule 6 of the 1988 Regulations, therefore, certain specific deposits are exempt. The most important exemption in the present context is that in paragraph 4 which exempts from the need for a licence:

> (1) ". . . the deposit on land of wastes of the descriptions set out in paragraphs 6 and 7 of Schedule 3 or of ash, slag or clinker, provided that the deposit is made for the purposes of construction currently being undertaken on the land on which the waste is deposited
>
> (2) . . . the deposit on land, for a period not exceeding three months, of wastes of the descriptions mentioned in subparagraph (1) provided that the deposit is made for the purposes of future construction on the land on which the waste is deposited."

The waste described in paragraphs 6 and 7 of Schedule 3 is, as noted above, waste arising from construction and demolition (or preparatory works) and waste from tunnelling or from any other excavation. The condition to the exemption is that the waste must be deposited by, or with the consent of, the lawful occupier of the land.[22]

This exemption will clearly be helpful in terms of material produced on site and stored for future use and will also cover material produced off site

---

22 Subparagraph (3). "Lawful occupier" is not defined.

provided it is the result of construction or demolition or tunnelling or other excavation. There is a wide range of material, however, that the exemption will not cover. Does it, for instance, cover rubble or concrete removed from one site, recycled at another and delivered to a third ? Is that strictly waste arising from a construction or demolition process?

It is also interesting that the possibility of the exemption does not appear to have been raised in the *Queenborough Rolling Mill* case. This is possibly because, although the material had been removed from the site of a former factory it was not actually considered to be the product of demolition. It might, however, have been argued that it was the product of excavation.

A further important general exemption is contained in paragraph 14 of Schedule 6 to the Regulations. A licence will not be required for "the deposit of the waste on the premises on which it is produced, pending its disposal elsewhere". This will clearly cover most of the waste produced on site which is kept before eventual disposal off site and, therefore, the demolition example outlined above. Timing, however, may be a factor. The waste should not be kept for too long or it would be possible to argue that it is outside the exemption and has, in fact, been deposited.

Paragraph 15 also provides for an exemption for deposits on the site on which it is produced of certain volumes of special waste[23] in a secure container or place. Paragraph 16 allows exemption for a temporary deposit of solid waste not exceeding 50 cubic metres away from the site on which it is produced but in a secure container. The important qualification to all the exemptions is that they are not to apply if the presence of the waste on land is likely to give rise to an environmental hazard within the meaning of the Act[24] nor where the waste is special waste.

Use of plant or equipment for the disposal or treatment of waste

As discussed above, a waste disposal licence is also required under the second limb of section 3(1) of the Act for the use of any plant or equipment for the purpose of disposing of controlled waste or of dealing with it in a prescribed manner (or knowingly permitting someone else to do so).

The term "disposal" or disposing is not defined in the Act and, in any given case, there could, as with the meaning of deposit, be room for argument as to what was intended. In particular, this includes whether it was intended to denote final disposal or, say, the moving about of waste on a site by a bulldozer prior to it being stored or taken elsewhere.

---

23 For which see below.

24 Regulation 9(2). See above for the meaning of environmental hazard.

What constitutes dealing with waste in a "prescribed manner", however, is set out in the Collection and Disposal of Waste Regulations 1988. The Regulations again set out exemptions which will cover some of the activities carried out on a construction site. Regulation 8 and Schedule 5 provide that the following are included amongst the activities which will constitute treating waste in a prescribed manner:

1. Bailing, compacting, incinerating, pulverising, sorting or storing waste;
5. Producing fuel from waste;
8. Using untreated waste as fuel to produce electricity or heat.

By Schedule 6 paragraphs 19 to 23 the exemptions include:

19. Bailing, compacting, pulverising or sorting waste on the premises on which it is produced.
20. Bailing, sorting or shredding waste paper or rags.
21. Sorting waste of the description set out in paragraphs 14 and 15 on the premises on which it is produced.
22. Incinerating waste, which is not special waste, on the premises on which it is produced by means of plant with a disposal capacity of not more than 200 kilogrammes per hour.
23. Using waste oil as fuel to produce heat.

For paragraph 21 the waste described in paragraphs 14 and 15 is, as noted above, waste on the premises on which it is produced, and certain volumes of special waste in secure containers. Subject to paragraph 15 then, once more, the exemptions do not apply to waste whose presence on land is liable to give rise to an environmental hazard or which is special waste.[25]

The application for a licence

From the above it will be seen that, subject to the specific exemptions, there are a number of situations in which the handling of materials in the construction process requires, strictly, a waste disposal licence. Much depends on an analysis of the character of the material concerned, the nature of the treatment of it and as to whether the exemptions apply. If a licence is required then the application must be made to the relevant waste

25 Regulation 9(2) and (3).

disposal authority.[26] In the majority of cases this will be the relevant county council. The criteria for the issue of a licence are that an application shall not be rejected unless rejection is necessary for the purpose of preventing pollution of water or danger to public health.[27]

A qualification, however, is that a licence is not to be issued for use of land, plant or equipment for which planning permission is required unless planning permission is in force. This could, of course, create difficulties as it is unlikely that any planning permission that exists for the development of a site will specifically cover the use of the site for the disposal of waste. Were that problem to arise it would have to be argued that the particular act of disposal, or treatment, of waste was ancillary to the construction or demolition process (if not an integral part of it) for which permission exists so that a separate permission is not required.

If an application for a licence is refused then section 10 of the Act provides for a right of appeal to the Secretary of State. Any licence that is issued may, under section 6 of the Act, be subject to conditions. An interesting point is that the National Rivers Authority has to be consulted whenever it is proposed to issue a licence. If the National Rivers Authority requests the disposal authority not to issue the licence or disagrees over conditions then either may refer the matter to the Secretary of State and the licence will not be issued except in accordance with his decision.[28]

The Environmental Protection Act 1990

The provisions of the Control of Pollution Act on waste disposal will eventually be replaced by those of Part II of the Environmental Protection Act 1990. As previously mentioned, the majority of the provisions of Part II are not yet in force, implementation having been delayed on two occasions in April and June 1993.

Entitled "Waste on Land", Part II of the Act when in force will provide for a new system of waste management licences underpinned by a new prohibition on the harmful treatment, disposal or keeping of waste.

Section 33(1)(a) and (b): The requirement for a waste management licence

Section 33(1) of the Act provides that a person shall not:

"(a) deposit controlled waste, or knowingly cause or knowingly permit controlled waste to be deposited in or on any land unless a waste management

---

26 See ss 5 and 30 of the Act.

27 S5(3). Neither "pollution of water" nor "danger to public health" is defined.

28 S5(4).

licence authorising the deposit is in force and the deposit is in accordance with the licence;

(b) treat, keep or dispose of controlled waste, or knowingly cause or knowingly permit controlled waste to be treated, kept or disposed of:
 (i) in or on any land, or
 (ii) by means of any mobile plant

except under and in accordance with a waste management licence."

Though subsections 33(1)(a) and (b) are amongst those provisions not yet in force, it is worth commenting on them as their eventual implementation is inevitable.

By section 33(6) a person who contravenes subsection (1) or any condition of a waste management licence commits an offence. Summary conviction for such an offence may result in a fine up to a maximum of £20,000 (presently the statutory maximum) or imprisonment for a term not exceeding six months or both. Conviction on indictment may lead to a fine, imprisonment for two years (five years where the offence relates to special waste[29]) or again both.

Defences are provided for in section 33(7). The first defence is different from the corresponding defence under the Control of Pollution Act. It is a defence for a person charged with an offence under section 33 to prove: ". . . that he took all reasonable precautions and exercised all due diligence to avoid the commission of the offence." The defences of emergency and acting on the instruction of an employer remain as before.

Section 33 is clearly an extension of section 3(1) of the Control of Pollution Act. Subsection 1(a) reflects the prohibition on the deposit of controlled waste without a waste disposal licence. Subsection 1(b) is an extension of the previous provision at section 3(1)(b) of the Control of Pollution Act. No longer, however, is there a reference to the use of plant and equipment for the purpose of disposing of controlled waste or dealing with it in a prescribed manner. Instead, there is the much wider categorisation of the treating, keeping or disposing of controlled waste "in or on any land or by means of any mobile plant".

What constitutes waste and controlled waste will again be key issues in determining whether a waste management licence will be required for the handling of material on site. By section 75(2) of the Act waste is defined as it was in the Control of Pollution Act. Cases on the definition of waste under that Act will therefore remain relevant.

Similarly, controlled waste is defined by section 75(4) as meaning household, industrial and commercial waste or any such waste. The definitions of

29 See below.

each respective form of waste are again given extended meaning but this time under[30] the Control of Waste Regulations 1992.[31]

In the construction context, industrial waste is again the important category. Waste to be treated as industrial waste is set out in Schedule 3. The categories of waste included under the Collection and Disposal of Waste Regulations 1988 are relisted and by Regulation 5(2) waste arising from construction or demolition works (and preparatory works) is once more included.

As with the Control of Pollution Act, once the nature of the material being brought on to site or produced on site has been ascertained then the question is whether the handling of it is subject to control. As far as section 33(1)(a) is concerned, "deposit" is likely to be interpreted as it has been under the Control of Pollution Act and so similar considerations will apply. As far as section 33(1)(b) is concerned, "treat" and "dispose" are defined in section 29 of the Act. By section 29(6) the disposal of waste includes: ". . . its disposal by way of deposit in or on land."

By the same subsection, waste is "treated" when it is: "subjected to any process, including making it reusable or reclaiming substances from it." "Recycle" (and cognate expressions) are to be construed accordingly.

The Secretary of State has the power by section 29(7) to prescribe activities which constitute the treatment of waste but has not yet done so. What is meant by to "keep" waste is not defined. There may therefore be debate as to what time periods are involved.

Once more there are exemptions which will cover the construction process. By Regulation 9 of the 1992 Regulations, section 33(1) is not to apply in any case where a disposal licence under the Control of Pollution Act is not required by virtue of Regulation 9 of the 1988 Regulations. The existing exemptions to the requirement for a licence will therefore continue to apply.

If a waste management licence is required then, whilst the application process remains much the same as for a waste disposal licence under the Control of Pollution Act, the terms on which a licence would be granted are substantially different. Once more, the licence may be granted subject to conditions.[32] The matters that may be dealt with by condition, however, are extended.[33]

Otherwise, by section 36(3) the Waste Regulation Authority, to whom an application must be made,[34] is not to reject an application for a waste

30 See s75(5).

31 SI 1992/588.

32 S35(3).

33 See s35(3) to (7).

34 Which will again usually be the county council.

management licence, if satisfied that the applicant is a "fit and proper person", unless it is satisfied that its rejection is necessary for the purpose of preventing:

(a) pollution of the environment;[35]
(b) harm to human health; or
(c) serious detriment to the amenities of the locality.

These represent an extension to the previous criteria which, as noted above, referred simply to pollution of water and danger to public health. Subsection (3)(c) is inapplicable if planning permission is in force in relation to the use to which the land will be put under the licence. Who is a "fit and proper person" is defined in section 74 of the Act. In brief, this is to be determined by reference to the activities to be carried on under the licence and the fulfilment of the requirements of the licence. A person is not to be treated as fit and proper if it appears to the authority:

- that he or another relevant person has been convicted of a relevant offence;[36]
- that the management of the activities which are or are to be authorised by the licence are not or will not be in the hands of a technically competent person;[37] or
- that the person who holds or is to hold the licence has not made and has no intention of making or is in no position to make financial provision adequate to discharge the obligations arising from the licence.

A further qualification is (as before) that the licence is not to be issued for a use of land for which planning permission is required unless that planning permission is in force in relation to that use or there is an established use certificate.[38]

---

35 For the definition of which see below.

36 See subsections 6 and 7. A relevant offence would be an offence in connection with waste management. By subsection (4) the Waste Regulation Authority may overlook any offence.

37 The issue of technical competence is currently subject to consultation by the DoE. Technical competence is likely to revolve around a qualification issued by the Waste Management Industry Training and Advisory Board (WAMITAB).

38 S36(2) The section is not yet in force. It is possible, of course, that the reference to an established use certificate should be amended to make reference to the new certificate of lawfulness of existing use or development under the Town and Country Planning Act 1990 as amended by the Planning and Compensation Act 1991.

Section 33(1)(c): The offence of harmful treatment etc. of waste

Section 33(1)(c) is one of the provisions of Part II of the Act which *is* in force. It is important both because it represents an extension of control over waste disposal and more particularly because liability under section 33(1)(c) can be incurred even where a waste management licence is in force.[39]

Subject to Regulation 9 of the Controlled Waste Regulations 1992 (see above) (whereby section 33(1) is not to apply to situations where a waste disposal licence would not be or have been required) it will apply whenever controlled waste is received or produced on a site.

The offence under the section is to "treat, keep or dispose of controlled waste in a manner likely to cause pollution of the environment or harm to human health." The penalties are as for a breach of subsections 33(1)(a) and (b).

Treating and disposing are defined as above in section 29. Pollution of the environment and harm to human health are defined in the same section. Pollution of the environment means "pollution of the environment" (*sic*) due to the release or escape into any of the environmental media[40] from:

- the land on which controlled waste is treated;
- the land on which controlled waste is kept;
- the land in or on which controlled waste is deposited; or
- fixed plant by means of which controlled waste is treated, kept or disposed of;

of substances or articles constituting or resulting from the waste and capable (by reason of the quantity or concentrations involved) of causing harm to man or any other living organisms supported by the environment.[41]

By section 29(5) "harm" means harm to the health of living organisms or other interference with the ecological systems of which they form part and in the case of man includes offence to any of his senses or harm to his property.[42] "Harmless" has a corresponding meaning.

There is no doubt that section 33(1)(c) will be a useful weapon in the armoury of the Waste Regulation Authority. Although the fact that it is

39 The Environmental Protection Act 1990 (Commencement No. 10) Order 1991, SI 1991/2829. Subsections 6 to 9 are also in force insofar as they relate to s33(1)(c).

40 Defined by s29(2) as all or any of land, water and the air.

41 S29(3).

42 Thus the "harm to human health" limb of the section seems to be merely duplicative of "pollution of the environment".

not to apply to any case where a waste disposal licence would not be required will limit the operation of the section on a construction site, it will apply to the transfer of controlled waste away from the site and whenever a waste disposal or waste management licence is required and even where they are fully complied with. The defences under section 33(7) will apply as they do to section 33(1)(a) and (b).

Section 34 Environmental Protection Act 1990—The "Duty of Care"

Section 34 of the Environmental Protection Act represents another extension of the regulation of waste management over and above that contained in the Control of Pollution Act. As with section 33(1)(c) of the Act it is a provision which has a wide and general effect beyond the traditional waste disposal industry. Like section 33(1)(c) it is also one of the provisions of this part of the Act which is already in force.

Section 34(1) provides that:

> "It shall be the duty of any person who imports, produces, carries, treats, keeps or disposes of controlled waste or, as a broker, has control of such waste, to take all such measures applicable to him in that capacity as are reasonable in the circumstances
> (a) to prevent any contravention by any other person of section 33 [of the Act];
> (b) to prevent the escape of the waste from his control or that of any other person; and
> (c) on the transfer of the waste to secure
>   (i) that the transfer is only to an authorised person or to a person for authorised transport purposes; and
>   (ii) that there is transferred such a written description of the waste as will enable other persons to avoid a contravention of that section and to comply with the duty under this sub-section as respects the escape of waste".

By section 34(6) any person who fails to comply with the duty imposed by section 34(1) will be guilty of an offence. The duty is not a civil law duty in the sense that a breach will sound in damages. Liability on summary conviction is to a fine not exceeding £20,000. Liability on conviction on indictment is to an unlimited fine. However in this case, there is no risk of imprisonment. "Controlled waste" has the same meaning as for section 33.[43]

The extent of the duty of care imposed by section 34(1) has been explained both in Department of the Environment Circular 19/91 "Environmental Protection Act 1990 : Section 34 The Duty of Care" and more

43 See above and the Controlled Waste Regulations 1992.

particularly in "Waste Management : The Duty of Care : a Code of Practice" published jointly by the Department of the Environment, Scottish and Welsh Offices under section 34(7) of the Act. Section 34(7) allowed the Secretary of State, after consultation with interested persons and bodies, to prepare and issue a code of practice for the purpose of providing to persons "practical guidance" on how to discharge the duty imposed on them by section 34(1).

The Code of Practice is important not simply because it expands on the requirements of the duty of care but because, by virtue of section 34(10), whilst it is not a defence to any criminal charge, it is admissible in evidence and is to be taken into account in determining any question to which any provision of the code appears to the court to be relevant.

Who is subject to the duty?

Section 34(1), as noted above, provides that this is anybody who "imports, produces, carries, keeps, treats or disposes of controlled waste or, as a broker, has control of such waste." In a construction context this needs to be seen in terms of the employer/client, the various consultants, the contractor and sub-contractors. Clearly, anyone directly responsible for controlled waste (for example, a subcontractor carrying the material to or away from the site or the contractor itself handling the waste on site) will be subject to the duty. There is more room for doubt with those not directly involved. It is conceivable that a consultant, or even the employer/client, may be found subject to the duty if indirectly involved in the selection or approval of controlled waste as a construction material. Equally, it could be argued that the employer/client produces or keeps controlled waste to the extent that the construction is subject to its ultimate control and is for its benefit.

Department of the Environment Circular 19/91 recognises that these arguments will arise particularly in the construction and demolition industries and so gives special advice at paragraphs 16 and 17 as to who is to be considered subject to the duty. The advice is repeated in Annex B to the Code of Practice.

The starting point for deciding who is a "producer" is said to be in deciding how the material became waste. Where an action is involved the producer will be the person committing the act. Where no action is involved the producer will be the person holding the waste who decides that it is waste. The Department's view is that the producer is to be regarded as the person undertaking the works that give rise to the waste, not the person who issues instructions or lets contracts. Although the client for the works may issue instructions that give rise to waste he does not physically produce the waste.

Where there are several contractors on site the producer of a particular waste is the particular contractor who takes the action that produces the waste or who treats something as if it were waste.

A client or contractor may, however, act as a broker of waste, by letting a contract for its removal and disposal away from the site. Paragraph 17 of the Circular concludes that every contractor (*i.e.* the main and all sub-contractors) on site will either be producing or carrying waste and so will be subject to the duty.

Clearly all parties need to be aware of the potential liabilities. It needs to be ensured that, where necessary, warranties are given that the duty under section 34 will be complied with. The existing provisions of the ICE and JCT standard forms probably cover this point in general but it may be useful to include more specific provisions.

The extent of the duty

The duty itself is in three parts.

- obligations on the transfer of waste,
- prevention of contravention by any other person of section 33 of the Act,
- prevention of escape of waste.

Obligations on the transfer of waste

Taking the transfer of waste first, the duty is to ensure that waste is transferred only to an authorised person *or* to a person for authorised transport purposes, *and* to see that there is transferred with the waste a written description of the waste sufficient to enable other persons both to avoid contravention of section 33 of the Act and to comply with the duty under section 34 as regards the escape of waste. The duty to provide a written description is supplemented by the requirement to provide a transfer note under the Environmental Protection (Duty of Care) Regulations 1991 (see below). Authorised persons for the purposes of section 34(1) are set out in subsection (3). In brief these are the Waste Collection Authority,[44] holders of waste management or waste disposal licences, persons to whom section 33(1) of the Act does not apply, and anyone registered as a carrier of controlled waste under the Control of Pollution (Amendment) Act 1989[45] (or a person who is not required to be registered).

---

44 Once more, usually the county council.

45 For which see below, p. 101.

Authorised transport purposes are described in subsection (4). These are:

- the transport of controlled waste within the same premises between different places in those premises;
- the transport to a place in Great Britain of controlled waste which has been brought from a country or territory outside Great Britain not having been landed in Great Britain until it arrives at that place; and
- the transport by air or sea of controlled waste from a place in Great Britain to a place outside Great Britain.

In the majority of cases, where controlled waste is being taken off a construction site (or is collected to be taken to a site)[46] then the transfer is likely to be to a contractor who is either a registered waste carrier or the holder of a waste disposal licence or waste management licence. The point is to ensure that this is the case.

Whether a carrier contracted to take waste from a site which is registered is revealed by inspection of the Waste Regulation Authority's register of carriers. Alternatively, the carrier can be asked to produce his registration certificate. If waste is collected on a regular basis or a number of trips are made to remove one load of waste by the same carrier then it may not be necessary to repeat these checks for each collection. They should, however, be repeated if collections are more irregular. The Code of Practice specifically recommends[47] that evidence of registration or exemption should be obtained afresh:

- whenever a new transaction is involved *i.e.* if the description or destination of the waste has changed;
- where several different carriers or disposers are collecting waste at one place and there might be a danger of an unauthorised carrier collecting a load (the specific example given is a construction or demolition site, where a number of sub-contractors may be involved);
- once a year even where there has been no change in a series of repeated transfers;
- where there has been change in the licence conditions of the destination.

The Code of Practice is clearly suggesting that these are the steps necessary to show that the person subject to the duty of care has taken all

---

46 If it is, then the subcontractor needs to be registered under the Control of Pollution (Amendment) Act 1989 for which see below, p. 101.

47 Paragraph 3.14.

measures applicable to him as are reasonable to ensure the transfer to an authorised person for authorised transport purposes.

The duty to provide a written description on transfer needs, as noted above, is to be considered in conjunction with the Environmental Protection (Duty of Care) Regulations 1991.[48] These Regulations were made under section 34(5) of the Act which enabled the Secretary of State to make provision imposing requirements on any person who is subject to the duty imposed by section 34(1) as respects the making and retention of documents and the furnishing of documents or copies of documents. The Regulations deal solely with that issue. Failure to comply with regulations made under section 34(5) is itself a criminal offence,[49] subject to the same penalties as failure to comply with the duty.

The Regulations refer to the Act and define the transferor and transferee of waste as, respectively, the person who in compliance with section 34(1) of the Act transfers a written description of waste and the person who receives that description. Note the definition by reference to the document rather than the product.

Regulation 2 then provides: "(1) The transferor and the transferee shall, at the same time as the written description of the waste is transferred, ensure that such a document as is described in paragraph (2) ("a transfer note") is completed and signed on their behalf".

By subsection (2) a transfer note shall:

(a) identify the waste to which it relates and state
  (i) its quantity and whether on transfer it is loose or in a container;
  (ii) if in a container, the kind of container; and
  (iii) the time and place of transfer;

(b) give the name and address of the transferor and the transferee;

(c) state whether or not the transferor is the producer or importer of the waste and, if so, which;

(d) if the transfer is to a person for authorised transfer purposes specify which of these purposes; and

(e) state as respects the transferor and the transferee which, if any, of the categories of person [authorised persons under section 34(3) of the Act] describes him.

If the transferee is a registered waste carrier then the transfer note must specify the name of the Waste Regulation Authority with whom he is regis-

48 SI 1991/2839.

49 S34(6).

tered and his registration number. If the transferee is the holder of a waste management or waste disposal licence then the transfer note must, if that person is to keep, treat or dispose of the waste, state the relevant licence number and name of the licensing authority.

Each of the transferor and transferee is to keep the written description of the waste and the transfer note (or at least copies) for a period of two years from the date of the transfer of the waste.[50] The Waste Regulation Authority may by notice require a transfer note to be produced within a period of not less than seven days to the authority's office.[51]

A precedent transfer note is set out in the Code of Practice. The Code recommends that the written description of the waste is either provided separately to the note or, perhaps more usually, as part of the note. Circular 25/91 simply advises that the Regulations do not prevent the description and transfer note being combined into one document where that is convenient.[52]

What the written description should contain clearly depends on the individual situation. The Code recommends that any special problems, requirements or knowledge should always be identified and that the description should include some combination of:

- the type of premises or business from which the waste comes;
- the name of the substance or substances comprised in the waste;
- the process that produced the waste; and
- a chemical and physical analysis.

The aim is for the written description to provide enough information to enable subsequent holders to avoid mismanaging the waste.[53] Clearly, some types of waste will require a fuller description than others. Obviously, not all waste will require a chemical and physical analysis. The Code suggests at paragraph 1.6 that questions which might be asked are:

- whether the waste needs a special container to prevent its escape;
- whether it can be safely mixed with other waste and whether there is anything with which it should not be mixed;
- whether it can be safely crushed and transferred from one vehicle to another;
- whether it can safely be incinerated or whether incineration is subject to certain requirements;

50 Regulation 3. There appears to be no particular reason for the time limit chosen.

51 Regulation 4.

52 Paragraph 20.

53 Paragraph 1.10.

- whether it can safely be buried in a landfill site with other waste; and
- whether there are significant quantities of an unexpected substance or even unusual amounts of an expected substance.

Details of any problems previously encountered with the waste should be identified as should changes to the description since any previous load was collected.[54] The Code also recommends that it is good practice to label drums and other closed containers with a description of the waste. Though only a recommendation, labelling would actually seem to be fundamental in most cases.

The duties of transfer will apply not only to waste removed from a site, but also to any waste *received* on site. Any contractor bringing waste to the site will want to ensure that the contractor or person responsible for its receipt is an "authorised person" (which may present difficulties in the absence of a waste disposal licence[55]) and that a transfer note is produced. The person receiving the waste should check back through the transfer note chain and also see that the transferor is a registered carrier.

Preventing the contravention of section 33

The Code of Practice concentrates principally on the specific duties on the transfer of waste and the prevention of its escape rather than this more general duty. Essentially, however, compliance with those aspects of the duty should be enough to fulfil this element.

Ensuring transfer to an authorised person with an adequate written description should be sufficient. As the Circular points out, a person to whom the duty applies is only expected to take such measures as are "applicable to him" in his particular capacity as producer, importer, carrier or broker, and "reasonable in the circumstances". The Code[56] states that a producer is under no specific duty to audit the waste's final destination although periodic site visits would be "prudent" to demonstrate the steps taken to prevent subsequent illegal disposal. Where there are two contracts with the producer, one for carriage and one for disposal, then the producer should establish that the waste reached the disposal point. As with other examples of regulation by code of practice, this places the burden on those in the waste chain to determine what action they need to take to be reasonable and applicable.

---

54 Paragraph 1.11.

55 Unless the contractor actually receiving the waste is a registered waste carrier. This would appear to satisfy the duty even if that particular contractor were not transporting the waste.

56 Paragraph 2.2.

The Code does, however, indicate that it may be necessary to consider what will happen to the waste further along the disposal chain where, for instance, waste needs to reach its final disposal or treatment place in its original container. Then the holder will need to satisfy himself that that will happen.

Otherwise, the Code recommends[57] that every waste holder should be alert for evidence that his waste is not being dealt with properly, including where they become aware of problems further down the waste chain over which they may have no control. If unsatisfied, the holder should refuse to continue transferring or accepting waste, ensuring that waste disposal contracts allow termination in this situation.[58] Stringent precautions should be taken if the arrangements do have to continue. The relevant authority should be informed by those involved in the waste chain of any suspected breach of the provisions of the Act.[59]

Preventing the escape of waste

Advice on this aspect of the duty is contained in section 2 of the Code of Practice. The advice is to protect against:

- corrosion or wear of waste containers;
- accidental spilling or leaking;
- accident or weather breaking contained waste open and allowing it to escape;
- waste blowing away or falling while stored or transported; and
- scavenging by vandals, thieves, children, trespassers or animals.

Waste being transferred should be packed well enough to ensure it reaches its next destination safely and, as above, its final destination if that is important.

Paragraphs 2.3 to 2.7 have particular implications for the construction industry. Construction waste will, in some circumstances, be attractive to scavengers and so it should be stored securely. Loose waste should not be transferred unless it is immediately transferred to a vehicle and then covered sufficiently to prevent escape. Otherwise it should be in some form of container which should suit the particular type of waste. Waste left for collection outside premises should be in secure, sealed containers and

57 Paragraph 5.5.

58 Paragraph 5.8.

59 There will be an obvious reluctance to do so unless the holder is certain that he will not himself be charged with a breach of the duty of care.

should not be left longer than necessary. Different categories of waste should, where necessary, be segregated to prevent the mixture of wastes that are incompatible.[60]

Department of Environment view

Annex B to the Code of Practice provides a helpful summary of what the Department of the Environment at least sees as the responsibilities under the duty. The advice for the construction and demolition industries contained in Circular 19/91 is repeated.

Waste producers are said to bear the main responsibility for:

- care of the waste while they hold it;
- the description of the waste which leaves them;
- if they select a final treatment or disposal destination, for ensuring that the waste falls within the terms of any licence or exemption (jointly with the waste manager); and
- packing the waste to prevent escape in transit.

A producer is said to be responsible "according to what he knows or should have foreseen". He should take note of anything he learns about the handling of his waste, particularly if he learns or suspects that it is not being taken to a legitimate destination.

The example given is where a carrier's vehicles are seen returning for collection in a shorter period than would be required to reach the correct disposal site, or where the producer becomes aware that a carrier is illegally disposing of someone else's waste. This evidence is ignored at the producer's peril.

Those importing waste are advised to act in most respects as if they were the producer. A waste carrier should ensure that packaging is adequate and make at least a visual inspection to see that the waste complies with the written description. Only if the waste alters in any way will a new description be necessary on the next transfer. The carrier will need to check the terms of any licence or exemption where he transfers waste for disposal or treatment.

Waste brokers (which, as noted above, could include in the construction context the employer/client) are advised to act as if they were both producer and the final waste manager. Ultimately, they need to be sure of the legality of the whole waste chain from "cradle to grave".

---

60 It is left to the holder to determine what is incompatible.

Control of Pollution (Amendment) Act 1989: the registration of waste carriers

Mention has already been made of the Control of Pollution (Amendment) Act 1989 and the registration of waste carriers. This Act is another measure which needs to be taken into account in the disposal of waste from a construction site.

In brief, section 1(1) of the Act provides that it is a criminal offence for any person:

> "who is not a registered carrier of controlled waste, in the course of any business of his or otherwise with a view to profit, to transport any controlled waste to or from any place in Great Britain".

The offence is triable only summarily. Liability is to a fine not exceeding £5,000.

There are a number of exceptions to the requirement to register. By section 1(2) of the Act a person is not to be guilty of an offence in respect of the transport of waste for what are effectively the authorised transport purposes under the Environmental Protection Act.

The details of the registration process are prescribed in the Controlled Waste (Registration of Carriers and Seizure of Vehicles) Regulations 1991.[61] These also provide for other exemptions. By Regulation 2(1)(b) the *producer* of the controlled waste in question is exempt from the requirement to be a registered carrier, but *not* where the controlled waste is building or demolition waste. "Building or demolition waste" is defined as waste arising from works of construction or demolition, including waste arising from work preparatory thereto, and "construction" is to include improvements, repairs or alterations.[62]

The defences available to the person charged with an offence under section 1 of the Act are listed in section 1(4):

(a) that the waste was transported in an emergency of which notice was given as soon as practicable after it occurred to the waste regulation authority;
(b) that the person neither knew nor had reasonable grounds for suspecting that what he was transporting was controlled waste and took all such steps as it was reasonable to take for ascertaining whether it was such waste; or
(c) that he acted under instruction from his employer.

---

61 SI 1991/1624 made under powers conferred on the Secretary of State under the Control of Pollution (Amendment) Act 1989.

62 Regulation 2(2).

Otherwise it is likely that any contractor working on a construction site who transports controlled waste away from that site or any contractor coming to the site to collect waste will need to be registered. Controlled waste is given the same meaning for the purposes of this Act as for the Control of Pollution Act.[63]

Registration can be refused by the Waste Regulation Authority, to whom application must be made, where either the applicant or another relevant person[64] has been convicted of a "prescribed" offence and in the opinion of the authority it is undesirable for the applicant to be authorised to transport controlled waste. Existing registration may be revoked on the same grounds.[65] Prescribed offences for the purposes of the Act are listed in Schedule 1 to the Controlled Waste (Registration of Carriers and Seizure of Vehicles) Regulations 1991 and in the main involve offences in relation to the handling of waste.

The details of the application process are also outlined in those Regulations. Section 4 of the Act provides for a right of appeal against refusal of registration.

Another provision of the Act which is of interest is section 5 by which the police and duly authorised officers of waste regulation authorities are given the power to stop anyone appearing to be transporting controlled waste in contravention of section 1 of the Act and to require that person to produce his or his employer's authority for transporting that waste. Powers are also given to search the vehicle and take away samples for testing of anything that is found. It is an offence intentionally to obstruct either the police or such an officer in the exercise of their powers.[66]

Section 6 of the Act is headed "Seizure and disposal of vehicles used for illegal waste disposal". By section 6(1) power is given for the issue of a warrant for the seizure of any vehicle if the Justice of the Peace issuing the warrant is satisfied, on sworn information in writing, that there are reasonable grounds for believing that an offence under section 3 of the Control of Pollution Act 1974, or section 33 of the Environmental Protection Act has been committed, that the vehicle was used in the commission of the offence, that proceedings for that offence have not yet been brought against any person and that the Waste Regulation Authority have failed, after taking prescribed steps to ascertain the name and address of any person

---

63 See s9.

64 For which see s3(5).

65 S 3(2).

66 Provided s5(5) that it is shown that the waste in question was controlled waste and that the person did transport it to or from a place in Great Britain, the authority to be produced is the certificate of registration as a carrier of controlled waste.

who is able to provide them with the prescribed information about who was using the vehicle at the time when the offence was committed.

By section 6(2) and (3) power is given to stop and seize the vehicle which is the subject of the warrant together with its contents subject to the proviso that a waste regulation officer may not stop and seize a vehicle unless a constable is present. Once more it is an offence to intentionally obstruct any authorised officer or constable in the exercise of their powers.

Regulation of "special waste"

Under section 17 of the Control of Pollution Act 1974, the Secretary of State was given power to make special provision for the regulation of the disposal of controlled waste that is "so dangerous or difficult to dispose of" that special provision should be made.

This the Secretary of State did by the Control of Pollution (Special Waste) Regulations 1980.[67] Under the Regulations, controlled waste is to have the same meaning as under the Control of Pollution Act.[68] By Regulation 2(1) "special waste" is controlled waste but distinguished by reference to the fact that it consists of or contains any of the substances listed in Part 1 of Schedule 1 to the Regulations *and*, by reason of the presence of that substance is dangerous to life, or has a certain flashpoint, or is a certain type of medicinal product. The substances listed in Part 1 of Schedule 1 includes acids and alkalines, asbestos, lead and mercury compounds. What is meant by dangerous to life is described in Part 2 of Schedule 1 by reference to volume and the effect of ingestion or exposure.

The duties on the producer of special waste are similar to those imposed on the transferor of controlled waste under the duty of care under the Environmental Protection Act (which may therefore be seen as elevating what was formerly the duty only for special waste, to apply to *all* controlled waste).

By Regulation 4 of the Regulations, any person who produces special waste must, before the waste is removed from the premises on which it is produced, prepare six copies of a "consignment note" in the form set out in Schedule 2 to the Regulations.

One copy of the consignment note must then be sent to the "disposal authority" (now the waste regulation authority) for the area in which the waste is to be disposed of. The note must be sent to the authority not more than one month and not less than three clear days before the removal of

67 SI 1980/1709.
68 Regulation 1.

the waste. One copy of the consignment note must be retained by the producer. All the remaining copies of the consignment note are to be given to any carrier removing the waste from the site.

The purpose of the Regulations is to allow the waste regulation authority to trace the progress of the waste to its final destination. Hence under Regulation 5, the carrier of the waste, having completed various parts of the note, is to furnish copies of the consignment note to the disposer of the waste. Keeping one copy for himself, the disposer of the waste must then produce a copy of the consignment note to the disposal authority, again retaining copies for himself.

The producer of special waste is to keep, at each site at which it is produced, a register containing copies of all consignment notes relating to special waste produced at the site. A carrier is to keep a register of consignment notes relating to all special waste he has transferred for disposal. A disposer at each disposal site is to keep a register containing copies of all consignment notes relating to special waste disposal at that site.

The records are to be kept for two years in the case of producers and carriers. Disposers are to keep copies of consignment notes until such time as the relevant waste disposal licence is surrendered or revoked.[69] A disposer of special waste is also to keep a record of where precisely on site the special waste is disposed of.

It is probably unlikely that special waste will be received on a construction site for what amounts to a disposal. It is more likely, however, that it may be produced, perhaps through demolition or excavation of a contaminated site, and that the duties under the Special Waste Regulations will need to be complied with.

Failure to comply with the Regulations is once more a criminal offence.

The important point is that compliance with the Special Waste Regulations does not obviate the need to comply also with the duty of care under section 34 of the Environmental Protection Act in respect of a written description and transfer note. This is an issue which experience shows is one likely to be misunderstood and overlooked in practice. The fact is[70] that compliance with the Regulations in the production of a consignment note will go a long way to satisfying the requirements under the duty of care for a written description and transfer note. In practice, the additional information required in a transfer note could simply be added to the consignment note.

Although the power is given in the Environmental Protection Act for the Secretary of State to make further provision as to the control of the

69 Regulation 13.

70 This is recognised in Circular 19/91 paragraphs 26 and 27.

disposal of special waste, he has not yet done so and, for the moment, the provisions of the duty of care and those of the Special Waste Regulations overlap.

Civil liability for damage caused by waste

Much of this paper has concentrated on the potential criminal liabilities in the management of waste either brought on to a construction site or produced on a site. However, damage caused by that waste may also give rise to civil liability. This may arise either by statute or under the common law.

The Control of Pollution and Environmental Protection Acts

Section 88(1) of the Control of Pollution Act provides:[71]

> "Where any damage is caused by poisonous, noxious or polluting waste which has been deposited on land, any person who deposited it, or caused or knowingly permitted it to be deposited, in either case so as to commit an offence under section 33(3) . . . of this Act is liable for the damage except where the damage
> (a) was due *wholly* to the fault of the person who suffered it; or
> (b) was suffered by a person who voluntarily accepted the risk of the damage being caused."

By section 88(2) the defences available under section 3(4) of the Act on a prosecution for an offence under section 3(1) are available to a claim of civil liability for damage under section 88(1). Liability is not, therefore, strict.

What is meant by "poisonous, noxious or polluting waste" is not defined (but it should be noted that liability is not restricted to damage covered by controlled waste). It may be thought that, if damage were proved ("damage" being defined as including the death of, or injury to, any person—including disease and any impairment of physical or mental condition), then the nature of the waste would be presumed.

That issue will not arise when the replacement section in the Environmental Protection Act is brought into force. Section 73(6) provides:

> "Where any damage is caused by waste which has been deposited in or on land, any person who deposited it, or knowingly caused or knowingly permitted it to be deposited, in either case so as to commit an offence under section 33(1) . . . is liable for the damage except for the damage
> (a) which is due *wholly* to the fault of the person who suffered it; or
> (b) was suffered by a person who voluntarily accepted the risk of the damage being caused."

71 By s105(2) no other action lies for breach of statutory duty.

As with section 88(1) of the Control of Pollution Act, the provision is without prejudice to any other claim that may arise from the damage caused. Damage is defined as previously and again, liability is not strict as the defences available under section 33(7) of the Act are again available in a claim under this section.

The important point with both provisions is that they apply to the "deposit" of waste and not apparently to the other forms of treatment which might require authority. This will limit the situations in which the section will apply to the construction site. Liability will in this context, however, attach not just to the contractor who may directly make the deposit but to any person who knowingly permitted the deposit. An addition in the Environmental Protection Act is "knowingly" before "caused".

Interestingly the subsection does not cover damage resulting from the failure to comply with the duty of care under section 34 of the Environmental Protection Act. It is likely, however, that where there has been a failure to comply with that duty, the enforcing authority may also bring a prosecution under section 33(1)(c) of the Act thereby remedying the position.

Both civil liability provisions need to be viewed together with the power of the waste regulation authority to enter a site to clean up illegally deposited waste and recover the cost of doing so from either the occupier of the land or, in certain circumstances, the person who made the deposit or knowingly caused or knowingly permitted the deposit of the waste to take place.[72] Similar powers are given to the National Rivers Authority under section 161 of the Water Resources Act 1991 where it appears that any poisonous, noxious or polluting matter or any solid waste is likely to enter, or to be, or to have been, present in any controlled water.

Common law

An analysis of the possible common law liabilities for damage caused by the handling of waste is outside the scope of this paper.

Potential actions in nuisance, negligence, the rule in *Rylands* v *Fletcher* and even trespass clearly exist, however, if waste is not handled correctly. There are limitations on the efficacy of the common law in actions for environmental damage, largely due to the elements necessary to make out the cause of action itself. The potential, however, is there and should not be ignored.

---

72 S16 Control of Pollution Act and ss 59 and 42 Environmental Protection Act 1990.

EC proposals on civil liability

Liability for damage caused by waste is also very much an issue at European Community level and an area where a number of proposals are under consideration. The Council of Europe has published a circular on Civil Liability for Damage Resulting from Activities Dangerous to the Environment (which the United Kingdom does not propose at the moment to sign) and the Commission has issued, for discussion, a Green Paper on remedying environmental damage.[73]

The most important proposal, as far as waste in particular is concerned, is the draft directive on Civil Liability for Damage Caused by Waste.[74] The directive proposes a system of strict liability for "damage" (defined as damage resulting from death or physical injury or damage to property) *or* "impairment of the environment" (defined as any significant physical, chemical or biological deterioration of the environment, insofar as it does not also constitute "damage"), from waste generated in the course "of an occupational activity". "Waste" is defined as in the Waste Framework Directive.

Liability is imposed on the producer of the waste (which includes the person with control of the waste if he cannot, within a reasonable period of time, identify the producer) from the moment that waste arises until its final disposal (provided that disposal is at a properly licensed site or installation and the disposer of the waste has not been misled as to its character).

Member States, by national laws, are to determine the remedies available but these must include injunctions restricting the act causing the damage or impairment or ordering reinstatement, and damages. Further, and importantly, common interest groups must be given the right to take or join an action. Exclusion clauses will be prohibited and the existence of a licence or permit will not be a defence. Issues of contributory fault will, however, arise.

A limitation period will be imposed of three years from the date of awareness (or deemed awareness) of the damage or impairment and thirty years from the date of the incident giving rise to the damage or impairment.

Finally, producers will be required to be insured against liability under the directive and to include a note of the insurance in any annual report. The directive provides that the Commission is to study the feasibility of a European Fund for Compensation where the person liable cannot be identified or is unable to compensate fully.

73 Com (93)47.

74 Com (91)219.

Personal liability

As a final point, the directors and managers of construction companies should not sit too comfortably behind the corporate veil. In a provision familiar from the Health and Safety at Work Act 1974 both the Control of Pollution Act[75] and the Environmental Protection Act[76] provide that where an offence has been committed under the Act by a body corporate and

> "is proved to have been committed with the consent or connivance of, or to have been attributable to any neglect on the part, of any director, manager, secretary or other similar officer of the body corporate or a person who was purporting to act in any such capacity, he as well as the body corporate shall be guilty of the offence and shall be liable to be proceeded against and punished accordingly."

Experience shows that the enforcing authorities are already taking advantage of these provisions and will increasingly do so under public pressure to prosecute those seen as truly responsible for environmental offences and damage.

75 S87(1).
76 S157.

5 Hazardous substances and clean-up

Dr Stephan A Jefferis

Introduction

The purpose of this paper is to give an overview of the engineering and technical issues associated with contaminated land and landfills. There are of course social as well as technical issues that must be debated and answers must be formulated to questions such as:

- What is an acceptable level of contamination?
- How clean is clean?
- Should every contaminated site be cleaned?
- Should landfills be sited only in geologically suitable areas despite the extra haul costs?
- What price should we be prepared to pay for landfill?
- How should toxic and hazardous wastes be disposed?
- What proportion of the national budget should be spent on the clean-up of past pollution and the prevention of new pollution?

At the present time there are no simple answers to these questions. Furthermore there are not even generally accepted definitions of basic terms such as "hazardous" and "toxic". However, two definitions can be advanced:

- hazard is the property or characteristic of a material, situation or activity which gives it potential for harm; and
- risk is the likelihood or expected frequency of a specified adverse consequence.

Thus the purpose of engineering work associated with contaminated land and landfills should be to reduce the risk posed by the hazardous substances that may be present as contaminants in soil or which are being or have been disposed to landfill and to do this at a reasonable cost. Unfortunately the techniques of risk analysis are relatively new and although they are very useful for identifying relative risks associated with different actions/remedial measures *etc.* the evaluation of absolute risks still leaves much room for debate.

At the present time perceived hazard tends to be the driving force for much pollution control whereas risk ought to be the controlling factor. Designers should be required to ensure that their facilities meet realistic risk criteria (which may in themselves be difficult to accept) and, for example, could take the form that a site should not cause more than 1 extra cancer per 100,000 of the exposed population (the chance of death from cancer in the general population is probably in the range 1 in 3 to 1 in 7).

Because there is currently no generally accepted definition of what is hazardous in this paper the term contamination will be used to describe all materials that could be hazardous.

It is often held that contamination may be present in all formerly used industrial land. However, if all materials which may be damaging to man, his structures or the environment are regarded as contaminants then it must be accepted that all land is potentially contaminated. Nature has produced more toxic chemicals than man and even in England very aggressive natural soils can be found.

However, when considering the contamination of land it is usually the chemicals etc. that have been brought onto the site by past or current users that are of the most immediate concern. Some of the major problems associated with contaminated land and landfills are:

- threats to human health;
- damage to flora and fauna;
- contamination of ground water;
- damage of underground foundations and structures;
- settlement of the ground as a result of degradation of deposited materials; and
- migration of contaminants to adjacent land.

Contaminant migration

The migration of contaminants is possibly one of the most serious issues associated with contamination. If contaminants remained where they were initially deposited and did not move the only necessary preventive measures would be to limit direct contact with or ingestion of the contaminant. However, the contaminants do move and contamination will always tend to spread. In this respect contamination can be likened to heat. If a rod is heated at one end then the heat will be conducted along it and the heat flow can be stopped only if it is cut and an insulator is interposed in the bar. If contamination is present in the soil it will tend to spread outwards unless stopped by some barrier. To control the spread of contamination it is therefore necessary to identify the mechanisms by which contamination may spread in the ground and what may form a barrier. Contamination may move as a result of:

- solution in ground water and movement with the water or diffusion through it;
- solution in rain water percolating down through the soil;
- density differentials between liquid contaminants or solutions; and the soil pore fluid;
- the generation and migration of gases;
- dust blown from the surface of soils especially if poorly vegetated;
- uptake by plant roots etc; and
- human activity.

Fundamentally all natural processes tend to reduce differences of potential in the environment. These potentials may be of temperature, water pressure, chemical concentration etc. The process of diffusion noted above is a typical example of such a levelling process. Molecules in a liquid are in continual movement and this movement will tend to smooth out any differences in concentration. For example, tea will diffuse from a tea bag immersed in water and the solution will take on a uniform colour after a few minutes even without stirring. Thus the spread of contamination is a natural process and to stop it will require either that the source is removed or the continued operation of some control system.

When considering contaminant migration it is also important to keep in mind that some materials, either natural or man made, which are initially harmless may become toxic or hazardous as a result of deposition/reaction with the ground water etc. A trivial example of such a process is the generation of methane and carbon dioxide from rubbish deposited in a landfill. These gases may be generated from the degradation of paper which in itself is harmless. Another example is the generation of sulphuric acid and the release of heavy metals from some mine spoils as a result of oxidation of materials such as iron sulphide by atmospheric oxygen (these materials are stable at depth in the ground where oxygen is not available). Interestingly both methane generation and mine spoil oxidation are bacterially mediated and when considering any contamination present in the ground it is important to keep in mind that bacteria may create niche environments where the chemical conditions and thus the reaction products are quite different to those that would be expected in the bulk soil.

It must also be noted that very small amounts of a contaminant may "pollute" very large volumes of soil or ground water. For example the guide level for many chlorinated solvents in drinking water is 1 part per billion. These materials typically have a solubility in water of 1 part in one thousand.

Thus a spill of 1 kg of solvent could saturate 1000 litres of ground water with the solvent and as it spread out into the surrounding ground water it could contaminate a total 1,000,000,000 litres of ground water to the guide level.

Finally not all chemicals will behave in the same way in the soil and it is useful to distinguish a number of material types.

Physical properties of contaminants

Solid materials of low solubility

These are materials of low solubility in ground water. They may move only slowly from the region where they were deposited. However, caution is necessary when describing any contaminant as of low solubility. For, as shown above, materials can be unacceptable in water when present at concentrations much below their solubility limit. Thus solubility is mainly of concern as regards the rate of migration from the site of deposition and says nothing about the resulting risk.

Many heavy metals in the soil may be in low solubility forms but are still capable of rendering any ground water with which they come in contact unfit for use as drinking water.

Soluble materials

Soluble materials are those which can dissolve in and move with the ground water and thus may move relatively rapidly from the point of deposition if there is a significant flow of ground water or infiltration of rain water. However, if water movement is limited, for example in clay soils, even highly soluble chemicals may remain as solids. The author has seen examples of highly soluble and even hygroscopic chemicals which have remained as bulk solids in the soil for many decades.

Light non-aqueous phase liquids

These are liquids which are of low solubility in water (non-aqueous phase liquids) and which are less dense than water. These liquids when spilled or released into the soil will sink downwards through unsaturated soils until they meet the ground water table. At this point they will cease to sink and will float on the water and then spread laterally from the point of release. In this way light non-aqueous phase liquids can travel substantial distances horizontally from the point of release. An example of this type of liquid would be petroleum spirit and spillages from garage forecourts have caused problems in basements at some considerable distance.

Dense non-aqueous phase liquids

There are also non-aqueous phase fluids which are denser than water and which will sink down through the soil but will not stop when they meet the ground water but continue to sink through it. An example of this type of contamination would be the chlorinated solvents that caused the problems in Eastern Counties Leather. A feature of dense non-aqueous phase liquids (dnapls) is that they can move down through sands and gravels but may not penetrate finer soils such as silts and clays. Thus dnapls may sink until they meet a fine soil layer. They will then move horizontally following any natural slope of the layer and finally pond in any natural depressions in the layer. Thus dnapls may end up as discrete pools at considerable distance from the original point of release. These pools may be very difficult to locate or remediate.

Gases

Gases can move only through soils which have a continuous system of air voids unless the gas pressure is sufficient to blow water out of the soil and force a path through it. A soil can be likened to a system of fine capillary tubes and the pressure necessary to blow ground water out of these 'tubes' can be relatively high – especially in fine soils. Thus, in general, gases will move through soil only in the region above the ground water table. Below the ground water table gas migration can be only by solution in and movement through or with the ground water unless high driving pressures are available.

The movement of air/gases (for example landfill gas) through the soil may be strongly influenced by the prevailing weather conditions.

- In wet weather the surface may be flooded thus limiting vertical gas escape which may lead to a pressure build up and a tendency for greater lateral migration of the gas.
- In dry weather the soil may dry and crack thus opening up large channels for gas flow.
- In periods of low pressure gases may tend to be drawn out of the soil and in periods of high pressure air may be forced in.

It should be noted that there is a continual movement of air into and out of soils near the ground surface. This movement is driven by diffusion and changes in atmospheric pressure. If this movement were to cease much plant life would die.

Tars and semi-liquids

A number of former industrial processes and especially those involved in coal gasification produced tars as by-products. The heavier tars may at first sight appear to be solids but under sustained pressure they will flow. Thus if a tar is covered with soil it may slowly squeeze through the soil and at some much later time may break out at the surface.

Sorbed materials

Many soils are relatively inert and when chemicals are deposited in them they act merely as a "sponge" holding liquids but not reacting with or modifying them. However, for some combinations of soil type and contaminant the soil may act as a chemical as well as physical sponge. That is the chemicals may bind to the soil. For example, organic soils such as peat may very effectively bind organic chemicals such as petroleum spirit and clays may very effectively sorb some heavy metals. In general finer soils will be more effective chemical sponges than coarser soils as the chemicals are sorbed on the surface of the particles (if a coarse particle is cut into pieces its surface area will increase rapidly but the total weight of material will remain unchanged). Thus fine soils have much higher surface areas per unit weight than coarse materials.

Sorption can very substantially retard the migration of chemicals through the ground and much use has been made of the sorption characteristics of clays when designing repositories for nuclear and toxic waste. Sorption is particularly useful for the control of materials which will decay naturally such as radioactive waste and some organic materials. The hold up introduced by sorption may ensure that substantial degradation has occurred before any material reaches the biosphere.

It is also important to keep in mind the effects of sorption when undertaking site investigation work as certain parts of the soil profile may be much more heavily contaminated than others.

As a final point it should be noted that any chemical which is sorbed and does not decay naturally will ultimately move forward with the ground water. Thus sorption results in the slowing down of migration but not an absolute stop. However, with strongly sorbed materials the retardation may be by a factor of 1,000 or more and in clays or other soils where the ground water is only very slowly moving sorption may provide an effective barrier for centuries.

The chemistry of contaminants

The above classification is fundamentally based on physical rather than chemical properties of the contaminants. Chemically contaminants can be very diverse and it is not possible to give even an overview of chemical phenomena in a short paper. However, it is appropriate to note some general chemical types.

Inorganic chemicals

Inorganic chemicals include such materials as sodium chloride (table salt), calcium carbonate (chalk) etc. The heavy metals chromium, nickel cadmium etc. are inorganic chemicals. A particular feature of inorganic chemicals is that they cannot be broken down to harmless sub-constituents. Cadmium will remain toxic regardless of the other chemicals with which it is associated though it may be made less available if it is precipitated from solution or absorbed into a clay or other solids (contaminants are said to be available if there is an easy pathway between the source of the contamination, and the potential receptor or target under consideration, see below).

Organic chemicals

Carbon is unique amongst the chemical elements in the range of compounds that it can form. Chemicals containing carbon and hydrogen are collectively known as organic chemicals and they are the basis of all living organisms and many industrial processes including the plastics and petrochemical industries.

Aliphatic organic chemicals

Aliphatic organic chemicals are materials which contain the basic elements carbon and hydrogen either as straight or branched chains. Ethyl alcohol and butane are examples of such materials. Aliphatic hydrocarbons tend to be of low solubility in water unless they contain elements which promote solubilisation such as oxygen, nitrogen, sulphur etc.

Aromatic organic chemicals

Aromatic organic chemicals are similar to the aliphatics save that the chains are closed to form ring structures. Benzene with a single six membered carbon ring is the simplest aromatic chemical. Coal tars such as are found on old coal gasification sites may contain several interlinked rings.

As a general guideline aromatic chemicals tend to be more toxic and/or carcinogenic than aliphatic materials. They also tend to be slightly more soluble. As a result aromatic chemicals may pose a greater environmental/ health threat than aliphatic chemicals. However, on many contaminated sites both types of chemical will be found and thus the distinction between aliphatics and aromatics may be of limited significance.

Toxicity

A fundamental concern about contamination is that it may cause harm to human health. Many different classes of individuals may be at risk from the contamination present on a site. These may include site workers, neighbours, those who use ground water from neighbouring wells etc. Exposure to the contaminants may be by contact, inhalation, direct ingestion of contaminated soil, drinking or bathing in contaminated water, consuming meat or milk etc. from cattle which have grazed on the site etc. As a result it can be extremely difficult to quantify the dose received by any class of individuals and exposure may have to be assessed on the basis of worst credible levels. For populations living adjacent to sources of contamination it also may be necessary to consider lifetime average doses.

Once some measure of exposure has been established it is then necessary to establish the response. For this, dose-response relationships are necessary. However, establishing the response is complex. At the simplest, chemicals may have two types of toxic effect: acute and chronic. Acute toxics will produce immediate symptoms (such as are identified in the definition of special waste, see below). Data on acute toxicity actually determined for man are quite limited and are mainly based on accidental ingestion of chemicals though some data have been provided by methodical murderers. The bulk of acute toxicity data are in fact extrapolated from animal tests.

Chronic toxicity is that arising from continued exposure to low concentrations (below the acute level). The data on chronic toxicity are even more limited than for acute toxicity. Most of the data on chronic toxicity relate to exposure in the workplace where workers have been subjected to relatively high levels of contamination over many years. This type of exposure may have little relevance to contaminated land where the dose may be much lower and possibly over a shorter time span. Indeed very often the doses will be so small that they produce no measurable effect. The fundamental issue is then whether very small doses have a cumulative effect so that continued exposure or repeated doses ultimately cause damage. For some chemicals it would seem that there is a minimum dose level below which there is no effect but for others and especially carcinogens it is generally held that they can produce additive effects at all concentrations. This may be an overstatement of the real situation but at least it is conservative.

The situation is further complicated by the fact that there may be substantial variations in response between individuals. The balance between intake and elimination of chemicals from the body may be age-dependent and there may be threshold effects and possibly a long time lag between exposure and appearance of symptoms (*e.g.* asbestos). Also there may be strong synergistic effects (where the total effect of a combination of constituents is greater than the sum of their individual effects) or antagonistic effects (the functional opposite of synergistic effects, where the total effect is less than the sum of effects of the constituents). A further problem is that symptoms may be non specific. For example the human body seems to have a limited number of ways to react to insults. Thus many chemicals may produce the same clinical manifestation.

The Control of Pollution (Special Waste) Regulations 1980 provide one of the few legal definitions of a waste type. In these regulations a special waste is defined as any material containing substances listed in Part 1 Schedule 1 of the Regulations and which by reason of the presence of the substance is dangerous to life. Dangerous to life is defined as follows:

(a) single dose of not more than five cubic centimetres would be likely to cause death or serious damage to tissue if ingested by a child of 20 kg body weight; or
(b) exposure to it for 15 minutes or less would be likely to cause serious damage to human tissue by inhalation, skin contact or eye contact.

These definitions are cited as examples of the difficulty of defining hazard. Clearly any deliberate testing would be quite unacceptable.

Waste Management Paper No. 23 gives a substantial body of toxicity data and examples of its application to the identification of special wastes.

Even for inanimate matter such as building structures or services there are minimal data on the effects of contamination. There is currently research work under way at the UK Building Research Station but it will be some time before sufficient data are available to assess the effects of even a small fraction of the wide range of chemicals that may be found on a contaminated site.

Source-path-target models

From the preceding discussion on contaminant migration and toxicity it can be seen that there are many uncertainties associated with the analysis of the effects of contamination. These include:

- uncertainties relating to contaminant migration;
- uncertainties regarding the effects of chemicals both singly and in the complex mixtures typical of landfill leachate or contaminated land; and
- the multiplicity of targets that may be affected by the contamination including fauna, flora, structures etc.

Because of these uncertainties it is now recognised that for most situations it is necessary to adopt techniques of probabilistic risk analysis. In general these techniques will seek to analyse the situation by considering:

- the sources of contamination;
- the pathways by which the contamination may reach the targets; and
- the targets.

The source is thus the contamination which may include many different chemicals. The pathway is the route by which the contaminant reaches the target which may be human, the environment generally or part of a structure. Examples of pathways include: drinking contaminated ground water or bathing in it, direct ingestion of contaminated soil by a child suffering from pica, eating of meat from cattle which have grazed on a contaminated site or breathing air contaminated with vapours from the site.

To do a full analysis of the potential effects of contaminated land it is necessary to consider the many possible sources that might be on a site, the multiple pathways that may exist to the many different targets. The situation is thus exceedingly complex and it is for this reason that it is necessary to adopt statistical techniques of risk analysis.

Using such procedures it is possible to investigate "what-if" situations and in particular to identify significant and insignificant chemicals, pathways, targets etc. From the results of this type of analysis it may be possible to set limits on contamination so that the risk of harm to specific targets in a number of generic situations is acceptably low. Thus it may be possible to produce tables of acceptable levels for various contaminants. Many countries including the UK already have tables giving guidance on acceptable levels of contamination etc. However, for the most part they are not based on a common level of risk and in a number of countries the figures are now being re-worked to put them on a more formal risk based footing. Previously the tabulated values may have been dictated by many different issues including aesthetics as well as toxicity.

In principle a full risk analysis will always be preferable to an analysis by reference to generic tabular values as individual site specific data can be included. However, a full risk analysis may be very expensive and also currently the number of suitably qualified individuals to carry out such analyses is limited.

Clean-up of contaminated sites

There are a large number of proven and developing soil and ground water remediation technologies but as yet rather few have been employed in the UK with the exception of digging up and removal of the contamination to a landfill. However, removal to landfill merely transfers the problem to a new (though it is to be hoped more secure) location. Thus there is pressure to adopt procedures which do not involve transfer.

The suitability of a treatment method at any given site will be influenced by the characteristics of the site and the remedial technologies that are available. Important characteristics of the site will include:

- the types of contaminants at the site, their distribution and depth;
- the subsurface conditions (type of soil, depth to the water table);
- the surrounding environment (houses, parks, industry); and
- the time available for remediation.

Significant factors in evaluating any potential treatment option will include:

- its availability;
- its state of development;
- its demonstrated reliability and effectiveness;
- its perceived environmental impacts; and
- its cost.

Large sites may permit the use of relatively new technologies after suitable testing, while small sites will generally be remediated using proven, easily available techniques.

The source-pathway-target model is useful when categorising clean-up technologies. Thus clean-up may involve removal of the source, cutting of pathways, for example by mechanical barriers, or hardening the target (for a structure this could involve using more chemically resistant materials).

Source removal

As already noted source removal can be achieved by digging out the contamination and removing it to a landfill. Removal to landfill is not properly a clean-up procedure as it merely transfers the problem. However, it is practised very widely though its use may decline as landfill costs rise and actual clean-up technologies become more cost effective. An important point to note for disposal to landfill is that the chemical data used to assess the significance of the contamination at the original site (for example the parameters listed in the Interdepartmental Committee on the Redevelopment of Contaminated Land, ICRCL guidance notes) may not be sufficient to enable its disposal to landfill. Landfill disposal licences may pose quite different controls from those used to assess contamination in-situ. For example, the licence could limit the total amount of a rather short list of contaminants that may be accepted in the landfill per day or week but not the maximum acceptable concentration in the soil. Thus, for example, on site a soil might be designated as contaminated as a result of the concentration of organic material in it but the rate at which it could be accepted into a landfill might be controlled by another constituent, for example mercury.

If the source is to be treated rather than removed then there are three options. It may be treated in situ, it may be dug up and treated on-site, or it may be taken to a remote treatment facility. Ideally contamination would be treated in-situ as digging it up will always involve some spread of the contamination and exposure of workers to physical contact, dust, vapours etc.

Source clean-up procedures include:

Bioremediation

The fundamental concept of bioremediation is the use of bacteria to destroy organic contaminants. Bacteria may use organic contaminants as food for their activity and in so doing break down the contaminants to simpler molecules and ultimately to carbon dioxide, methane and water etc. Bacteria cannot destroy inorganic contaminants such as heavy metals though they may be used to extract or immobilise such materials. Bioremediation is still a quite young technology but has great potential in terms of cost and effectiveness for certain chemicals including petrol, diesel fuel, light mineral oils, and aromatic chemicals such as benzene, toluene etc. The basis of the process is to establish conditions in the soil which will enable those bacteria which can break down the organic materials to flourish. If the appropriate conditions are not established the numbers of bacteria may remain small and the rate of clean-up may be unacceptably slow. In general, establishing the right conditions will involve getting oxygen in the soil. Many natural organic chemicals such as oils will have survived for millennia in oxygen free environments and thus are effectively immune to bacterial attack in such environments. However, if oxygen and water are present they may be quite rapidly decomposed. At the present time only bacteria naturally present in the host soil are used for bioremediation as there is concern about the introduction of "foreign" bacteria into the soil. However, it may be necessary to boost the numbers of bacteria present in the soil by adding bacteria drawn from the site but cultured in the laboratory.

The rate of degradation decreases as chemical compounds become more complex, so that PCBs (polychlorinated biphenyls which can bio-accumulate in living tissue), carbon tetrachloride, trichloroethylene and similar chemicals and pesticides are not readily biodegradable. Some companies have developed specific micro-organisms to attack some of these chemicals, but as already noted the use of imported bacteria is considered to be doubtful.

In-situ bioremediation works best in sandy soils, at sites where the geology is uniform. Sites with well-defined point sources of contamination (*e.g.* a leaking tank) are more amenable to in-situ bioremediation than sites with multiple and ill-defined sources of contamination. It is often a preferred approach when the contamination is on-site, not affecting any off-site location and there is time available to use bioremediation (probably in the order of 6 months to several years).

When contaminated ground water is being bioremediated, it is usually recirculated, with oxygen or hydrogen peroxide and/or nutrients being added before the water is re-injected. In-situ bioremediation is being increasingly used in conjunction with other techniques such as vapour extraction and sparging (see below) to provide overall remediation of a site. However, it should be noted that bioremediation cannot reduce the concentrations of many contaminants to the levels that would be required for drinking water. As the concentration of the contaminants drops so will the number of bacteria and at some point the rate of breakdown may become very slow and effectively zero. If further breakdown is required it may be necessary to provide additional non-toxic organic material to maintain the bacterial numbers so that the contaminants are removed by co-metabolism of the contaminants and added materials.

Soil vapour extraction

The techniques of soil vapour extraction, forced air venting, and in-situ air stripping all revolve around the extraction of air containing volatile chemicals from unsaturated soil. The vapour laden air is withdrawn under vacuum from extraction wells, while fresh air is either injected or allowed to flow into the subsurface around the area that is impacted. It was initially used in the early to mid 1980s at petrol service stations where there had been spills or leaks of fuel, but its use quickly spread to the remediation of other chemical compounds including chlorinated solvents (though as was noted earlier such solvents tend to be denser than water and thus cannot be removed as vapour unless the local ground water level is lowered or air is injected under pressure so that it displaces the ground water).

Vapour extraction is only applicable to relatively volatile compounds and this restricts its use. It could not be used to remove heavy oils and tars etc.

Soil vapour extraction is particularly attractive at sites where areas of contamination are large and deep (greater than about 6 m), or when the contamination is beneath a building in relatively permeable soils.

The recovered gases also may need to be treated prior to discharge to atmosphere (for example by carbon absorption) and this can significantly increase the cost of the process. On some sites it may be possible to reduce costs by venting the gases into an existing industrial furnace or similar unit.

An alternative to soil vapour extraction is air sparging. In this process air is injected into the soil rather than extracted from it. The air may be injected either into the saturated or unsaturated zones of the soil. An advantage of the process is that the provision of air compressors is generally cheaper than vacuum pumps. Treatment of contamination below the water table (that is the saturated zone) is only possible in sands or coarser soils as the pressure required to force water from finer soils would be excessive.

Steam stripping

In-situ steam stripping is effectively a similar procedure to air sparging save that the soil is heated to encourage volatilisation of the contaminants. The procedure was first used in the Netherlands in the early 1980s, with steam being injected to treat 2 m by 2 m columns of soil at a former gas plant. Steam stripping has not become widely used as an in-situ remedial method but it is used in a commercial ex-situ process.

Soil washing

The basic principle of in-situ soil washing (sometimes called soil flushing) is the injection of clean water adjacent to the contamination and the extraction of contaminated water. In principle any reasonably soluble material may be removed by in-situ soil washing and even some non aqueous liquids may be removed if a surfactant is added to the injected water. However, field tests have shown the process to be less effective than was first hoped. It would seem that the problem lies in the fact that almost all real soils are significantly heterogeneous. The injected/abstracted water thus follows preferred flow paths through the soil. These paths are rapidly cleaned but much contamination remains in the adjacent slower flow paths. When washing is stopped the contamination diffuses back from the slower flow paths thus re-establishing a significant overall average level of contamination in the soil. In principle if the process is regularly repeated the average level of contamination could be reduced to an acceptable level but in many soils this would take an unacceptable time. Soil washing is now seldom used as an in-situ process but once again the process is available as an ex-situ technique.

Electrokinetics

From the foregoing discussion it can be seen that many remedial methods are limited to permeable sandy soils. One method which has been used with some success to treat contamination at sites on clayey/silty soils is electrokinetics. In this process electrodes are placed in the soil and an electrical current is passed through the soil to be treated. This induces a flow of both charged ions and water through the soil. The process can remove inorganic contaminants such as heavy metals, cyanides, nitrates and some organic materials may be carried out with the water that is extracted from the soil. The process may be substantially slowed by any buried metal in the ground and it may remove buried plumbing!

Vitrification

In-situ vitrification is a thermal treatment process which converts contaminated soil into a durable glass by melting the soil electrically. The process has been under development in the USA since about 1980 when it was initiated as a method to stabilise high level radioactive wastes in-situ. Electrodes are placed in the soil and the soil heated to over 2000°C, well above the initial melting temperature of soils. A hood placed over the area being treated is used to draw off gases for treatment. There have been only limited full size applications (400 to 800 ton); these demonstrated some problems in recovering all off-gases, and the process is still under development, although it has apparently been selected to remediate some sites impacted with organic contaminants, herbicides, pesticides, PCBs, dioxins and heavy metals. The vitrified product is about ten times stronger than unreinforced concrete and largely unaffected by weathering.

Radio waves

This process is still at the development stage but in a trial demonstration 30 tons of soil impacted with jet fuel, chlorinated solvents and waste oil were heated by radio frequency waves prior to soil vapour extraction the effect of which was considerably enhanced by the heating.

Ex-situ treatment

In-situ treatment may seem to be the ideal remedial strategy as it minimises the exposure of workers to contamination and the generation of secondary waste etc. However, it has been found that the natural heterogeneity of soils has lead to rather poor overall clean-up performance. There is now a movement towards ex-situ technologies. These may be carried out in plant specially established on the site or at a centralised treatment centre. In such plants the contaminated soil is treated as the feedstock of a chemical process plant. A wide range of processes may be employed but the basic technology is often a development of that used in-situ.

With all clean-up technologies and especially those that involve severe treatment of the soil (e.g. incineration) it is necessary to consider the final state of the soil. Severe treatment may leave it in a biologically dead state and furthermore a state which may not be readily colonised by living organisms. Also the processing may tend to release heavy metals naturally present in the soil and make them more available.

Pathway interdiction

Cutting the pathway involves placing some form of barrier between the source and the targets. The barrier may need to be horizontally across the source as a cap, underneath it and vertically around the periphery. Capping is discussed at page 127 and need not be considered further. Installing a barrier underneath a large area of contamination can be very difficult and techniques currently available are limited to the injection of grouts (fluid materials which will set) underneath the contamination. The effects of these techniques may be rather limited and there may be some residual escape of contamination. However, many sites are underlain by natural low permeability materials such as clays. Thus if vertical walls are installed around a site to a sufficient depth to intersect a low permeability layer then the source can be contained. Vertical walls are now widely used especially to prevent the migration of landfill gas. The most popular method is the slurry trench cut-off wall. In this process a trench is excavated in the ground and as the excavation progresses a slurry of cement and clay is pumped into the trench. This slurry is designed to exert sufficient pressure to keep the trench from collapsing during excavation and to set and harden at the end of excavation to form a barrier. Typically the width of the trench may be 0.6 metres and the depth may be of order 10 metres though much deeper walls have been installed to intersect deep clay layers. Individual walls may be several kilometres long and may take some months to install. The permeability of the barrier can be such that the velocity of water movement through it can be of the order of millimetres per year. A problem with clay-cement slurries is that they can shrink substantially on drying. Thus such walls may not be suitable for landfill gas migration control. For gas control the technique has been developed to include the installation of a high density polyethylene membrane into the trench as excavation progresses and prior to set of the slurry. At the present time these walls are in regular use particularly for the control of gas migration from old landfills. There are a number of other techniques for wall installation and there is particular interest in techniques which do not involve excavation as this not only reduces the exposure of site workers to contamination but also eliminates any need to dispose of contaminated arisings.

Hardening the target

This can only be considered for inanimate targets such as foundations though it could be extended to include flora which can be very useful in reducing problems associated with old spoil heaps such as dusting and soil erosion by rainwater. In general it will not be appropriate to try to harden human targets – though the regulations specifying acceptable exposure levels may change with time. However, the general trend of such regulations is towards lower acceptable levels and thus major clean-up programmes may need to assess the potential for regulatory softening of the targets during the clean-up process.

Landfill

As well as the contamination of land, issues related to landfill must be addressed.

All man's activities generate waste and this waste must be disposed in a manner such that it does not degrade the quality of life or pose health and safety problems. Volumes of waste are large and must be disposed in a rapid and efficient manner. Until quite recently landfills were focused on available holes and rather little attention was paid to contamination issues. The general by-word was "dilute and disperse". It was assumed that provided there was sufficient ground water available any contaminants would be rapidly diluted to insignificant levels. On many occasions this philosophy appears to have worked to an acceptable extent – though quantitative data are few. From dilute and disperse we have now moved to containment, the aim being to ensure that there are no uncontrolled escapes to the environment of landfill gas or leachate (leachate is the complex chemical solution that is produced if water comes into contact with decomposing waste and leaches soluble material from it).

Landfill gas

The fundamental processes in a landfill involve the breaking up or lysis of large molecules by bacteria to form simpler molecules, generally organic acids. These materials are then in turn decomposed and the final reaction products are predominantly methane and carbon dioxide. Thus in principle any organic material may be broken down methane and carbon dioxide. Both of these gases can be asphyxiant if they are present in sufficiently high quantities that the available oxygen is reduced and methane is also potentially explosive.

In practice the rate of breakdown of organic material in a landfill may be relatively slow so that methane and carbon dioxide are still being evolved many tens of years after placement of the original waste in the landfill. Also some organic materials may be relatively refractory and remain little changed.

Landfill gas is one of the major concerns in landfill design and in the remediation of old landfills. It can kill neighbouring vegetation and cause explosions if it builds up within buildings etc. Procedures for the control of landfill gas are now becoming more widely understood and it is to be hoped that there will be few problems with gas escape from new landfills and that the gas derived from landfills can be put to economic use for power generation etc. However, in power generation terms the quantity of gas available on most landfills will be quite modest when compared with a major power station. As a result power generation may not be commercially viable without some measure of subsidy.

Ironically many of the major problems of gas migration relate to landfills where the technology had developed from loose tipping in any available hole to controlled tipping, with compaction and daily cover layers of soil to control vermin, odours etc. The effect was to produce landfills in which the free vertical escape of gas to the atmosphere was hindered and thus lateral migration was encouraged. "Technical advances" do not always produce the desired results.

Leachate generation

Leachate generation is also a major issue in landfill design and licensing. As waste degrades it produces gases and also soluble by-products which themselves may be degraded during later stages of the reaction. If water is available these by-products will dissolve as also will any soluble inorganic materials such as heavy metals. The resulting leachate may be a noxious and polluting liquid that can cause much damage to aquatic life in a stream or pollute water abstraction wells. In many countries there are now regulatory controls on leachate escape and landfills must be lined to prevent such escape.

For the most part the water component of leachate is not derived from the waste itself but comes from infiltration of rainwater or ground water into the landfill. Thus landfills must be sited in a suitable hydrogeological setting to avoid ground water inflow.

Landfill caps

They must also be capped and sloped so as to shed water and not pond it (prevention of ponding can be quite a problem as the waste may settle by the order of 15% of its depth in the years following placement and there may be substantial local differential settlements due to the inherent heterogeneity of wastes). Capping is every bit as complex as lining a site save that the cap remains accessible for maintenance or renewal if there are problems. In contrast the liner may be impossible to replace without digging out the entire contents of the landfill. The principal elements of a landfill cap working from the top surface downwards will be:

- a layer of soil to support vegetation. This may need to be in the order of 1 metre thick.
- a drainage layer to remove rain water which percolates down through the vegetation layer.
- an impermeable layer to prevent water entering the body of the landfill. This layer may be formed from special polythene sheet or compacted clay.

Landfill caps must be of very high impermeability if they are to shed a significant proportion of the incident rainfall and if they do not shed this rainfall very substantial quantities of leachate will be generated. An uncapped or poorly capped landfill in the UK might generate 3000 cubic metres of leachate per hectare per annum.

Thus in effect a landfill becomes a closed tomb into which water should not enter and from which no water should escape. Gas, of course, must be allowed to escape but only via controlled routes such as flares, power generators etc. Unfortunately if there is no water in a landfill the degradation processes are enormously slowed and the waste may remain unchanged for many years retaining its potential to pollute the environment or release gas if, or, more realistically, when the cap and liner ultimately fail (it must be assumed that a landfill containment system will fail unless there is some ongoing maintenance – and it can be difficult to ensure the continuance of maintenance of a non-income producing structure for long periods of time).

To permit significant depths of water to build up within a landfill may be an anathema to those charged with protecting the aquatic environment for the greater the depth of leachate the greater the rate of escape at leaks or through clays barriers etc. However, there will always be some materials that must be disposed to landfill and it is important that as much degradation as possible occurs before such material ultimately is in a position to escape to the environment.

Thus it may be preferable to ensure that there is always some water in a landfill and in particular it can be advantageous to recirculate the leachate from the base of the landfill to just under the cap to ensure that the waste is continuously wetted with water.

The debate on the permitted water levels within landfills is set to continue. However, in many countries the maximum permitted depth is 1 m although landfills may be over 100 metres deep. Without leachate recirculation much of the material in such landfills may degrade extremely slowly if at all.

Landfill liners

It is appropriate to note that there have been major technical developments in landfill lining and capping in recent years. It is not now normal practice to rely on a single liner. In normal practice there will be at least two and often three barrier elements to a liner. Thus there might be a layer of natural clay. A mat of special low permeability clay sandwiched between two textile layers (to hold the clay during placing) and a layer of high density polyethylene sheet which is laid in strips and welded together on site. The use of composite liners recognises the fact that all liners will leak but that properties of different liner systems are different and the overall performance of a composite system can be much better than the sum of the parts.

Of course such composite liner systems are expensive and thus the landfilling of waste is becoming progressively more expensive. We must be careful to check that the money spent on controlling leachate escape etc. produces commensurate environmental benefits.

The future

Much of the technology associated with the clean-up of contaminated land is relatively new and new developments are regularly appearing. Thus there can be no doubt that technology can be developed to achieve any realistic level of control that is demanded. However, the costs are high. It is therefore always necessary to ask whether the money is being well spent.

Environmental awareness seems to be well correlated with per capita income. Individuals appear to become more conscious of their environment as their quality of life improves. Those living at subsistence level may have little interest in environmental quality and certainly no means of influencing it. Clearly environmental quality is of great importance. However, a moral balance must be struck between the spending of large sums of money on clean-ups where risks are already minimal. Pollution can spread between countries by air, seas and river waters. Even purely selfishly we should consider diverting some of the funds that are spent on clean-up (and the associated litigation) in the developed world to improvements in developing countries. Also we must be careful not to export pollution by setting up or encouraging production in manufacturing plants etc. which do not meet basic environmental standards.

As a final note we must ensure that any environmental initiative brings real benefits. For example at the present time there is a substantial focus on recycling. However, it is now coming to be accepted that the recycling of glass and paper may give only marginal benefits. Indeed any benefits will be negated if a special car journey is made to the recycling point. At the present time car exhaust emissions are probably the single most important environmental issue in the developed world. Despite this there is much greater public pressure to deal with other more marginal pollution issues such as contaminated land, recycling of wastes etc. than to reduce car use. Fundamentally this is entirely selfish. To restrict car use would impact on lifestyle. Recycling has minimal impact on lifestyle and is an easy sop for the conscience. Sadly it may produce no environmental benefit at least until there is a stable market for recycled paper, plastic, glass etc.

6 Contaminated land and groundwater problems

Michael Renger

Introduction

The environment, as with the construction process itself, may be divided into sectors or phases, but there is inevitably an overlap and inter-relationship between different parts of the environment, in the same way as with different parts of a building. The purpose of this paper is to address those environmental issues which are relevant at and, in particular, below ground level.

The redevelopment of contaminated land is a matter that is increasingly being considered by contractors and developers as the availability of alternative sites for development become restricted as a result of the adoption of policies for preserving virgin greenfield sites. However, in these circumstances, there is a dilemma presented to potential developers. On the one hand, the redevelopment of contaminated sites is encouraged by initiatives such as the Derelict Land Grant, the Urban Development Corporations and the embryonic Urban Development Agency. On the other hand, developers and landowners—and their financiers—are wary of possible clean-up costs and liabilities associated with the development of sites that have been subject to contaminative uses or land that may have been contaminated historically.

The concept of contaminated land is not new. In 1977 the Government issued guidance in the form of Circular 49/77 which announced the establishment of the Interdepartmental Committee on Redevelopment of Contaminated Land (ICRCL) to provide general guidance on the assessment and redevelopment of contaminated land. The ICRCL subsequently published a number of papers dealing with the problems of particular types of contaminated sites.[1]

Subsequently, the Government issued specific guidance on the development of contaminated land in the form of Circular No. 21/87. The purpose

1 ICRCL 17/78 Notes on the redevelopment of landfill sites, ICRCL 18/79 Notes on the redevelopment of gasworks sites, ICRCL 23/79 Notes on the redevelopment of sewage works and farms, ICRCL 42/80 Notes on the redevelopment of scrap yards and similar sites, ICRL 59/83 Guidance on the assessment and redevelopment of contaminated land, ICRCL 61/84 Notes on the fire hazards of contaminated land, ICRCL 64/85 Asbestos on contaminated sites, and ICRCL 70/79 Notes on the restoration and aftercare of metalliferous mining sites for pasture and grazing.

of this Circular is to provide advice and guidance to local authorities and developers on the identification, assessment and development of contaminated land. The approach taken in this Circular is effectively reactive in that it relates to proposals for the redevelopment of contaminated land and advises that contaminated land is identified at an early stage in the planning process, that appropriate policies are developed for its use and that planning applications are decided on the basis of adequate information. Contamination therefore only became an issue when it had to be taken into account during redevelopment. The treatment of the contaminated material was an integral part of the development process, as with the treatment or compaction of unstable ground. The Welsh Office in conjunction with the Welsh Development Agency undertook a survey in the mid-1980s to record information about sites in Wales thought to be contaminated. However it was the House of Commons Environment Committee on Contaminated Land that processed the extension of this approach, to the identification of all sites that have been subject to contaminative uses within Britain. The first report of the Environment Committee on Contaminated Land, published in January 1990 made a number of recommendations relating to contaminated land including registers of contaminated land, the powers of enforcement bodies, and civil liability for damage.

Definition

What constitutes "contaminated land"?

Whilst we now have a statutory definition of "pollution of the environment"[2] (namely—pollution of the environment due to the release into any environmental medium from any process of substances which are capable of causing harm to man or any other living organisms supported by the environment), we do not have a statutory definition of "contaminated land". In their evidence to the Environment Committee, the Department of the Environment stated that "at present, it is not possible to define contaminated land unambiguously". At least some things have not changed!

Dr Fisk, Chief Scientist at the Department of the Environment, reminded the Committee that the public used the word "contaminated" rather loosely with respect to land. In other areas of pollution control, a scientific distinction exists between "contamination" (*ie* the mere presence of a foreign substance, possibly harmless) and "pollution" (which poses or causes harm).

---

2 S1, Environmental Protection Act 1990.

In their evidence to the Environment Committee, the Department of the Environment rightly drew the distinction between "derelict" and "contaminated" land.

> "Derelict land is currently defined as 'land so damaged by industrial or other development that it is incapable of beneficial use without treatment'. Contaminated land is more difficult to define, but may be regarded as land which represents an actual or potential hazard to public health or the environment as a result of current or previous use."[3]

Land may thus be derelict but not contaminated, such as a disused limestone quarry; alternatively, land may have been previously derelict, but now restored without the removal of the underlying contamination.

Indeed the Department of the Environment themselves provide an example with their Marsham Street office of a site which is not derelict (at least not for the present), but nevertheless would be classified as contaminated, the site having been previously used for a gas works.

Policy and statistics

There is a clear contrast in the historical treatment of derelict and contaminated land in this country. There have been three exhaustive studies of derelict land in the United Kingdom, the surveys having been published in 1974, 1982 and 1991. The report of the most recent survey, published in two volumes, categorises the amount of derelict land and the area justifying reclamation both by type of dereliction and location for each region of the country. The stock of derelict land recorded in 1988 (to which the 1991 report refers) comprised 40,500 hectares which represented an 11% reduction in the derelict land recorded in 1982.

In contrast to the published detail available for derelict land, the Department of the Environment in their evidence to the Environment Committee were only able to offer the following broad statement as to the amount of contaminated land within the United Kingdom:

> "Contamination is best regarded as a general concept, rather than as something capable of exact definition and measurement. For these reasons, there is no easy method to estimate the total area of contaminated land. From a sample of cases dealt with by ICRCL, the Department estimated in 1986 that there were at least 10,000 hectares of contaminated land in England. But, if all contaminated land was required for the most sensitive use, i.e. housing, the significance of contamination (and hence the area of such land) would be greater".

Dr Fisk in his evidence used an oil refinery as an example:

---

3 Paragraph 3.1—Department of Environment Evidence to Environment Committee.

> "Crucially, if nobody is ever going to build a housing estate on that oil refinery land, in our definition it would not be viewed presently as contaminated land".[4]

Some of the major environmental consultancies have attempted to produce their own estimate of the amount of contaminated land within the United Kingdom. One consultancy, extrapolating from a pilot study in Cheshire, estimated that there was something of the order of 50,000 to 100,000 potentially contaminated sites in the United Kingdom.

The Development Director of the Black Country Development Corporation identified the problem of contamination as one of the biggest single issues in the process of regenerating the area. His own estimate was that there were over 300 hectares of contaminated land within the Corporation's area alone.

HMSO published in 1992 a statistical volume entitled "The UK Environment" which Michael Howard QC, MP, in his capacity as Secretary of State for the Environment, described as bringing together "both the major long term statistical series and also less readily available data from other areas and research programmes". The volume contains numerous graphs and pie charts, but there is a notable lack of statistics in the brief section on "contaminated land". Significantly, contaminated land is simply treated as a sub-category of derelict land and the depth of Government information on the subject is summarised as follows:

> "Major industrial conurbations of the North, the Midlands, South Wales and Scotland have large areas of land formerly used by industry and now derelict or reclaimed for other uses. Much of this land may be contaminated. However, many other parts of the country are or were centres for industries or trades which may cause contamination of the soil, and the sites of former town gas works, scrap yards and waste disposal facilities, for example, are found throughout the country.
>
> Neither the total area of contaminated land nor the number of sites in the UK can easily be quantified at present. Current independent estimates suggest that there may be 50,000 to 100,000 hectares of contaminated land, but this should be regarded as no more than a broad estimate".[5]

Identification of contaminated sites

Each owner, purchaser and financier has his own concept of what constitutes a "contaminated site", with a consequential impact upon the perceived value of that site.

4 Page 24—Volume II—Minutes of Evidence to Environment Committee.

5 *The U.K. Environment* published by HMSO, (1992).

The Government's proposed register under section 143 of the Environmental Protection Act 1990 was for a register of land which was being or had been put to a contaminative use.

Notwithstanding the Government's decision to call for a wide ranging inter-departmental review of contaminated land rather than to implement the provisions of section 143 of the Environmental Act 1990, in my experience, the market place still has regard to the Government's original proposals for the register published in a Consultation Paper in May 1991. The original proposals would have placed sites that had been subject to a very wide range of uses, ranging from the manufacture of pet foods to dry cleaners, on the register. For ease of reference the full schedule of contaminative uses designated in the first Consultation Paper is set out in full in Appendix A to this paper.

Delegates will be aware that the second Consultation Paper drastically reduced the range of uses which would have been subject to registration, and the Government's own estimate was that only 10–15% of the land originally destined to be placed on the register would initially appear there.

However, it is of the first, rather than the second, Consultation Paper that the market place has most regard, because the letter accompanying the draft regulations and second consultation paper stated that the Government "has it in mind" to extend the list of contaminative uses "in due course in the light of experience". Quite apart from the Consultation Paper and draft regulations published under section 143, the Government has also produced other lists of potentially contaminated uses.

The 1991 Building Regulations, which have not changed in this respect from the 1985 Regulations, suggest various other categories of sites which may contain contaminants including:

(1) chemical works;
(2) industries making or using wood preservatives;
(3) munitions production and testing sites;
(4) nuclear installations;
(5) paper and printing works;
(6) railway land, especially the larger sidings and depots; and
(7) tanneries.

The ICRCL Guidance on the Assessment and Redevelopment of Contaminative Land published in 1987, included a similar list of uses:

(1) railway land, especially large sidings and depots;
(2) chemical works;
(3) munitions production and testing sites;

(4) tanneries;
(5) paper and printing works; and
(6) industries making or using wood preservatives.

The Guidance emphasises that this list should not be regarded as exhaustive.

Legal liability—common law

No single body of law deals with the issue of liability for injury caused by contaminated land. Instead, the law that can be applied is drawn from both common law principles and a range of legislation.

The common law principles relevant to the protection of the environment derive principally from the law of tort. The law of tort can provide protection for the private interests of individuals and can therefore provide private individuals with redress for injury caused by contamination.

Rule in Rylands *v* Fletcher

The rule in *Rylands* v *Fletcher* contains a principle upon which action can be taken in relation to contamination. The principle, first expounded by Blackburn J is:

> ". . . that the person who for his own purposes brings onto his land and collects and keeps there anything likely to do mischief if it escapes, must keep it in at his peril, and, if he does not do so, is *prima facie* answerable for all the damage which is the natural consequence of its escape".[6]

This principle has been applied to the escape of water, gas, chemicals, colliery spoil and numerous similar matters. However, it is not of such wide application as may first appear as the rule is hedged in by limitations.

(1) *Non-natural user:* The most important limitation on the principle is that there must have been a non-natural use of land. Therefore, for the rule in *Rylands* v *Fletcher* to apply with regard to contaminated land, the use that produced any contamination must be a "non-natural" use. To assess whether the use is a non-natural use, there must be consideration of "all the circumstances of time and place and produce of mankind" *Read* v *Lyons*[7] (1947) House of Lords. It is now

6 *Rylands* v *Fletcher* (1868) LR 3HL 330.
7 *Read* v *Lyons* [1947] AC 156, [1946] 2 All ER 471.

common for an ordinary industrial use to be considered as a natural use if it is sited with due care and consideration.

Therefore, contaminated uses that have taken place in heavily industrialised areas may well be considered to be the result of a "natural" user of the land and, as such, the rule in *Rylands* v *Fletcher* will not be applicable.

(2) *Escape:* There is a requirement that the substance must escape from the land where it is kept before the rule in *Rylands* v *Fletcher* will apply. In relation to contamination, escape can be considered widely so that seepage to groundwater through, say, a defective tank, can be regarded as an escape from the land.

The rule in *Rylands* v *Fletcher* is further restricted by the availability of a number of defences to an action brought under the rule. It is a defence if statute allows for the activities to be undertaken e.g a discharge consent or waste disposal licence, both of which can be controlled by conditions and therefore allow a certain level of contamination to take place. In addition, there is a defence of common benefit where a party derives some benefit from the harmful activities.

These defences, together with the above limitations have diluted the liability imposed by the rule in *Rylands* v *Fletcher*. The rule was considered by the Court of Appeal in the recent case of *Cambridge Water Company* v *Eastern Counties Leather plc* (1992)[8] with which I will deal later.

The common law also provides other remedies for instances of contamination. The relevant branches of law are trespass and negligence.

Trespass

Trespass involves direct interference with another person's rights without lawful excuse. In relation to contaminated land, trespass may be a possible cause of action where there has been an unjustifiable intrusion by one person upon the land in the possession of another. However, in terms of environmental law, trespass has been construed narrowly. There must be a causal link between the directness of the act and the inevitability of its consequences.

In *Esso* v *Southport Corporation* (1956) an oil tanker was grounded and discharged much of its cargo of oil to lighten the ship. This was then carried on to Southport's beach by the tides and the wind. The House of Lords

8 *Cambridge Water Company* v *Eastern Counties Leather plc*—Court of Appeal—*The Times*, 29 December 1992. See also postscript.

considered this could not be trespass as there was no inevitability about the oil being deposited onto the shore as it depended upon the action of the tide and wind. Applying this principle to other environmental media such as the air and soil, means that an action in trespass is unlikely to be a source of redress for environmental pollution. However, it may be possible to argue that for land contamination or contamination of groundwater geological and hydrological conditions make contamination an inevitable consequence of a particular act.

Negligence

The third area of common law that may provide redress for land contamination is that of the law of negligence. Liability in negligence arises when damage which is not too remote is caused by the breach of a duty of care owed to the injured party. The scope for liability in negligence is therefore very wide. However, the law of negligence is based on fault and in relation to contaminated land, fault may be very difficult to establish. This was considered in depth by the European Council when finalising the Green Paper on remedying environmental damage, to which I shall return later. However, negligence may provide an appropriate method of redress for one-off incidents where fault can be apportioned.

The difficulty in proving that contamination is caused by the fault of a particular person who owed a duty of care, means that negligence is rarely used to provide a cause of action. In addition, the availability of statutory remedies in relation to contaminated land means that this common law means of redress may not be pursued.

Nuisance

Liability in nuisance arises where there is interference with the lawful rights of another. The common law principles of nuisance, negligence and the rule in *Rylands* v *Fletcher* have recently been considered in the case of *Cambridge Water Company* v *Eastern Counties Leather plc* (1992).[8]

The water company supplied water to an area in Cambridgeshire and abstracted from a borehole located in a chalk aquifer. The company acquired premises, including the borehole, in 1976, to provide water for the public supply and commissioned a pumping station in 1979. A water quality directive issued by the Council of the European Communities in July 1980 specified the maximum permissible concentrations of compounds including PCE, a chlorinated solvent. The water company identified PCE in the water abstracted from the borehole above the permissible concentration and ceased pumping in 1983. It developed a new borehole at a cost of approximately £1 million. Having carried out a hydro-geological inquiry, the water company claimed the PCE had originated from the leather tannery of Eastern Counties Leather at Sawston and commenced proceedings, contending that the leather company was liable in nuisance and under the rule in *Rylands* v *Fletcher*.

Tanneries had been located at Sawston for over 350 years and Eastern Counties Leather was incorporated in 1879. It was found that spillages of PCE were likely to have occurred when drums of PCE were poured into a reservoir for pumping to de-greasing machines. The use of PCE ceased in 1976.

The High Court held that the actions in negligence and in nuisance failed because the leather company could not have reasonably foreseen in 1976, or before, that the spillages would result in detectable quantities of PCE being found in the aquifer. The High Court also rejected liability under the rule in *Rylands* v *Fletcher* holding that Sawston was an "industrial village" and that the storage of PCE at the leather company's premises was a natural use of the land.

The Court of Appeal considered that the rule in *Rylands* v *Fletcher* was inapposite in this case. It was held that the rule makes a person liable for the event of an escape rather than for his actions and in this case liability attached by reason of the actions of the leather company in spilling PCE. It did not escape into the aquifer through, for example, cracks in a negligently fabricated storage tank.

There was no appeal against the High Court finding that there was no liability in nuisance or negligence. However, the Court of Appeal did consider further the tort of nuisance and its application in *Ballard* v *Tomlinson*[9] to the right of an owner to naturally occurring water which comes beneath his land by percolation through undefined underground channels. The court held that interference with this "natural" right which resulted from the spillage of PCE was a nuisance. It was sufficient to say that the action of the leather company in spilling PCE caused the contamination and that where the nuisance is interference with a natural right incident to ownership, then liability is strict. The water company was awarded damages plus costs, but the leather company have been granted leave to appeal in the House of Lords.

This decision is significant in relation to the contamination of groundwaters. Contamination can percolate through soils over many years. Substances that may not be regarded as contaminative may now be considered

---

9 *Ballard* v *Tomlinson* (1885) 29 ChD, 115 (1881–5) All ER 88.

as such in future. The local geological and hydrological conditions are relevant to whether percolation can occur and affect water sources.

Legal liability—statutory remedies

There are a number of statutory provisions that can be applied to liability caused by contamination land. These can be divided into two: certain provisions impose a clean-up liability, whereas others impose a criminal liability.

Clean-up liability

As can be expected, the statutory provisions relating to clean-up liability centre around the deposit of waste and the pollution of water. Both are issues relating to contamination:

(1) *Deposit of waste:* Waste disposal was one of the uses identified as a contaminative use by the Government in its proposals for a register. In fact, the existence of the register would have provided the information for action with regard to the clean-up of waste.

Section 61 of the Environmental Protection Act 1990 imposes a duty on Waste Regulation Authorities to inspect land in their areas to see whether or not that land is in such a condition that it may cause pollution of the environment or harm to human health as a result of noxious gases or liquids caused by the deposit of controlled waste. In addition, where a Waste Regulation Authority considers that land is polluted, it is under a duty to inspect the land and to keep its condition under review.

The critical provision in section 61 is that where it appears to a Waste Regulation Authority that the condition of the land is such that pollution of the environment or harm to human health is likely to be caused, it is under a duty to carry out remedial works and to take such other steps as are reasonable to avoid pollution or harm. The statute entitles the authority as of right to carry out such works. Where such clean-up work is carried out the authority is entitled to recover the cost from "the owner of the land for the time being", provided that such costs were reasonably incurred. It is important to note that the authority will look to the owner for the time being. It is not concerned with who was the owner at the time when the pollution occurred; and is, regardless of responsibility for or knowledge of, the existence of the contamination.

Section 61 contains a provision that in deciding whether to recover the cost of clean-up and if so how much, authorities should have regard to any hardship which the recovery may cause. This may provide relief where contamination is historical and the present owner does not have the resources to pay for the clean-up. In these circumstances, the authority may realise that if it carries out the clean up, it will be unlikely to recover its costs from the present owner.

This section of the Act is not yet in force, and the powers of the Waste Regulation Authority to control and tackle land pollution are part of the interdepartmental review of contaminated land currently being carried out by the Government.

Section 42 of the Environmental Protection Act provides that the Waste Regulation Authority is under a duty to ensure "that the activities authorised by the [waste management] licence do not cause pollution of the environment or harm to human health or become seriously detrimental to the amenities of the locality affected by the activities". For the purpose of performing the duty, the authority has power to carry out an emergency clean-up and to recover the cost from the holder or former holder of a waste management licence. Like section 61, this section is not yet in force.

(2) *Statutory nuisances:* Section 79 of the Environmental Protection Act imposes a duty on local authorities to inspect the land in their area for "statutory nuisances" and to investigate any complaints about such nuisances made by the public. Statutory nuisances include a broad range of matters such as smoke, noise, smells and dust and also "any accumulation or deposit which is prejudicial to health or a nuisance". Section 80 of the EPA empowers a local authority to serve an abatement notice which requires the nuisance to be removed within a stated time period on either "the person responsible for the nuisance" or "where the nuisance arises from any defect of a structural character, on the owner of the premises". Section 81 of the EPA empowers a local authority to take steps to abate the nuisance and do whatever may be necessary in execution of the notice. This may involve extensive clean-up works.

(3) *Pollution of water:* Contamination of land can result in pollution of controlled waters which include rivers, streams, lakes, ponds, groundwater and coastal waters. In the context of this paper, it should be emphasised that "controlled waters" include any waters contained in underground strata. Section 161 of the Water Resources Act ("the WRA") empowers the National Rivers Authority ("the NRA") to carry out anti-pollution works and operations in relation to controlled waters. The NRA can take preventative action to forestall pollution of controlled waters or take remedial steps where pollution has already occurred. Remedial work may be undertaken for the purposes of preventing the matter from entering controlled waters, removing the matter, remedying or mitigating any

pollution caused by its presence in the waters, or the restoration of waters including flora and fauna to the state they were in before the pollution occurred. Where the NRA carry out work they are entitled to recover the expenses of so doing from any person who "caused or knowingly permitted" the matter to be present in controlled waters. These criteria are similar to that for criminal liability and are dealt with below.

Criminal liability

Criminal liability in relation to contaminated land is an area causing concern not only to industry, but also to financial markets, who finance the development and construction projects. Again, the two issues that the statutory provisions are directed at are the deposit of waste, statutory nuisance and the pollution of water.

(1) *Deposit of waste:* Section 33 of the EPA deals with the deposit of controlled waste on land. It provides that the person who knowingly causes or permits controlled waste to be deposited on any land or keeps any such waste on land commits an offence, unless it is deposited in accordance with the waste management licence. It is a defence for a person charged with an offence under this section to prove that he took all reasonable precautions and exercised all due diligence to avoid the commission of the offence; or that he acted under instructions from his employer and neither knew nor had reason to suppose that the acts done by him constituted contravention; or that the acts were done in an emergency in order to avoid danger to the public and that, as soon as reasonably practicable thereafter, particulars were furnished to the Waste Regulation Authority. Penalties that can be imposed by a magistrates' court are a fine not exceeding £20,000 and/or imprisonment for a term not exceeding six months. For a matter which goes to the Crown Court, there is an unlimited fine and/or a maximum period of imprisonment of two years.

Section 34 of the EPA imposes an obligation on all parties in the waste chain *i.e.* "any person who imports, produces, carries, keeps, treats or disposes of controlled waste or, as a broker, has control of such waste". Such persons have a duty of care as respects waste and this includes taking all measures "to prevent the escape of the waste from his control or that of any other person". In the context of contaminated land, the duty of care applies to waste that escapes and therefore results in contamination. Failure to comply with the duty is a criminal offence and an offender is liable to a fine.

With regard to statutory nuisances, under section 81 of the EPA, it is an offence to contravene an abatement notice served by a local authority without reasonable excuse, for which a fine not exceeding £20,000 may be imposed, where the offence is committed on industrial premises. There are a number of possible defences. It is, for example, a defence to prove that the best practical means were used to prevent or counteract the effects of the nuisance, where the nuisance is caused on industrial, trade or business premises. Best practical means is construed bearing in mind questions of cost. It has been accepted by the courts that the profitability of an operation, taking into account the cost of any further steps to be taken, is a relevant factor, but the mere fact of increased expenditure or even unprofitability is not sufficient on its own.

(2) *Statutory nuisance:* If a person on whom an abatement notice is served, without reasonable excuse, contravenes or fails to comply with any requirement or prohibition imposed by the notice, he is guilty of a criminal offence (section 80, Environmental Protection Act).

(3) *Water pollution:* Section 85 of the WRA provides that it is a criminal offence to pollute controlled waters. Section 85(1) states:

> "A person contravenes this section if he causes or knowingly permits any poisonous, noxious or polluting matter or any solid waste matter to enter controlled waters."

Again, the section makes reference to "causes or knowingly permits". In the recent case of *Wychavon District Council* v *NRA*[10] in 1992 the court held that generally "causes" requires a positive act rather than mere passive inaction. The extent of "knowingly permits" is still uncertain. The courts have indicated that constructive knowledge will suffice for a knowingly permitted offence under section 85, and that the defendant bears an evidential burden of proof to show that he did not have the requisite knowledge. However, it is not clear whether knowledge should extend beyond the mere discharge to the nature of the substance discharged and its polluting effect.

It is a defence to section 85 that there is a discharge consent, authorisation for a prescribed process under Part I of the EPA or a waste management or disposal licence. However, any discharge must be in accordance with the terms or conditions attached to such consents. There is also a defence that a discharge is made in an emergency in order to avoid danger to life or health, that all reasonable practical steps were taken to minimise the extent of the discharge and its polluting effects, and that details of the discharge were notified to the NRA as soon as reasonably practicable after the discharge occurred.

10 *Wychavon District Council* v *NRA* [1993] 1 WLR 125.

The penalties upon conviction by the Magistrates' Court are a fine up to £20,000 and/or a period of imprisonment of up to three months. Upon conviction by the Crown Court the penalties are an unlimited fine and/or a period of imprisonment of up to two years.

Under both the EPA and the WRA criminal liability of a body corporate can be extended to directors, managers, secretaries or other officers of the body corporate if the offence is proved to have been committed with "the consent, or connivance, or to have been attributed to any neglect on the part of" any such person.

Sources of practical guidance

Practical guidance on the investigation and treatment of contaminated land is available from a wide variety of sources.

A Code of Practice for the identification of potentially contaminative land and its investigation was published by the British Standards Institute in its Draft for Development series of publications. This publication should not be regarded as a British Standard and the Code of Practice should be applied on a provisional basis only. Nevertheless, the Code of Practice (DD175:1988) provides guidance on the identification and investigation of sites where contamination may exist and where hazards from undesirable substances may occur.

The Draft for Development adopts the definition of "potentially contaminated land" being "land that, because of its nature or former uses, may contain substances that could give rise to hazards likely to affect the proposed form of development".

Protection of workforce

Contamination may be a potential health risk to those working on a site and to members of the public unless adequate precautions are taken.

The Health and Safety Executive in October last year (1992) produced a guidance booklet entitled *Protection of Workers and the General Public during the Development of Contaminated Land* (ISBN 0–11-885657-X).

The Health and Safety Executive have also produced a video entitled *A Clean Sweep* which examines some of the main problems which may be encountered during the development of contaminated land. These include the need for a thorough pre-start survey and the use of personal protective equipment.

Petroleum based land contamination

Earlier this year (1993) the Institute of Petroleum published a Code of Practice for the investigation and mitigation of possible petroleum based land contamination. The Code of Practice, which has been written by experts from the oil industry and reviewed by both the Department of Environment and the National Rivers Authority, aims to provide site managers with an appreciation of the process of site assessment and remediation work.

The importance of such a code was highlighted in May this year by David Pirret, General Manager of Shell UK's retail division, who expressed the view that at least one third of British petrol stations would be producing some degree of ground contamination.

It is now Shell's corporate policy to undertake a pre-disposal survey of all sites and to remediate those found to be contaminated. It is reported that the cost for just one small site has been in the region of £¼ million, exceeding the site's market value.

It is thus not surprising that new petrol stations are now being designed with stricter safeguards so as to minimise the potential for contamination in the future. Again Mr Pirret indicated that "to build an average forecourt costs £92,000 per site more today than would have been necessary 10 years ago in order to comply with new environmental and safety standards and regulations".

The Construction Industry Research and Information Association has a number of projects under way in relation to contaminated land, including:

- COSHH in construction;
- safe working practices on contaminated sites;
- remedial treatment of contaminated land; and
- urban hydrology.

The Building Research Establishment (BRE) has also produced a number of relevant documents, including:

(1) Building on contaminated land—which is an assessment of geotechnical methods of preventing the migration of gases and liquids in the ground;
(2) Contaminated land—site surveys and assessment of the effectiveness of barriers;
(3) Structures on contaminated land—external protection measures; and

(4) Fire and explosion hazards associated with the development of contaminated land.

The National Rivers Authority (NRA) set out their policy to protect the quality of groundwater in their publication *Policy and Practice for the Protection of Groundwater.*

The NRA is currently preparing detailed maps, to be published over the next three years, identifying abstraction points throughout England and Wales. The authority is establishing source protection zones (SPZs) around abstraction points. There are to be three zones, with zone one being closest to the abstraction points. The zones will relate to the time groundwater takes to travel to the point of abstraction. The NRA is a statutory consultee on a wide range of development control matters, and the establishment of the SPZs may affect the development potential of many areas, including the redevelopment of contaminated land within an SPZ or on a major aquifer.

Government strategy

In the statement of policy contained in the first Consultation Paper, the Government affirmed the view of the Royal Commission on Environmental Pollution that "contamination is not synonymous with pollution". The Commission regard a contamination as "a necessary, but not a sufficient condition for pollution" and also noted that "what today is regarded as no more than contamination may tomorrow be pollution, and as substance accumulates to . . . harmful concentrations or as knowledge is gained of hitherto unsuspected effects". The Commission therefore used "contamination" to denote the presence in the environment of certain substances, without making a judgment on whether they are actually harmful. The use of the term in the Consultation Paper follows this principle. (The Royal Commission Report referred to here is the 10th Report of the Royal Commission on Environmental Pollution entitled *Tackling Pollution—Experience and Prospects*). Annex C to the Consultation Paper which sets out the schedule of contaminative uses is set out in full for the sake of completeness as an appendix to this paper.

The Government's most recent strategy on dealing with the legacy of contaminated land was outlined in a speech by David MacLean, Minister of State for the Environment and Countryside, on 14 May 1993. The speech contained an invitation to let the Government know "what you think about liability for pollution of our land . . . at a simple level, the problem with contaminated land is 'who should pay for it when the polluter has gone away?' ".

The issue of contaminated land is important and needs to be tackled. In the Minister's words "it figures in urgent projects for the regeneration of our urban and industrial areas; it figures in negotiations between businessmen and their bankers where land is used as security for working capital; and it figures when the directors of companies, large and small, have to sign their annual accounts showing the value of their operational land and of their contingent liabilities, including clean-up costs".

The key to contamination is to make it a matter of risk analysis and risk management. The Government wish "to see contaminated land kept or brought back into beneficial use wherever practicable, as long as there are no unacceptable risks to human health or the environment, taking into account the actual or intended use or uses of the land. This is the 'fitness for purpose' standard for reclamation which (the Government) have applied for many years".

The Minister stated two policy objectives namely:

(1) actual contamination problems to be tackled in a sensible way; and
(2) the avoidable pressures for new development in the countryside to be minimised.

He considered that the matter required:

(1) vigilance to identify the risks;
(2) a considered appraisal of the actual hazards; and
(3) if it is appropriate under the fitness for purpose standard, the use of well thought out and cost effective measures to contain, control or eliminate those risks.

The Minister went on to commit the Government to delivering "a policy of rising environmental standards; in the context of a better informed public; but only where the benefits exceed the costs". The starting point for the Government review is "the legislation and controls relevant to contamination". However, the review is not restricted to the legislation and the Government are looking to achieve their environmental goals by other means. These include:

(1) relieving industry and commerce of the burden of regulation; and
(2) the use of economic instruments to influence behaviour.

The Government wish "to get away from imposing controls to prohibit action, with the attendant bureaucracy and inflexibility that always involves. We want to get into place the right mixture of pro signals, incentives and penalties, to reward environmental improvement and penalise environmental impairment . . . in effect, we want deregulation plus economic instruments to provide a market method for applying the 'polluter pays' principle".

The Minister went on to state that the Government had "no intention of going down the Super Fund road. We do intend to take into account its lessons—about unrealistic clean-up standards for land contamination and about excessive legal bills incurred as people fight over whose pocket is deep enough to pay for the work". The Government have thus reaffirmed their traditional policy of "fitness for purpose" as contained in the ICRCL guidance.

The Department of the Environment has also initiated a programme of research projects into contaminated land. As at June 1993, the Department of the Environment had commissioned no less than 19 research projects into contaminated land, namely:

Risk assessment and prioritisation procedures for sites

Treatment technologies for contaminated land; guidance

Contaminative uses of land; technical guidance

Biological remediation of contaminated soils

Generic guideline values for contaminants, or "trigger levels"

Review of technologies for monitoring remediation of contaminated land

Preliminary site inspection of contaminated land

Sampling strategies for site investigations

Framework for assessment of impact of contaminated sites on water environment

Collation of toxicological data on contaminated land

Aggressive soils

Framework for risk assessment

Blight and risk communication

Analysis of asbestos in soils and loose aggregates

Investigation of fire and explosion hazards

Section 143 Registers: management of register information and use of information technology

Guidance on protection of housing and associated developments on contaminated land

Section 143 Registers: use of historical information in compilation

Evaluation of remedial measures for contaminated land

In conclusion, the Minister stated that "buyers, lenders and insurers need to assess the risks of contamination before committing their money in relation to any land whose current or past uses may have left contamination behind. 'Caveat emptor' still applies; where contamination is concerned, it is 'let the *informed* buyer beware' ".

Future European developments

The Government's role is "to provide guidance on methods and standards for addressing the problems. A particular priority is to provide authorities, developers and consultants with guidance on a common basis for risk assessment and the evaluation of solutions". There have been two recent European initiatives, namely the Council of Europe's Convention on Civil Liability for Damage Resulting from Activities Dangerous to the Environment and the Commission of the European Community's Green Paper on Environmental Liability.

The cost of clean-up liability associated with contaminated land and the experience of the USA Super Fund in this context has led the UK and Europe to consider the establishment of civil liability for environmental damage. The first report of the Environmental Committee on Contaminated Land recommended that attention be given to the question of creating statutory liability for damage caused by contamination to land, particularly where this causes damage to neighbouring property or the environment.

On 14 May 1993, the European Commission published a Green Paper on remedying environmental damage ("the Green Paper"). The Green Paper envisages the introduction of a harmonised strict liability regime, coupled with a compensation mechanism for cases of environmental damage when no liable party was identified or was able to pay. The Commission considered formulating fault based liability for environmental damage. Such liability requires proof that the liable party committed a negligent or otherwise wrongful act which caused damage, fault being dependent upon a duty of care or rule of law. Strict liability eases the burden of establishing liability because fault need not be established. However, potentially liable parties need to know the scope of the costs they would be expected to pay in cases of damage. The European Commission identified a trend in both national legislation and international instruments regarding environmental damage towards a strict liability regime for certain activities dangerous to the environment.

The Green Paper also considers the difficulties arising from the question of determining how to apportion liability where more than one party is responsible for the damage, determining who and what is damaging the environment and in defining environmental damage.

Insurance is considered to be a means of controlling the risk of economic loss, but the uncertainties which make civil liability for environmental damage difficult also create problems for environmental insurance. The type, extent and probability of environmental damage are unpredictable and the level of cover to be provided cannot be determined easily. The Green Paper points out that some insurers have sought to limit coverage of accidental losses to damage occurring by a "sudden" event, excluding damage caused gradually such as a slow leak from an underground tank. The possibility of particularly hazardous industries or activities posing particular hazards providing insurance to cover their potential liability is considered and the proposed directive for civil liability for damage resulting from waste would require the liability of the producer and the eliminator to be covered by insurance or other financial security.

The purpose of the Green Paper is to stimulate community wide discussion among parties with an interest in the issues raised. Various bodies in the UK have responded. The Commission's consultation period ends on 1 October 1993, to be followed by a joint hearing with the European Parliament.

CBI response to the Green Paper

In formulating their response to the Green Paper the Environment Policy Group of the CBI recognised that a business should face court action under civil laws where it is at fault and causes damage to persons and property. But uncertainty about the extent of businesses' environmental liabilities and worry that they will be unaffordable is now hampering normal commercial transactions. Meanwhile, public concern about the consequences of historic pollution is increasing. Uncertainty leads to reluctance to develop on contaminated land, which in turn puts more pressure on greenfield sites. The potential cost of cleaning up the past is enormous and the extent of present liabilities is only just beginning to be recognised'.

The CBI calls for certainty and predictability about the extent of its major liabilities so as to foster the innovation and commercial risk-taking so essential to business investment, growth and employment. Business needs Government and the EC to resolve the uncertainties, and create a clear and equitable framework of law and policy which will protect the environment and enhance industrial competitiveness. It comments that civil law has been developed to allow individuals to obtain compensation for damage to property and persons. There is nothing to suggest difficulties with the existing liability laws in EC Member States on the scale which would justify attempting to harmonise them, with all the difficulties in trying to ensure parity in practice, between fundamentally different judicial systems.

In addition the CBI point out that the past and present should be treated separately. This generation can help to put right the damage caused by previous generations, but it cannot afford to do more than make a start.

The CBI urges the Government to rule out any possibility of retroactive environmental liability for damage caused by lawful activities which the perpetrator could not, at the time, have known were harmful and which complied with the accepted standards of the day. The CBI further recommend the introduction of a limit to the period of liability of 3 years from the time when the damage was discovered and the creation of a 30 years' long stop.

The CBI are opposed either to an extension of strict liability or to any attempt by the EC to introduce joint and several liability into the regulatory or public law.

Advisory Committee on Business in the Environment (ACBE)

The Financial Sector Working Group of the Advisory Committee on Business in the Environment in their report published in February 1993 concluded that there was no clear evidence to support the case that the United Kingdom's existing large default based legal framework was inadequate and should be extended to include a greater element of strict liability.

British Bankers Association ("the BBA") response to the Green Paper

The BBA comment that "if lenders are confronted with potentially unlimited contingent liability for the clean-up costs of borrowers then this could have a major impact upon capital adequacy requirements. This may also, as a consequence, inhibit lenders from supporting certain sectors of the economy, restrict the flow of funds available for environmentally beneficial technology and overall affect the ability of lenders to support industry in general."

The BBA go on to state that "We therefore believe that EC and UK environmental legislation should contain appropriate exemption from liability for lenders who have acted in the ordinary course of their business and have not directly attributed to environmental damage caused by their customer."

The BBA go on to advocate wide consultation with the financial services industry throughout the development of legislation and discussion with financial experts in respect of market mechanisms. They also advocate that future legislation should be clear and unambiguous particularly with regard to the concept of the "person primarily responsible". In addition, Government should clearly define what constitutes pollution, the clean-up standards which should be applied and how business may expect to be held accountable for its environmental performance going forward.

Council of Europe's International Convention on Civil Liability for Damage Resulting from Activities Dangerous to the Environment

The Convention applies the mechanism of strict liability to a wide range of dangerous activities. This is because the EC considers that in environmental matters the risks attendant on some occupational activities are such that the traditional system of fault is clearly inadequate.

Broadly, the activities regarded as dangerous to the environment are activities which produce or use dangerous substances, such as toxic substances, activities which make use of genetically modified organisms and waste treatment activities and waste dumps. Under the Convention, liability rests with the person who controls the dangerous activity and where several installations are implicated, all the operators concerned are jointly and severally liable.

Under the Convention, operators are liable for damage arising from an accident. They are also answerable for creeping pollution and it is noted that the long term consequences of creeping pollution sometimes prove very serious.

The Convention covers personal injury, damage to property, damage by impairment of the environment, financial loss resulting from impairment of the environment and, in particular, the Convention requires operators to take any reasonable measures designed to restore and reinstate the damaged environment. The Convention requires that where some particularly dangerous activities are concerned, States will have to require operators to take out compulsory insurance as soon as the environment insurance market is sufficiently developed.

To obtain compensation, the victim must prove that he or she has suffered damage and that the damage was caused by one of the activities covered by the Convention. The Convention provides that anyone may have access to information on the environment held by the authorities and persons who have suffered damage may request, through the courts, that the operators concerned provide them with the specific information they hold, for inclusion in their files with a view to possible legal proceedings.

Voluntary organisations are given a key role. They may request the courts to prohibit a dangerous activity which is unlawful, order an operator to take measures to prevent damage or order an operator to take reinstatement measures.

To date, seven states have signed the Council of Europe's Convention. Neither the European Community nor the United Kingdom has signed. It is unlikely that the European Community will now sign as they have published the Green Paper on remedying environmental damage.

Conclusion

In conclusion the way ahead is still not clear. The need for information on the extent and nature of contamination is urgent at all levels—government, regulator, owner, financier. The current lack of clarity creates uncertainty, to the detriment of society as a whole.

Both the European Green Paper and the Government review offers all interested parties an opportunity to contribute towards the development of future strategy and policy. Full advantage *must* be taken of this opportunity.

Appendix

Extract from First Consultation Paper on section 143 EPA 1990, published in May 1991.

Annex C: Schedule of contaminative uses

Notes:

(a) "Contaminative use" is defined in section 143 of the Environmental Protection Act 1990 as "any use of land which may cause it to be contaminated with noxious substances".

(b) "Land" includes: any ground, soil or earth; houses or other buildings; the air space above it; but excludes all mines or minerals beneath it. It also includes land used for integral, partial and ancillary processes which form part of the primary use.

(c) A contaminative use is not to be taken to fall into the description if it is carried out as a domestic activity in connection with a private dwelling.

(d) The uses of land in this Annex have been included because they may make use of or give rise to noxious substances which may persist in the land where the use took place. It is intended that land uses which may have been contaminative in the past, but are not now, will be covered by the definitions of specific processes below.

(e) It is proposed that certain uses of land which may be contaminative are excluded from section 143 registers because the location of use cannot be defined sufficiently precisely. For example, it would be impossible to establish all locations where asbestos products have been used.

(f) The title of the main profiles relevant to each description of use are given in brackets.

Uses for the following purposes are contaminative:

C.1 Agriculture

(a) Burial of diseased livestock
(Profile: to be determined)

C.2 Extractive industry

(a) Extracting, handling and storage of carbonaceous materials such as coal, lignite, petroleum, natural gas, or bituminous shale (not including the underground workings)
(Profiles: Coal mines and coal preparation plants; Oil refineries and petrochemicals)

(b) Extracting, handling and storage of ores and their constituents.
(Profiles: Mineral workings; Mineral processing works)

Note: Handling includes loading, transport, sorting, forming and packaging and similar operations. Ore means any mineral, including non-metal bearing, except fuels.

C.3 Energy industry

(a) Producing gas from coal, lignite, oil or other carbonaceous material (other than from sewage or other waste), or from mixtures of those materials.
(Profiles: Gasworks and coal carbonisation plants; Oil refineries)

(b) Reforming, refining, purifying and odorising natural gas or any product of the processes outlined in C.3. (a) above.
(Profiles: Gasworks and coal carbonisation plants; Oil refineries)

(c) Pyrolysis, carbonisation, distillation, liquefaction, partial oxidation, other heat treatment, conversion, purification, or refining of coal, lignite, oil, other carbonaceous material or mixtures and products thereof, otherwise than with a view to gasification or making of charcoal.
(Profiles: Gasworks and coal carbonisation plants; Oil refineries; Coal mines and coal preparation plants)

(d) A thermal power station (including nuclear power stations and production, enrichment and reprocessing of nuclear fuels).
(Profiles: Power stations; Radioactive materials; Asbestos works)

(e) Electricity sub-station.
(Profiles: Power stations; Electrical equipment)

C.4 Production of metals

(a) Production, refining or recovery of metals by physical, chemical, thermal or electrolytic or other extraction process.
(Profiles: Metal processing; Heavy engineering)

(b) Heating, melting or casting metals as part of an intermediate or final manufacturing process (including annealing, tempering or similar processes).
(Profiles: Metal processing; Heavy engineering; Miscellaneous (High Street) trades)

(c) Cold forming processes (including pressing, rolling, extruding, stamping, forming or similar processes).
(Profiles: Metal processing; Heavy engineering; Electroplating and metal finishing)

(d) Finishing treatments, including anodising, pickling, coating, and plating or similar processes.
(Profiles: Metal processing; Heavy engineering; Electroplating and metal finishing; Miscellaneous (High Street) trades)

Note: Metals are taken to include metal scrap.

C.5 Production of non-metals and their products

(a) Production or refining of non-metals by treatment of the ore.
(Profile: Mineral processing works)

(b) Production or processing of mineral fibres by treatment of the ore.
(Profiles: Mineral processing works; Asbestos works)

(c) Cement, lime and gypsum manufacture, brickworks and associated processes.
(Profile: Mineral processing works)

C.6 Glass making and ceramics

(a) Manufacture of glass and products based on glass.
(Profile: Glass manufacturing)

(b) Manufacture of ceramics and products based on ceramics, including glazes and vitreous enamel.
(Profile: To be determined)

C.7 Production and use of chemicals

(a) Production, refining, recovery or storage of petroleum or petrochemicals or their by-products, including tar and bitumen processes and manufacture of asphalt.
(Profiles: Oil refineries and petrochemicals; Mineral processing works; Drum and tank cleaning)

(b) Production, refining and bulk storage of organic or inorganic chemicals, including fertilisers, pesticides, pharmaceuticals, soaps, detergents, cosmetics, toiletries, dyestuffs, inks, paints, fireworks, pyrotechnic materials or recovered chemicals.
(Profiles: Bulk inorganic and organic chemicals; Fine chemicals; Fertiliser manufacture; Pesticides' Pharmaceuticals; Textile and dye industry; Paint and ink manufacture; Miscellaneous (High Street) trades; Drum and tank cleaning)

(c) Production, refining and bulk storage of industrial gases not otherwise covered.
(Profile: Fine chemicals)

C.8 Engineering and manufacturing processes

(a) Manufacture of metal goods, including mechanical engineering industrial plant or steelwork, motor vehicles, ships, railway or tramway vehicles, aircraft, aerospace equipment or similar equipment.
(Profiles: Heavy engineering works; Engineering works; Car manufacturing works; Shipbuilding)

(b) Storage, manufacture or testing of explosives, propellants, ordnance, small arms or ammunition.
(Profile: Heavy engineering)

(c) Manufacture and repair of electrical and electronic components and equipment.
(Profiles: Electrical and electronic equipment manufacture; Miscellaneous (High Street) trades)

C.9 Food processing industry

(a) Manufacture of pet foods or animal feedstuffs.
(Profile: Food preparation and processing)

(b) Processing of animal by-products (including rendering or maggot farming, but excluding slaughterhouses, butchering).
(Profile: Animal processing works; Miscellaneous (High Street) trades)

C.10 Paper, pulp and printing industry

(a) Making of paper pulp, paper or board, or paper or board products, including printing or de-inking.

(Profiles: Pulp and paper manufacture; Printing works; Miscellaneous (High Street) trades)

C.11 Timber and timber products industry

(a) Chemical treatment and coating of timber and timber products.
(Profiles: Wood preservative industry and timber treatment works; Miscellaneous (High Street) trades)

C.12 Textile industry

(a) Tanning, dressing, fellmongering or other process for preparing, treating or working leather.
(Profiles: Animal processing works; Miscellaneous (High Street) trades)

(b) Fulling, bleaching, dyeing or finishing fabrics or fibres.
(Profiles: Textile and dye industry; Miscellaneous (High Street) trades)

(c) Manufacture of carpets or other textile floor coverings (including linoleum works).
(Profile: Textile and dye industry)

C.13 Rubber industry

(a) Processing of natural or synthetic rubber (including tyre manufacture or retreading).
(Profiles: Fine chemicals; Tyre manufacture)

C.14 Infrastructure

(a) Marshalling, dismantling, repairing or maintenance of railway rolling stock.
(Profile: Heavy engineering; Docks and railway land)

(b) Dismantling, repairing or maintenance of marine vessels, including hovercraft.
(Profiles: Shipbuilding and shipbreaking; Docks and railway land)

(c) Dismantling, repairing or maintenance of road transport or road haulage vehicles.
(Profiles: Road transport and road haulage; Garages and filling stations)

(d) Dismantling, repairing or maintenance of air or space transport systems.
(Profiles: Engineering works; Airports)

C.15 Waste disposal

(a) Treating of sewage or other effluent.
(Profile: Sewage works and farms)

(b) Storage, treatment or disposal of sludge including sludge from water treatment works.
(Profile: to be determined)

(c) Treating, keeping, depositing or disposing of waste, including scrap (to include infilled canal basins, docks or rivercourses).
(Profiles: Landfills and other waste treatment and disposal sites; Scrapyards; Drum and tank cleaning)

(d) Storage or disposal of radioactive materials.
(Profile: Radioactive materials)

C.16 Miscellaneous

(a) Premises housing dry cleaning operations.
(Profile: Miscellaneous (High Street) trades)

(b) Laboratories for educational or research purposes.
(Profiles: Research laboratories; Miscellaneous (High Street) trades)

(c) Demolition of buildings, plant or equipment used for any of the activities in this schedule.
(Profile: Demolition)

7 Hazardous waste liability issues for construction contractors and design professionals in the US

Jack S Kannry, PE

Introduction

Construction contractors and design professionals (principally engineers and architects) throughout the United States have a common growing concern as to an emerging problem that ultimately could be very costly, if not handled properly during the planning, design and construction phases of a typical building or heavy construction project. That is the encountering of unanticipated hazardous wastes at the construction site.

Aside from the fact that an awareness of this problem is relatively new to the construction site, it is particularly alarming to the typical foundation, highway or site work construction contractor due to a lack of critical knowledge and understanding. Familiarization is necessary as to: responsibility for dealing with this problem under a maze of federal and state legislation; methodology and specialty equipment and training needed in handling such materials; and the nature and scope of potential and perhaps uninsurable liability exposure upon becoming involved in any related physical activities. Similar concerns exist for the design professional in the pre-construction stages as well.

This paper will review the legal aspects of potential liability for the construction contractor and design professional, as well as offer some practical suggestions for protection against a calamity, upon encountering hazardous wastes at the jobsite.

Nature and scope of the hazardous waste problem at the construction site

Since the 1970s, there has developed a keen national environmental awareness in the United States, which led to a number of federal and state statutes of growing significance. These have and will continue to impact upon construction projects, as distinguished from those contracts specifically designated for removal and disposal of hazardous substances, which are not really the focus of this paper. Although such construction projects will look very much like those of the past, the hazardous waste factor adds a new dimension. It might arise, for example, on a highway being built through an old dump, a pipeline installed through an existing refinery, a housing project constructed in an abandoned cement quarry, or site work at an existing industrial location.

During excavation and other subsurface operations, workmen may confront buried leaking oil drums, strange coloured soil with unpleasant odours, gaseous vapours or other suspicious looking liquids, any or all of which may indeed constitute potential hazardous wastes and/or toxic substances. The immediate question to be answered in those situations is what to do in the field. Should all operations be stopped in the area, should attempts be made to move or isolate the potentially hazardous substances, should they be transported off the site?

Clearly, what is to be done by the construction contractor largely depends upon the risks of imminent danger to personnel, as well as the contractual provisions that may possibly cover this type of problem. However, even if the contract contemplates additional compensation when dealing with hazardous waste, that may be insufficient. A typical construction contractor is likely to be ill-equipped to remove such waste, in terms of personnel, availability of support facilities, actual know-how and the legal requirements involved in that type of operation.

What is hazardous waste?

As to what actually constitutes hazardous waste, one federal statute (the Resource Conservation and Recovery Act[1]) defines it as solid wastes, excluding domestic sewage, mixtures of domestic sewage and other wastes which pass through a sewer system to a publicly owned treatment facility, and certain industrial point source discharges. Specifically, the statute states that a hazardous waste is a:

> "Solid waste, or combination of solid wastes, which because of its quantity, concentration or physical, chemical or infectious characteristics may (a) cause or significantly contribute to an increase in mortality or an increase in serious irreversible, or incapacitating reversible, illness, or (b) pose a substantial present or potential hazard to human health or the environment when improperly treated, stored, transported, or disposed of, or otherwise managed."[2]

The federal regulations promulgated under this statute define hazardous wastes more specifically by characteristics, including ignitability, corrosivity, reactivity and toxicity, each of which has specified limitations beyond which it is deemed a hazardous waste.

---

1 42 U.S.C. §6901 *et seq.*

2 42 U.S.C. §6903.

A subsequent federal statute (the Comprehensive Environmental Response, Compensation and Liability Act[3]) broadened the scope of hazardous wastes by adding materials prohibited under pre-existing statutes, such as the Federal Water Pollution Control Act and the Clean Air Act, as well as substances specified by the United States Environmental Protection Agency ("EPA"), and exceeding a thousand in number.[4] All of these were then grouped under the broad heading of hazardous "substances". Some classic examples of these are the so-called PCBs (polychlorinated biphenyls) and asbestos materials, about which much has been written, but there are, of course, many more. Hazardous substances do not include petroleum, crude oil and natural gas.

Potential liability under federal statutes

To the uninitiated, the federal statutory scheme in the United States for hazardous wastes, which has developed over the past two decades, appears to be a maze of acronyms, such as "RCRA", "CERCLA", "SARA" and "Superfund". Most of this legislation is fairly recent, and the cases interpreting it are not plentiful on issues of liability for those other than owners and operators of hazardous waste facilities. As to potential construction contractor and design professional liability under these statutes, there is little determinative case law to date, although the issue has arisen of late in courthouses throughout the country with increasing frequency. Add to that the basic premise that many federal statutes are extremely difficult, complex and cumbersome for the legal community to comprehend, let alone the uninitiated, the task is quite formidable.

However, reduced to its minimum significant aspects, for purposes of this paper, the initial legislation on the scene was the Resource Conservation and Recovery Act of 1976 ("RCRA"). This statute represented an attempt by the U.S. Congress to deal with problems posed by the general disposal of wastes in our country, as well as the particular problems associated with the disposal of hazardous wastes. It provides what the U.S. Congress has called a "prospective cradle-to-grave regulatory scheme governing the movement of hazardous waste in our society".[5]

The statute authorizes the EPA to identify hazardous wastes; to promulgate standards for transporters of hazardous wastes and operators of hazardous waste facilities; and to issue permits for the operation of hazardous

3 42 U.S.C. §9601 *et seq.*

4 42 U.S.C. §9601(14).

5 H.R.Rep. No. 1016, Part 1, 96th Cong. 2d Sess. 17, reprinted in 1980 U.S. Code Cong. & Admin. News 6119, 6120.

waste disposal facilities. In addition, it authorizes suit when the past or present handling, storage, treatment, transportation or disposal of any hazardous waste may present an imminent and substantial endangerment to health or to the environment. Such suit is permissible against any person who has contributed or who is contributing to such handling, storage, treatment, transportation or disposal, to restrain such person or to order such person to take such other actions that may be necessary, or both. That requirement has been interpreted to impose strict liability[6] and to apply to persons who in the past contributed to the handling, storage, treatment, transportation or disposal of hazardous waste, regardless of how far into the past those activities occurred.

The Comprehensive Environmental Response, Compensation and Liability Act ("CERCLA")[3] was enacted in 1980 in an effort to eliminate unsafe hazardous waste sites throughout the United States. Amended in 1986 by the Superfund Amendments and Reauthorization Act of 1986 ("SARA"),[7] CERCLA authorized the EPA to clean up hazardous waste sites itself and created a "Superfund" to pay for such EPA activities. Superfund is financed through a combination of appropriations, industry taxes and judgments obtained through legal actions to recover response costs from those found to be responsible for the hazardous waste problems.

The statutory scheme to facilitate the clean-up of hazardous toxic waste sites includes established procedures for either removal actions (clean-up and removal of released hazardous substances) or remedial actions (taken instead of or in addition to removal actions, generally to prevent or minimize the release of hazardous substances). Although the line between removal and remedial actions has not been precisely drawn by the U.S. Congress, removal actions are typically short-term measures taken to prevent immediate harm, whereas remedial actions are generally long-term projects designed to effect permanent solutions (*e.g.*, perimeter protection using dykes, trenches or ditches; clay cover; neutralization of hazardous substances; and monitoring to assure that such actions protect the public health and welfare, and the environment).

CERCLA places the ultimate responsibility for clean-up on those responsible for problems caused by the disposal of chemical poisons, by authorizing suit against four classes of parties: (1) the owners and operators of a facility at which there is a release or threatened release of hazardous

---

6 For the non-attorney reader, "strict liability" is the imposition of absolute liability for resulting damages without any necessary showing of actual negligence or other wrongdoing by the party held liable, and generally is applicable to abnormally dangerous activities, *e.g.*, hazardous waste removal.

7 42 U.S.C. §9601–9675.

substances; (2) the owners or operators of such a facility anytime in the past when hazardous substances were disposed of; (3) any person who arranged for transport, treatment or disposal of a hazardous substance; and (4) the persons who transported hazardous substances to sites where there is a release or threatened release of such substances.[8]

The preponderance of court decisions interpreting this statute have held that CERCLA imposes strict liability, and joint and several liability,[9] on those various categories of parties, with only a limited number of statutorily prescribed defences being available. In considering the breadth of CERCLA's reach, one need merely review the statutory definitions provided for certain of its terms: "Facility" is any site or area where a hazardous substance has been deposited, stored, disposed of or placed, or otherwise comes to be located, and specifically includes any building, structure, installation, equipment, pipe or pipeline, well, pit, pond, lagoon, impoundment, ditch, landfill, storage container, motor vehicle, rolling stock or aircraft.[10] "Release" is any spilling, leaking, pumping, pouring, emitting, emptying, discharging, injecting, escaping, leaching, dumping or disposing into the environment.[11] "Disposal" is the discharge, deposit, injection, dumping, spilling, leaking or placing of any hazardous substance such that the substance may enter the environment.[12]

Strict liability under CERCLA is subject only to three potential defences: (1) an act of God; (2) an act of war; or (3) where the release is caused by the act or omission of a third party and (a) the third party does not have a direct or indirect contractual relationship with the defendant and (b) the defendant establishes that (i) he exercised due care with respect to the substance concerned and (ii) he took precautions against foreseeable acts and omissions of the third party.[13]

Additionally, in an attempt to respond to the potential liability concerns of Superfund clean-up contractors (the "response action contractors"), the U.S. Congress exempted such contractors from strict liability under federal law, and also provided EPA with discretionary authority to indemnify such contractors for hazardous substance releases arising out of negligent response action activities, all under the 1986 Superfund Amendments and

8 42 U.S.C. §9607(a).

9 Again, for the non-attorney reader, "joint and several liability" connotes a liability which may be imposed against each of several defendants, both individually for all claimed damages, as well as jointly, together with the other defendants, for such damages.

10 42 U.S.C. §9601(9).

11 42 U.S.C. §9601(22).

12 42 U.S.C. §6903(3); see also, 42 U.S.C. §9601(23).

13 42 U.S.C. §9607(b).

Reauthorization Act ("SARA").[14] However, it should be noted, albeit beyond the scope of this paper, that under new EPA guidelines for response action contractors, effective in early 1993, such indemnification has been significantly limited, both in duration and amount, as well as imposing stringent conditions on its inclusion in future contracts.

The existence of any such statutory exception to liability is perhaps more troublesome to the construction contractor than if the U.S. Congress had done nothing at all so to limit the broader liability of the original statutory language. It demonstrates that the legislature has considered the problem and established only very specific limitations, with the construction contractor not at all being among the protected class.

Illustrative of the prevailing policy to maintain the broadest classifications of potentially responsible parties, because of the enormous costs involved in hazardous waste clean-up, is the commentary a few years ago in the well known U.S. construction industry periodical, *Engineering News-Record:*

> "The critical issue of 'who pays' has also come before Congress. A proposal to amend the law and exempt lenders narrowly missed enactment in the closing days of the last Congress, and Hill staffers say the issue is likely to be the first order of Superfund business next session—if not the only one. 'We would fight that very hard,' says Linda Greer, an attorney for the National Resources Defense Council. '*The liability scheme is why we're getting voluntary cleanups and good behaviour.*'" (emphasis supplied).[15]

Such broad liability schemes, extended beyond those who have contributed by generating the waste, may well include the designer or builder of the facility at which the waste is stored or disposed. If it is found that such parties *contributed* to the handling, storage or disposal of that waste, they are very definitely at risk.

There can be little doubt as to the viability of persuasive arguments distinguishing the type of contribution made by a generator of hazardous wastes from the contribution by a contractor who builds the waste facility. However, the statutory language is, as previously noted, not self-limiting in that regard, nor has it as yet been limited by judicial interpretation. Indeed, in one case in the U.S. District Court of Pennsylvania, a motion to dismiss a complaint against an engineering firm that designed a portion of a landfill, on the ground that such defendant was not a person contributing to the disposal of waste which endangered health, was denied by the court,

---

14 Superfund Response Action Contractor Indemnification, 58 Fed. Reg. 5972 (25 January 1993).

15 Rubin and Setzer, "The Superfund Decade: Triumphs and Troubles", *Engineering News-Record*, Vol. 225 No. 21 at 38, 44, 26 Nov 1990.

suggesting at least a potential liability, depending upon resolution by trial of the relevant fact issues.[16]

In a similar vein, the question arises as to the liability exposure of a construction contractor who, as an incident of excavation or other subsurface operation in which he is engaged on a major underground project, moves a quantity of hazardous waste or substance out of the way of such operation. Does he thereby becomes a transporter, handler and/or disposer of such hazardous waste, so as to subject him to the statutory liability under discussion? Such questions are of great concern, and a number of recent decisions by federal courts in various locations throughout the United States suggest that there is definitely potential liability for the construction contractor.

In broad context, a federal appellate court in Texas expressed the view that CERCLA does not automatically exclude the imposition of "chilling liability on the defendants' businesses: banking, real estate, *construction*, and development"[17] (emphasis supplied). The same court also noted, albeit in the context of ownership or operation of a facility at which hazardous wastes are disposed, that:

> "This definition of disposal does not limit disposal to a one-time occurrence; there may be other disposals when hazardous materials are moved, dispersed, or released during landfill excavations and fillings."[18]

Another federal court, this time in North Carolina, citing *Tanglewood, supra*, held that an adequate claim was pleaded by the federal government against a construction contractor, as follows:

> "Through defendants' construction of roadways directly over areas of wastepits, redisposal of the hazardous substances has occurred. The kind of activity in which the defendants were allegedly involved may be interpreted as 'disposal' activities within the meaning of CERCLA 107."[19]

In yet another recent federal case, in New Jersey at the pretrial stage,[20] a public authority brought an action to recover costs for the clean-up of a contaminated site. The defendants included the waste generator, the current owner of the property, a company that sold contaminated mud for fill

---

16 *DesJardiens* v *Strasburg Landfill Assoc.*, (E.D.Pa. 1985), n.o.r., Civ. Action No. 85–2801, 24 September 1985.

17 *Tanglewood East Homeowners* v *Charles-Thomas, Inc.*, 849 F.2d 1568, (5th Cir. 1988); accord, *Guidice* v *BFG Electroplating and Mfg. Co., Inc.*, 732 F.Supp. 556 (W.D.Pa. 1989).

18 849 F.2d at 1573.

19 *United States* v *Skipper*, n.o.r. (E.D.N.C., 14 August 1990, U.S.M. Leonard, Civ. Action No. 89–102).

20 *Jersey City Redevelopment Authority* v *PPG Industries*, 655 F.Supp. 1257 (D.N.J. 1987), aff'd 866 F.2d 1411 (3d Cir. 1988).

material, and a construction contractor hired by the authority to perform excavation and filling work at the site being developed by that authority. Various defendants moved for summary judgment to dismiss the claims against them, including an initial count for clean-up liability under CERCLA. Notably, however, the excavation contractor, although moving for summary judgment on a number of other counts, did not separately seek dismissal of the CERCLA count as to it.

On the lengthy trial that followed, this contractor was successful in escaping liability to the plaintiff. The indicated reasoning of that court was that such contractor was not a responsible party under CERCLA, 42 U.S.C. 9607(a), because its transportation of hazardous substances was to a residential development site, which the court distinguished from a disposal or treatment facility, and that it had not selected the site.[21] Although such fine distinction saved that contractor, one might possibly question such judicial interpretation when viewed in the context of the statutory definitions of "facility" and "disposal" (see p 165). Moreover, might not disposal of a hazardous waste at a residential development site be considered by the environmentally oriented to be even a more serious matter to public health and safety than disposal of such substance at a waste disposal or treatment facility?

The principal import of that case for construction contractors, generally, is that a legally viable cause of action under CERCLA was asserted against such a contractor, that the contractor was at risk on this issue through trial, and that the judicial reasoning which led to it being found not liable under CERCLA might not necessarily exonerate the next similarly situated contractor. Clearly, these must be points of concern for construction contractors.

Even more disturbing to the construction contractor and its counsel, with potential ripple effects against the design professional as well, are a series of very recent federal appellate decisions in cases originating in the states of California, Missouri and Illinois.[22] In each of these, the courts, in very direct and clear determinations, held that construction contractors involved in excavation and related sitework are potentially responsible parties under the CERCLA definitions.

---

21 *Jersey City Redevelopment Authority* v *PPG Industries*, n.o.r. (D.N.J., 3 September 1987, J. Sarokin, Civ. Action No. 85–2014).

22 *Kaiser Aluminum & Chemical Corp.* v *Cattelus Development Corp.*, 976 F.2d 1338 (9th Cir. 1992); accord, *Danella Southwest, Inc.* v *Southwestern Bell Telephone Company*, 775 F.Supp. 1227 (E.D. Mo. 1991), aff'd w/o opinion 978 F.2d 1263 (8th Cir. 1992); *Environmental Transportation Systems, Inc.* v *Ensco, Inc.*, 763 F.Supp. 384 (C.D. Ill. 1991), aff'd 969 F.2d 503 (7th Cir. 1992).

In the most widely reported of these cases, *Kaiser Aluminum*, *supra*, the defendant in a CERCLA action had been a prior owner of the contaminated site, which then impleaded as third-party defendant the construction contractor retained to excavate and grade part of the property for a proposed residential development. During performance of that work, the contractor spread some excavated soil over other portions of the property. That soil was subsequently determined to contain a number of hazardous substances, including paint thinner, lead, asbestos and petroleum hydrocarbons. The defendant alleged in its third-party complaint that the construction contractor had exacerbated the contamination by spreading such soil over previously uncontaminated parts of the property. The federal district court dismissed the impleader action, finding that such contractor was not a potentially responsible party under the CERCLA definitions. However, the appellate court reversed, holding that allegations that the contractor "excavated the contaminated soil from one area of the property and moved it to another are sufficient to allege potential liability."[23] By virtue of those acts, the contractor was considered an operator of a facility at which it disposed of hazardous substances and it also accepted hazardous substances for transport to sites selected by it.

Statutory settlement procedures

One of the purposes of the most recent federal statute ("SARA") was to implement a detailed settlement procedure designed to help facilitate negotiated settlements between the EPA and potentially responsible parties ("PRPs"). The intent here is to recover and conserve federal Superfund monies.

PRPs are defined in CERCLA to include any and all parties who are responsible for the release of hazardous waste, such as current owners and operators of hazardous waste facilities, past owners and operators who accepted the waste on-site, generators of hazardous waste, and transporters of waste to a disposal facility. Once a hazardous waste site becomes listed on the EPA's National Priorities List, established under the National Oil and Hazardous Substances Pollution Contingency Plan,[24] the PRPs are given the option to enter into a settlement agreement with the EPA. The EPA is not obliged to enter into such an agreement, and any decision to do so is wholly discretionary. The settlement agreement occurs in the form of a court ordered consent decree and contains promises by the PRPs to

---

23 976 F.2d at 1343.

24 40 C.F.R. §300.

perform and finance the clean-up, pursuant to a clean-up plan approved by EPA. Where the parties have failed to settle, the EPA may commence the clean-up, using Superfund monies. Once the clean-up is completed, the EPA generally seeks recovery of all costs from the PRPs under CERCLA's cost recovery provisions.

It is also noteworthy that the federal statutory scheme does not prohibit any party, potentially responsible for response or remediation costs in cleaning up a hazardous waste site, from seeking contribution from other potentially responsible parties in an action brought by the federal government to recover such costs. Moreover, a party potentially responsible for such costs may also maintain a separate private suit against another potentially responsible party to recover such costs.

State "Mini-Superfund" statutes

The federal legislative scheme in the United States for clean-up and liability with respect to hazardous wastes is carried forward in many states through so-called "Mini-Superfund" statutes. There is not really any general rule of thumb which would be applicable throughout all jurisdictions in the country. However, construction contractors and design professionals should be aware of the existence of such statutes, which would have to be reviewed by their counsel in contemplation of performing any work at potential hazardous waste sites, either in their home venues or out of state.

Illustrative are the statutes in the metropolitan New York, New Jersey and Connecticut area, with which the author is most familiar. The State of New York has a Mini-Superfund statute, generally tailored after the federal CERCLA statute, and referred to as the Hazardous Waste Remedial Fund.[25] Decisions in the New York courts suggest that a standard of strict liability would be imposed against property owners and generators of hazardous waste. However, an interesting 1987 amendment to that statute, apparently intended to limit liability for clean-up contractors in performing hazardous waste remediation contracts for the New York State Environmental Conservation Department, actually contains wording that may also protect the design professional involved in such projects. Thus:

> "The liability of any person *designing*, implementing or otherwise performing services related to clean-up or restoration work pursuant to a contract with the department, or an order of the department or a court for any injury to a person or property caused by or related to such services, shall be limited to acts or omissions of the person during the course of performing such services which are

25 New York Environmental Conservation Law 27–0916.

shown to have been the result of negligence, gross negligence or reckless, wanton or intentional misconduct." (emphasis supplied)[26]

In New Jersey, the comparable statute is known as the New Jersey Spill Compensation and Control Act,[27] which imposes a general strict liability on any person who discharges a hazardous substance or is responsible for a hazardous substance which the state has removed; however, clean-up or response action contractors have been excepted and held to a negligence standard in that jurisdiction. As to Connecticut, that state's general statutes, under its Water Pollution Control Act,[28] have created an Emergency Spill Response Fund, with liability generally appearing to be based on a negligence rather than strict liability standard.

For the construction contractor and design professional alike, the concern here should nevertheless be, as it is under federal law, that in dealing with hazardous wastes at the construction site, extreme care must be exercised to avoid being categorized as an operator, generator, transporter, handler or disposer of hazardous wastes, or one who has "contributed to" or "arranged for" one or more of such activities. Any of these could trigger some degree of liability to the federal or state government, or to another potentially responsible party in a private litigation.

Implications for the construction contractor of response action contractor liability and indemnification

Previously mentioned was the limited liability of Superfund clean-up or response action contractors, both under federal and some state laws. The prospect of liability under CERCLA had been a significant deterrent to prospective clean-up contractors, and had threatened to delay or disrupt the CERCLA clean-up programme. As noted, the U.S. Congress responded to such problem under SARA by limiting the liability of response action contractors to circumstances in which their grossly negligent or intentional misconduct caused the release of hazardous substance. SARA also provided that response action contractors could be further indemnified against liability where they could not obtain adequate liability insurance at a fair and reasonable price.

Although it would appear reasonable that the typical construction contractor, ill-equipped to deal physically with hazardous wastes at the jobsite,

---

26 New York Environmental Conservation Law §27–0916, subd. 3, see also 17½ *McKinney's 1993 Cumulative Annual Pocket Part* 224–225, 1988 Supplementary Practice Commentaries.

27 New Jersey Statutes, §58:10–23.11.

28 Connecticut General Statutes, §22a-416 to 22a-471.

should be legislatively insulated, at least to the extent of the response action contractor (if not more), as earlier stated, that simply is not the case at present. Thus, the lack of such statutory protection underscores the need for construction contractors to exercise extreme vigilance in this area as work progresses on the deep foundation or other subsurface site, where unforeseen hazardous wastes may be encountered.

There can be no argument with the proposition that clean-up contracting is a dramatically growing business throughout the nation, and opportunities in that field may appear quite attractive to the aggressive U.S. construction contractor, particularly for one who has heavy earthmoving experience and is understandably concerned about the lengthy and continuing downturn in the construction industry. However, as to those commentators who suggest that there exists a natural transition from construction to clean-up contracting, it should be emphasized that the nature of a response action contractor's business is dramatically different from that of a construction contractor. A response action contractor has know-how, experience, facilities and personnel well-equipped to deal with hazardous wastes in a safe, efficient manner, and thereby to limit potential liability exposure. Such a contractor is further buttressed, as noted above, by statutory liability limitation and even statutory indemnification if adequate insurance coverage is unavailable.

A notable trend in recent years, underscoring the sharp dichotomy between these two types of businesses in the United States has been the recent public sector trend of treating the clean-up contract as a professional services contract, requiring a high order of technical field engineering and laboratory testing prequalifications, and thereby avoiding the customary competitive bidding statutes applicable to most public construction contracts.

Pre-bid inquiries

Having now reviewed the broad statutory scheme and types of potential hazardous waste liability for the construction contractor and design professional on a subsurface project, the focus of this paper shifts to consideration of what these entities can do to minimize the risks and protect themselves during the design and bidding period, as well as in the construction phase itself.

The previously mentioned cradle-to-grave concept of owner liability for hazardous wastes under RCRA was softened under SARA, wherein an "innocent purchaser" defence was established to environmental liability, applicable if the owner, at the time of acquisition, made "all appropriate inquiry into the previous ownership and uses of the property" and conducted "appropriate inspection".[29] This duty of inquiry led to the development of a new branch of environmental engineering services for owners, known as the site assessment. It can be a very valuable tool for the construction contractor during the pre-bid period. Briefly, the site assessment typically comprises three components: an audit, an assessment and a report.

Audits typically include a review of available historical records and regulatory files, which would involve checking the ownership of the site for the past 50 years or more to see how the land was used. For example, was it a manufacturing plant employing hazardous substances, some of which may have been disposed at the site? The audit would also include a walking tour of the property, an automobile tour of the immediate vicinity, interviews with property owners, and a report documenting activities on the property and providing an opinion on actual or potential contamination.

One of the difficulties with this phase of site assessment is that a potential owner may not want to tip its hand to the existing owner as to its intentions prior to negotiating a purchase price, and hence there may be a tendency to tiptoe around what really needs to be done in an environmental assessment to make a valuable judgmental determination. This problem particularly arises where a prospective purchaser is contemplating assembling a series of contiguous parcels for a large development such that, if existing owners get wind of that intention, the prices can soar.

An engineering firm represented by the author was recently involved in that type of situation, where the prospective purchaser wanted a limited site assessment, excluding actual entry onto the land or into the buildings under consideration. Subsequent to purchase, when potentially hazardous substances were discovered at the site, there was one very unhappy purchaser. This led to significant litigation against prior owners, as well as against the engineering firm, for the diminution in property value, prospective cleanup costs and related damages, the outcome of which is far from certain.

The assessment phase, which involves a more detailed and specific fact-finding effort, generally includes field sampling, laboratory analyses and other testing to investigate specific concerns identified during the audit. The purpose of such assessment is to confirm or refute suspected contamination with real data. However, that does not necessarily mean that such sampling and testing will eliminate all uncertainty. It is fairly common that the extent of sampling activities is balanced against the owner's willingness to assume risk, as compared to the amount of time and money available for such detailed assessment.

29 42 U.S.C. §9601(35)(B).

The results of the above fact-finding are incorporated by the environmental engineer into a site audit and assessment report for the owner. This is an extremely valuable document, which the construction contractor should seek to obtain and review prior to entering into a construction contract on any project where there is the remotest possibility of the existence of hazardous wastes. Even if there has been no site assessment undertaken by an engineer on behalf of the current or a prior owner, the mere fact that the contractor is on record as having requested a copy of any such report, or that a site assessment be made prior to contracting if no such report exists, could stand it in good stead if problems of this type develop during construction.

In the situation where the owner of the project is a public body, it is recommended that requests for such site assessment reports be in the form of a federal Freedom of Information Act and/or state Freedom of Information Law request. This should be done at the earliest possible time, probably as soon as the contractor takes out a set of plans and specifications, and even before it determines if an actual bid is to be submitted. That lead time could be important, inasmuch as FOIA and FOIL requests generally necessitate several weeks, at best, before one is likely to obtain any of the requested documents.

Beyond this type of pre-bid inquiry, the prudent construction contractor should also review the plans, specifications and other contract documents scrupulously, with a focus on any provisions relating to hazardous waste at the site. Such indications could include, for example, references on soil boring logs or other subsurface data included in the contract documents with respect to decomposed matter or degradable materials encountered during the subsurface investigation phase.

The contractor should also pay particular attention to provisions in the general or special conditions, dealing with site investigation responsibilities on its part, setting forth the steps to be taken in the event that hazardous wastes are encountered, which may or may not require the contractor to be responsible for their removal; any special insurance requirements with respect to hazardous wastes; and any exculpatory language, such as in the areas of unforeseen conditions and damages for delay, which the owner may have inserted to insulate itself from liability with respect to hazardous wastes, as well as from the more traditional type of construction problems that often arise.

Obviously, if the potential contract is with a public body, the contractor is facing what is legally referred to as a contract of adhesion, *i.e.*, take it or leave it, with no opportunity to negotiate any more favourable terms. On the other hand, if the contractor is dealing with a private owner, an awareness as to the significance of these type of provisions can be extremely helpful to it and counsel in negotiating a more favourable and fair balancing of the risks in the area of hazardous waste.

Another recommended pre-bid area of inquiry is the contractor's own investigation of the project site, as well as that of the surrounding land and water bodies near the project location. Thus, *e.g.*, if the nature of the project is that of covering over an old garbage landfill, that may put the contractor on notice as to the possibility of initial exposure, since of necessity it may have to move or relocate some of the decomposed matter in that landfill to fulfil the contractual obligations. Similarly, if the project is adjacent to muck swampland, and one can hardly see the colour of the water, with nonaromatic vapours arising from the surface, the contractor may well be in for a very unpleasant water table condition and a significant problem, of not just dewatering, but of how to dispose of the dewatered material.

To illustrate the potential extreme of this type of situation, a contractor client recently consulted the author on a problem that had him running in circles. It seemed that his project called for the construction of a sewer line in an area adjacent to an extremely stagnant body of water that contained, in this instance, not hazardous waste, but oil and grease. Clearly, his dewatering operations, in order to perform the deep sewer installation, involved the removal of water containing that oil and grease. The New York State Environmental Conservation Department, however, would not permit him to discharge that water back into the same contaminated adjacent body of water which had generated this oil and grease, but rather insisted that it be disposed of elsewhere by very expensive means.

In that situation, while there may have been no way of totally avoiding such result, surely it is far better to recognize it at the pre-bid stage, so the contractor is aware of what could be a very costly risk, and at least has the opportunity to consider that in its bid, rather than face a very unpleasant and unexpected surprise at a later point in time.

Thus, if the contractor is fortunate enough to have the opportunity to negotiate any of the contract provisions prior to entering into the construction contract where hazardous waste might be encountered during performance, the best rule of thumb is to minimize absolutely, if not eliminate, any responsibility on its part for handling, transporting or disposing of such waste, or even arranging for or contributing to any of those activities. Ideally, the contractor would seek to be in a position where, if hazardous waste is encountered during the job, it has the right to stop work and avoid the area until the owner makes arrangements with a third party (probably a clean-up or response action contractor) to remove and dispose of the hazardous waste, and with the construction contractor to be appropriately compensated for any delays and increased costs in construction work arising out of that particular situation.

With respect to the design professional's vulnerability in the pre-bid period, its likely direct involvement in site investigation, as part of the design function, and the preparation of construction contract documents, requires a different type of inquiry in that period from that of the construction contractor. It must scrupulously put the owner on notice, in very timely fashion, as to the need for various types of subsurface investigations and testing throughout the project site, particularly where there be any suspicion as to the presence of hazardous wastes. Should the owner baulk, due to economic or time constraints, or perhaps for other practical reasons, the design professional cannot afford the risk of getting caught up in the owner's problems where the price is inadequate site investigations data for a prudent design. Clearly, that situation creates a dilemma, requiring a balancing of legal and business factors for the design professional in determining how to proceed in performing professionally within the owner's less than palatable parameters.

Contractual liability and protective mechanisms

The spectre of potential strict liability for the construction contractor and, perhaps, the design professional as well, in handling or disposing of hazardous wastes, necessitates recognition and careful consideration of various contract provisions which can affect that type of responsibility.

There is often to be found a contract provision which requires a pre-bid investigation by the contractor and an acknowledgement in the contract that he is fully familiar with all existing conditions by virtue thereof. Yet, as a practical matter, the typical construction process provides the owner and its design professionals with many months, if not years, to consider the existing conditions in developing the contract documents. On the other hand, the prospective bidders will have a period of a few short weeks to do likewise. Hence, a bidder can usually do little more than rely on existing conditions, information furnished in the contract documents, or made available during the bidding period, coupled with cursory field visits to the jobsite. This can be a potentially troublesome area, particularly since the owner, seeking to bar a contractor claim in a contamination situation, will likely raise this clause as a defence.

Some public construction contracts provide that unforeseen subsurface conditions, which could not reasonably have been anticipated at the time of contracting, may entitle the contractor to an equitable adjustment for the additional costs arising out of encountering such conditions. While hazardous wastes may not be specifically identified as a potential source of unforeseen subsurface conditions, a strong argument could be made to that effect in contracts which provide the contractor with such type of relief.

A no-damages-for-delay clause, which prohibits the contractor's recovery for project delays from any cause whatsoever, is quite common these days in construction contracts throughout the United States, and generally has been found to be enforceable, with certain very limited exceptions. In some jurisdictions, depending on the representations and information contained in the contract documents, unanticipated hazardous substances causing project delays would likely be regarded as unforeseeable and outside the application of a no-damages-for-delay clause. Likewise, discovery of hazardous materials contrary to the express representations in the contract documents may also be a basis for escaping application of such exculpatory provision.

On this point, in New York, for example, delays resulting from the owner's breach of a fundamental obligation of the contract have also been considered an exception to exculpatory language that there shall be no damages for delay.[30] Active interference by the owner has been held to be such a type of breach, with a number of courts holding that the failure timely to provide a site for project construction constitutes such interference. Recognizing that there as yet appear to be no judicial determinations in New York or elsewhere considering this issue in a hazardous waste context, the contractor deprived of his ability to proceed because of the discovery of hazardous waste may nevertheless have a compelling argument that the owner has effectively interfered with the contractor's entitlement to site access, and hence that the delay damages flowing from that condition are compensable.

Another significant area for the contractor to consider in seeking liability protection from the hazardous waste problem at the jobsite is whether or not it can obtain insurance coverage against this potentiality. Many carriers that provide contractor's comprehensive general liability coverage are insisting on pollution exclusion provisions, which essentially negate insurance coverage in this type of situation. Even where there is no express pollution exclusion in the comprehensive general liability policy, it is well to note that there have been a number of court challenges by insurance carriers in various jurisdictions, as to whether in fact the clean-up costs occasioned by the encountering of hazardous wastes actually constitute property damage, so as to be within the ambit of the provided coverage. However, the law is far from settled in this area, with, for example, New Jersey courts holding against coverage,[31] whereas in New York and several

30 *Corinno Civetta Construction Corp.* v *City of New York*, 67 N.Y.2d 297, 502 N.Y.S.2d 681 (1986).

31 *Atlantic City Municipal Utilities Authority* v *Cigna Companies*, (N.J. Super.Ct. App.Div. 1987), n.o.r., Case No. A-1320–8477, July 2, 1987).

other jurisdictions coverage is generally supported,[32] in the absence of an express exclusion.

Generally, complaints in hazardous waste actions seek the repayment or restitution of funds expended or to be expended investigating and cleaning up a contaminated site or preventing further contamination of a site. Various courts have held these claims are not for damages resulting from property damage, since they have no relationship to the actual diminution in land value, for which that coverage is intended. In fact, there have been instances where the total bill for clean-up costs far exceeded the overall value of the land involved, let alone any diminution in value; in one such Pennsylvania federal case, the court limited damages to the value of the property.[33]

The time has not yet come where any federal or state legislature has indicated a receptiveness to insulate the construction contractor in the same manner as the clean-up or response action contractor, due to an inability to obtain adequate insurance coverage. However, this may well be due to the lack of much significant litigation to date over claims for clean-up costs against the construction contractor.

Some enlightened owners, seeking to maintain a healthy competitive bid environment on their construction projects, have recognized the need to provide contractual indemnity to the construction contractor, in view of the lack of any real involvement in the hazardous waste process and impropriety of liability for that contractor. While it is premature to suggest that this is a mushrooming trend, nevertheless it does afford some degree of comfort to the construction contractor in knowing that such protection is at least possible, particularly in a negotiated contract context.

Illustrative is a provision recently promulgated by a major utility company in its construction contract form. Although such contractual language may not fit the bill in every situation, and the reader is cautioned to consult with counsel prior to drafting or proposing any comparable provision, it is offered here simply to show the breadth of potential protection in this area, which one owner deemed to be fair and reasonable:

> "It is recognized that certain federal statutes related to hazardous waste work, including the Comprehensive Environmental Response Compensation and

---

32 *Bankers Trust Co.* v *Hartford Accident & Indemnity Co.*, 518 F.Supp. 371 (S.D.N.Y. 1981), vac on other grds, 621 F.Supp. 685 (S.D.N.Y. 1981); accord, *Savoy Medical Supply Co., Inc.* v *F&H Mfg. Corp.*, 776 F.Supp. 703 (E.D.N.Y. 1991); *Boyce Thompson Institute* v *Insurance Co. of N.A.*, 751 F.Supp. 1137 (S.D.N.Y. 1990); *Claussen* v *Aetna Cas. & Sur. Co.*, 754 F.Supp. 1576 (S.D.Ga. 1990); *Unigard Mut. Ins. Co.* v *McCarty's, Inc.*, 756 F.Supp. 1366 (D.Idaho 1988).

33 *Bogar* v *Sperry Rand Corp.*, 504 F.Supp. 872 (E.D.Pa. 1980), aff'd 671 F.2d 495 (3d Cir. 1981).

Liability Act of 1980 (CERCLA) and the Resource Conservation and Recovery Act of 1976 (RCRA), provide that individuals and firms may be held liable for damages and claims related to such work under a doctrine of joint and several strict liability. It is not the intention of this contract that the contractor be exposed to any hazardous waste liability arising out of pre-contract site contamination, the activities of others, including the owner, or for any hazardous waste liabilities which may arise from the non-negligent performance by the contractor of any work hereunder. Accordingly, for purposes of this contract only, excepting the wilful negligent performance by the contractor or its subcontractors, the owner shall reimburse the contractor and/or its subcontractors for, or otherwise indemnify, defend and save the contractor harmless from, any and all demands, suits, judgments, expenses, attorney's fees and losses arising out of, or in connection with, bodily injury (including death) to persons or damage to property which may arise from the presence or origination of hazardous substances, pollutants or contaminants on the site, irrespective of whether such materials were generated or introduced before or after execution of this contract and irrespective of whether the owner was aware of, or indirectly involved in, the generation or introduction of such materials.

The contractor and/or its subcontractor shall, under no circumstances, be considered the generator of any hazardous substances, pollutants or contaminants encountered or handled in the performance of the work. Without contradiction of any assertion by the owner of third party liability, as described above, for the purpose of this contract only, it is agreed that any hazardous materials, pollutants or contaminants generated or encountered in the performance of the work shall be the responsibility of the owner."

Notwithstanding such favourable contract language, it should be borne in mind that the parties to such a contract cannot, by their agreement, override any contrary statutes with respect to liability, especially to the federal or state governments. Nevertheless, this type of provision can dramatically reduce the risk with respect to private parties' litigation.

Protecting the record during construction upon encountering hazardous waste

We next consider what the construction contractor and design professional should do when hazardous wastes are actually encountered, not only from the physical standpoint, which is likely simply to mean the stopping of work and notifying the owner of the problem, but rather from the perspective of protecting the record and the rights of the parties.

In virtually every construction contract, there are a series of notice provisions, which require the contractor to apprise the owner of problem areas being encountered, may require decisions of the architect or engineer, and may also serve as a prelude for seeking additional compensation for the associated increased costs. Such notice requirements typically deal with the subjects of unforeseen conditions encountered at the jobsite (such as hazardous wastes), disputed work notices and force account records, as well as notices of delay, disruption, work stoppages and the like, which also require maintenance of supporting cost records. The obvious purpose of these notice provisions is to enable the owner and its architect or engineer to be alerted in a timely fashion, and thereby to be able to maintain contemporaneous cost records to compare against the contractor's at such time as the problem is resolved, whether it be through a subsequent change order or a claim in litigation.

Failure to comply with such contractual provisions with respect to existing or potential claims can yield a very harsh result of being nonsuited on this procedural ground. The importance to construction contractors of complying with the contractual notice provisions cannot be overemphasized, since there are more than enough problems to be faced with litigating a substantial and complex construction claim on the merits without being barred at the threshold by procedural impediments.

Other steps which should be implemented in protecting the record are the maintenance of detailed job diary entries by the field personnel, setting forth the encountering of hazardous waste, in terms of what was seen, by nature, description and quantities, what, if anything, was disturbed or touched, as well as the substance of field discussions with other parties. Timely correspondence, apprising the other parties of this problem, which may well delay completion of the project and increase the costs, are also essential.

While a picture may be worth a thousand words in some fields of endeavour, it is probably worth much more than that in construction. A programme of periodic professional photographs is recommended, showing both existing and as-built conditions of major elements and items of the work, perhaps augmented by snapshots taken by field personnel of problem areas. This can ultimately be an invaluable record of what occurred, and could be particularly useful in connection with the encountering of hazardous wastes. Additionally, in recent years there has been an increasing use of video cassettes, narrated by the photographer, to show certain types of construction and related operations, and depending upon the nature of the hazardous waste encountered, this might be a good idea as well.

Claims against the construction contractor and design professional

As noted in the cited decisions from several courts throughout the United States, it is becoming increasingly common for the construction contractor to be a named party in hazardous waste litigation under CERCLA and exposed to serious liability. To a much lesser degree thus far, but nevertheless a very real risk, is the exposure of the design professional to such liability. In either instance, the claim would generally be for participating in or contributing to the handling, transporting or disposal of such wastes, or arranging to have others do it. The contractor or design professional might be a party defendant in an action by the government or by another potentially responsible party. While the experience in either situation is certainly not going to be pleasant, the contractor and design professional are not wholly without recourse.

In the first instance, even in the absence of a contractual indemnity provision, of the type reviewed earlier, the contractor should be able to claim over against the owner of the property, who more than likely played a significant role in the generation or storage of the hazardous waste or, if not, could be in a position to pass that exposure onto a prior owner. In either case, it would certainly help the contractor's cause.

As to the engineer who performed the site assessment or designed the project, while the construction contractor does not have any direct privity of contract with that party upon which a claim can be based, there is a limited body of law in some jurisdictions which may permit the contractor to implead such engineer as a third-party defendant, on the ground that it owed a duty beyond contractual that was certainly foreseeable, and that its negligent performance directly caused the complained of damages. At the very least, this potential avenue of liability should not be overlooked by prudent counsel for the construction contractor. Obviously, the design professional would have similar reciprocal rights.

Claims by the construction contractor

Regardless of how well the construction contractor may be protected in its contract for liability to others for clean-up costs and related damages that may occur due to hazardous wastes, the situation could occur where it has significant claims of its own arising out of delays, disruptions and increased costs from those circumstances.

Reported federal and state court cases considering such claims are few and far between to the present time, but logically should be on the rise in the future, as the encountering of hazardous waste on construction sites is expected to grow dramatically in the United States. However, there have been a number of federal agency Board of Contract Appeals ("BCA") administrative determinations which illustrate the point.

In one such BCA decision,[34] the Board held that, whereas the contract

34 *Darwins Construction Co.*, ASBCA No. 27596; 86–1 BCA (CCH) §18,645; accord, *Frank Lill & Son, Inc.*, ASBCA No. 35774; 88–3 BCA (CCH) §20,880.

documents indicated that certain ceiling tiles could be removed as ordinary construction debris, the construction contractor was able to show the existence of a latent condition of contamination with asbestos dust, and required much more expensive asbestos removal procedures to abate. The contractor recovered such unanticipated increased costs under the contractual differing site conditions provision.

Insofar as measure of damages is concerned in this area, the contractor may find that there are items of work, if not the contract as a whole, that may turn out to be performed precisely in the manner called for under the original contract documents, and with no design or other changes, but that the overall cost far exceeds that which was included in the lump sum price or applicable contract unit prices, as the case may be. In essence, there could be a loss of productivity claim.

The measure of these damages, which the courts of New York and elsewhere have been most receptive to, is *quantum meruit*, *i.e.*, the total actual job costs plus an allowance for overhead and profit, less the amounts paid to date by the owner for such items or elements of work. Where the contract is of a unit price type, the amounts paid for the items of work in question are clearly determinable. In a lump sum contract, the problem becomes a bit more difficult. However, in that situation, the contractor is usually required to submit at the start of the job a trade breakdown for partial payment purposes, which would allocate amounts for various items and elements of work, and to which the owner agrees. This would then constitute the basis for determining the amount paid in that type of situation.

One word of caution on such approach is that the courts in some jurisdictions, notably New York, will not allow the use of the pre-bid estimate to measure damages for labour inefficiency, in lieu of amounts paid. Thus, if it is not possible to determine the amounts paid needed to subtract from the total costs on the *quantum meruit* approach, the contractor may well have to consider the alternative and generally less preferred approach discussed below.

That would be to measure labour inefficiency, predicated upon an inefficiency percentage or factor, a method that has not been extensively adopted by courts in many jurisdictions. However, the contractor should be aware that there are a number of subcontractor trade association studies that provide such factors for various items and types of work which, together with appropriate contractor and expert testimony showing performance of similar elements of work on the same contract when unimpeded at a higher productivity rate, can nevertheless be viable. In a federal case decided under New York law, the court noted a loss of efficiency claim may be difficult to prove, but that a loss of productivity percentage, based upon a proper evidentiary foundation, may well be allowable.[35]

Sometimes the contract work may be delayed, interfered with and impeded by the encountering and disposing of hazardous waste, such that it is performed in later periods of time than originally contemplated under the original contract (even if not beyond the specified contractual completion date). It may well be the contractor is paying its labour higher wage rates pursuant to applicable union contracts, than would have otherwise been paid had the work been capable of being performed at the time periods contemplated, and upon which the contract price was based. Typically, in New York, many union agreements expire on 1 July, at which time higher rates go into effect. Although the *quantum meruit* approach to increased costs of contract work would actually have built into it such wage rate increases for those elements of work, it may be prudent to back out the wage rate increases as a separate claim item, on the principle that the chances of success are increased by not having all the contractor's eggs in the same basket.

Similarly, there may well be material and equipment cost escalations incurred by the contractor for the same reason as the labour escalations, and they as well would be claimable.

Depending upon the extent of the delay encountered, the contractor might also be entitled to claim extended field and home office overhead costs, the latter being a more difficult item to prove, because it is the rare contractor that is able to show direct home office overhead costs specifically attributable to the project. However, there are methods which have been permitted by some courts to establish an estimated, but acceptable, dollar value for that element.

Conclusion

This paper has been intended to acquaint the reader with the general legal scheme in the United States, both federal and state, affecting construction contractors and design professionals in the hazardous waste area. Contractual pitfalls and protective mechanisms, as well as broad claim parameters, have also been reviewed. The bottom line here, worth reiterating, is that if the contractor encounters unforeseen hazardous waste at its construction site, it should not be touched, the work in that area should be stopped and immediate notification given to the owner and its engineer, both orally and in writing.

---

35 *S. Leo Harmonay, Inc.* v *Binks Manufacturing Co.*, 597 F.Supp. 1014 (S.D.N.Y. 1984), aff'd w/o opinion 762 F.2d 990 (2d Cir. 1985).

Depending upon the specific contractual requirements which the contractor or design professional has agreed to, it should avoid, to the extent possible, being put into the position of having to handle, move, transport off the site, or otherwise dispose of, any such hazardous waste, either directly by the contractor, or arranged for or contributed to by it or the design professional. Any one or more of these activities can be a legal basis for the federal or state government, or for a private party, to claim against one or both such parties for all or part of the clean-up costs and related damages.

Moreover, the construction contractor should not assume the role of a clean-up contractor on a construction project, in the absence of qualified technical expertise and capabilities, which it likely does not possess. If it contemplates doing otherwise, before the first shovelful of hazardous waste is turned, the construction contractor had best be sure that its attorney is well qualified in this field.

8 Construction sites and the human factor: a challenge for the construction industry

Helen Garthwaite

Introduction

The last decade has seen a significant and sustained increase in society's concern for the environment including the protection of human health. From origins in the early pressure campaigns to "Save Moby Dick" and "Ban the Bomb" environmental issues have become recognised as key items on both the domestic[1] and international[2] political agenda. Much of society's environmental concern has been and continues to be directed at the construction industry as in the case of the on-going controversy over the construction of the motorway across Twyford Down.

This paper seeks to examine the nature of the challenge (and the consequential risks and liabilities) facing the construction industry as a result of today's raised environmental consciousness by focusing on recent and proposed developments in statutory control of construction sites with particular regard to those statutory controls which impact on human health and safety. In so doing, the paper considers emerging and associated trends with a view to identifying underlying policies and pressures and predicting future developments on the health and safety front as an insight into the parallel issues for the construction industry in the wider environmental context.

Construction sites and the human factor

Few would dispute that construction sites and construction activities present a significant risk to the health and safety of individuals, whether on-site construction workers or simply neighbours or passers-by. The health and safety record of the construction industry is notoriously poor.

1 The 1992 Election Manifestos of all the UK political parties included environmental protection proposals, the current Government affirming the principles set out in the White Paper on the Environment: *This Common Inheritance* September, 1990 Cm 1200 and more recently in *This Common Inheritance: The Second Year Report* published by HMSO in October, 1992 which considered Government performance against Government environmental objectives.

2 Illustrated by attendance at the Earth Summit in Rio de Janeiro in June, 1992.

> "... a worker is killed in the construction industry every three days and 59 construction workers are daily reported injured. One member of the public is killed by construction activities every month."[3]

The hazards to the health and safety of individuals from construction sites and construction activities are many and varied, immediate and long-term and include the following.

Occupational hazards

Occupational hazards are perhaps most commonly thought of, in particular, in more obvious short-term risk areas such as roofing which is currently receiving greater attention from the Health and Safety Executive (HSE) in view of the "black spot" nature of this trade:

> "Roofers' deaths in building accidents make them the largest single occupational group for fatalities. Construction itself is the most dangerous of all industry sectors."[4]

The more long-term occupational hazards in the industry have proved difficult to assess and control due to the transient nature of many construction activities and the workforce engaged in them, many of which are self employed.

Hazardous substances

Use or storage of hazardous substances on site or release of hazardous (or polluting) substances during demolition or stripping out such as asbestos fibres, can affect both construction site workers and individuals in the vicinity of the construction site as well as the natural environment.

Falling materials and plant

Another site risk is from construction activities involving demolition and also from unstable plant. A dramatic illustration of the latter was the crane collapse on St. James, Garlickhythe Church which received media and television coverage in September 1991.[5]

---

3 Tolley's *Health and Safety at Work Handbook 1993* by Malcolm Dewess published in association with the Royal Society for the Prevention of Accidents, p. 106, para. 7.1.

4 *Financial Times*, 8 May 1992.

5 *New Civil Engineer*, September 1991.

Noise and vibration

Construction activities are inherently noisy and often take place in areas which are usually quiet and so this is a frequent cause of public complaint. Problems also arise for employees working in confined spaces.

Dust and dirt

This may range from the unsightly and annoying to, in the case of hazardous dust or fibres, in sufficient quantities, the directly harmful, and is another common cause of public complaint. Effective site control has been identified as an essential means to control dust but in the absence of a clear publication explaining these site control techniques, the industry record in this area is poor.[6]

An entertaining illustration of the diverse nature of construction site risks and site prompted complaints was that recently encountered by an associate of the author. Asked for advice by a client conducting piling operations in the North of England in close proximity to a local TV transmitter, he armed himself with a copy of the Control of Pollution Act 1974 and BS.5228[7] and prepared himself to advise. Unfortunately, the problem did not relate to noise or vibration and he was slightly disconcerted to find himself discussing the possible consequences of the piling rig interfering with the reception of the latest episode of "Coronation Street"!

In passing, it is also worth noting that the permitted levels applied in assessing whether or not there is a construction site hazard are often higher than the permitted levels used when assessing hazards from permanent installations. A clear example of this is seen in the assessment of permitted levels of noise and concentrations of dark smoke as illustrated in *Figure 1* over.

Recent and proposed developments in statutory controls relating to site health and safety

Traditionally, health and safety legislation has been perceived as separate from and in many cases a precursor of environmental legislation. However,

---

6 CIRA Publication: *Environmental Issues In Construction – a review of issues and initiatives relevant to the building, construction and related industries* Volume 2—Technical Review at para. 5.3.4.

7 BS 5228 Part 4 concerns piling and covers both noise and vibration—see also BRE Digest 353 which gives information on damage to structures and ground borne vibration and BS 6472 (BSI 1984) which covers the evaluation of the human response to vibration although relating to permanent installations and not for short term vibration as in construction activities where higher levels have been established as permissible.

for the purposes of this paper it is proposed to focus on recent changes in health and safety legislation as a specific element of environmental legislation with a view to drawing parallels with the evolution and future development of environmental legislation.

The statutory measures relating to human health and safety in the context of the construction site comprise of a complex mesh of legislation structured around the Health and Safety at Work Act 1974 and the Factories Act 1961 (under which a series of regulations have been passed) as well as the Occupiers' Liability Act 1957. It is not proposed in this paper to review such existing legislation but rather to concentrate on recent and proposed developments in key areas with a view to identifying legislative policies.

Figure 1

Hazard	*Permanent installation*	*Construction site*
Noise	50dB–55dB (Batho Report 1991 and many planning enquiry decisions)	70dB–75dB (Wilson Report (1963) and many local authorities)
Dark smoke	No dark smoke from industrial or trade premises (Clean Air Act 1993)	Permitted from burning timber and certain other waste matter (excluding rubber) from demolition or site clearance (Clean Air (Emission of Dark Smoke) (Exemption) Regulations 1969)

Recent statutory developments, whether in the form of alteration to existing legislation or innovation, can be seen in relation to the control of noise, smoke and in respect of site practices and site management as follows:

Noise

Outline of existing legislation: Construction site noise is governed by one of the few parts of the Control of Pollution Act 1974 (COPA) which remain in force following the enactment of the Environmental Protection Act 1990. Section 60 of the COPA empowers local authorities to serve on persons carrying out or responsible for the carrying out of construction works a notice imposing requirements as to the way in which works are to be carried out. Notices can only control works within the perimeter of the construction site. It is not necessary for the local authority to establish nuisance and the Notice may be served prior to commencement of works. Appeal against a Notice lies to the Magistrates Court. Failure to comply with the Notice without reasonable excuse[8] is an offence punishable on summary conviction.

Under section 61 of the COPA it is possible to apply in advance to the local authority for consent to the carrying out of works. This affords a means of avoiding the risk of a section 60 Notice providing a route for dialogue with the local authority and an opportunity for early agreement on satisfactory noise control measures. Despite common reference to compliance with these provisions in the Preliminaries section of Bills of Quantities and Employer's Requirements this procedure is often not utilised on grounds of time, the cost of reaching agreement with the local authority and a feared reduction of the contractors' flexibility to control site operations (although the latter is probably misconceived as if good practices are not adopted a section 60 Notice would almost certainly result). Contractors seem to prefer taking the risk of delay following service of a section 60 Notice rather than a possible delay due to section 61 negotiations. Aggrieved neighbours occupying premises near construction sites affected by construction site noise may bring proceedings in the Magistrates Courts under section 59 or seek an injunction in the civil courts in respect of nuisance.

Other existing UK legislation with the aim of controlling noise includes legislation requiring employers to carry out an assessment of the exposure of employees to noise levels and provide personal protection where employees are exposed to noise levels in excess of specified levels[9] and legislation implementing the various directives which set emission standards for certain types of plant and equipment.[10]

Recent Developments: On 9 June 1993 the European Commission published a proposal[11] on the limitation of noise emitted by earth moving

---

8 "Nothing much short of an emergency, unless an event beyond the party's control, could in my view provide a reasonable excuse for contravention in a case such as this" Bingham L.J. *City of London Corporation* v *Bovis Construction Limited. The Times*, 21 April 1988. See also *A. Lambert Flat Management Limited* v *Lomas* [1984] 1 WLR 898 and *Saddleworth UDC* v *Aggregate and Sand* (1971) 60 LGR 103.

9 The Noise at Work Regulations 1989.

10 Construction Plant and Equipment (Harmonisation of Noise Emission Standards) Regulations 1985 and 1988.

11 COM (93) 9 June 1993 amending Directive 86/662.

machinery. The proposal includes a new noise test method which is closer to real operating conditions than existing methods and when implemented will set new noise limits of 4 decibels above stringent existing limits. The proposal is scheduled to take effect in December 1995.

The Noise and Statutory Nuisance Bill introduced in the Commons last year and which aims to provide local authorities with powers to control noise and nuisance in the streets completed its second reading and committee stages in the House of Lords during July. Although the main thrust of the Bill is to deal with noise from loudspeakers and faulty car and burglar alarms, proposed provisions will enable local authorities to deal with noise from stationary vehicles and equipment in the street.

Smoke

Outline of Existing Legislation: UK statutory control of air pollution is governed in the main by the Environmental Protection Act 1990 (EPA 1990) which deals with the authorising of polluting processes and emissions. The EPA 1990 also contains statutory nuisance powers under which the local authority can require (through issue of an Abatement Notice) the person responsible for dust, steam, smells or other effluvia prejudicial to health arising on premises such as harmful fumes and gases and accumulations of rubbish and (in some cases) smoke to stop such nuisance.

The primary legislative means of control over smoke, grit and dust also enforced by local authorities were the Clean Air Acts 1956 and 1968 since superseded by the Clean Air Act 1993 (see below).

Recent Developments: As noted above the recent development in this area of legislation is the consolidation of the Clean Air Acts of 1956 and 1968 in the Clean Air Act 1993. The 1993 Act preserves the provisions of the original Acts including the control of the emission of dark smoke from trade premises (which includes land) in section 2(1). The control of bonfires on a demolition site emitting dark smoke has been found to be within the ambit of the Acts and would still be covered by the new legislation. However, emissions from the burning of timber and most other site waste (except rubber) including waste from demolition of a building and emissions from resurfacing work are exempted from the ambit of the Act by specific regulations[12] as amended by the 1993 Act.

Also of relevance in this area are the Asbestos (Amendment) Regulations 1992 which came into force on 1 January this year, adding new and

12 Clean Air (Emission of Dark Smoke) (Exemption) Regulations 1969.

stricter requirements to The Control of Asbestos at Work Regulations 1987. The 1987 Regulations were already extensive, extending the employer's duty under the Health and Safety at Work Act 1974 not only to employees but to any other person who may be affected by the work including visitors, neighbours and even trespassers where the duty exists. The new amendments require the preparation of a written method statement before asbestos removal operations start which is to include details of location, nature and proper duration of the work, the methods to be applied in handling asbestos, the characteristics of protective equipment and decontamination of workers and the protection of other persons on or near the site. However, there is no duty to submit the method statement to an appropriate enforcing authority. The Regulations also require the notification of employees and other persons who may be affected in the event of any escape of asbestos.

The Regulations were driven by the need to implement a number of EC Directives in this area including the Directive covering Exposure to Carcinogens[13] which also was responsible for amending regulations[14] to the Control of Substances Hazardous to Health Regulations 1988 (COSHH).

Site activities and site management

As mentioned above, the framework for health and safety legislation in the UK is provided by the Health and Safety at Work Act 1974 (HSWA). The Act creates a number of general duties on employers to ensure that, so far as reasonably practicable, the health, safety and welfare of employees (and others who may be affected by their work) is safeguarded. A breach of any one of these duties (sections 2–4 and 7) is a criminal offence as is any failure to observe any requirement or prohibition contained in regulations issued under the HSWA. The HSWA was designed to allow the creation of supplementary or interpretive regulations initially to cover certain risks or activities. More recently the Act has become a channel for the UK implementation of the requirements of EC Health and Safety Directives as will be seen below.

The general duty placed on employers under section 2 is extended in section 3 towards non-employees who may be affected by the undertaking of an employer or self-employed person, other than in respect of welfare.

A director or manager will be personally liable (in addition to the company being liable) when the offence is proved to have been committed with

---

13 Directive 90/394/EEC.

14 The Control of Substances Hazardous to Health (Amendment) Regulations 1992—also brought into force 1 January 1993.

their consent or connivance or to have been attributable to their neglect (section 37). In the case of a health and safety breach, directors or managers can find themselves faced with a fine, imprisonment and (in the case of directors) disqualification.

As far as the general duties of the Act are concerned, civil actions for breach of statutory duty are excluded by section 47. However, breach of a duty imposed by regulations is actionable except where the regulations expressly provide otherwise (hence the controversy in relation to the possibility of increased civil liability under the proposed Construction (Design and Management) Regulations, see below).

The statutory duty is non-delegable. A sub-contractor cannot argue that the main contractor in control has sole responsibility[15] where the employer is not in control. It is a question of fact as to whether the employer took reasonable care for the safety of his employees in all the circumstances and this may involve site visits, co-operating with other employers and ensuring that his employees are aware of their safety responsibilities. However, there is a vital distinction between injury to a sub-contractor or employee and injury or damage to a third party caused by a sub-contractor's employee. In the former situation the employer cannot avoid liability by delegating it to the main contractor but in the case of the latter, the person responsible is the one who has the right of control over the employee. This distinction is also reflected in civil liability.[16]

In addition, the Occupiers' Liability Act 1957 places an employer under a common duty of care to take such care in all the circumstances as is reasonable to see that visitors will be reasonably safe in using premises. The 1957 Act applies not only to land and buildings but also to fixed or movable structures such as scaffolding. Further, an absentee owner may "occupy" notwithstanding that he has contracted to allow a third party to have use of the premises. This is a potential risk area for the freehold owner of premises granting a prospective tenant licence to fit out prior to grant of a lease. "Control" is what matters and therefore, a client who has entrusted work to a contractor will not be liable provided he has taken such steps as he reasonably ought to satisfy himself that the contractor is competent (section 2(4)(b)).

Numerous Regulations have been issued under the Health and Safety at Work Act 1974 to deal with specific site problems. An illustration of this is

---

15 *Morris* v *Breaveglen Limited* (1992) CA *The Times* 29 December. Where "An employer who under a labour only sub-contract, sent his employee to work on site under the direction and control of the main contractor, remains liable to his employee if the system of work was unsafe".

16 *Mersey Docks and Harbour Board* v *Coggins & Griffiths (Liverpool) Limited* [1947] AC 1, [1947] 1 All ER 478, [1946] 2 All ER 345.

the Construction (Head Protection) Regulations 1989 which places an obligation on employers and self-employed workers to provide and ensure that suitable head protection is worn by employees and other persons at work on operations or works over which they have control.

Recent developments: The Health and Safety at Work Act 1974 provides the statutory framework for the implementation of European Directives concerning health and safety in the form of subsidiary regulations supported by voluntary standards and approved codes of practice issued under section 15 of the Act. European legislation is more descriptive and detailed in approach than the newer UK regulations which are "object-setting". The UK emphasis is seen as more flexible and suited to keeping abreast of advances in technology. Standards and codes of practice are not legally binding but compliance with them will usually satisfy the requirements of the relevant regulations.

The period of the UK Presidency of the EC coincided with a significant increase in legislative activity in the health and safety arena with many of the regulations below coming into force at the beginning of 1993.

The various UK health and safety regulations affecting construction sites and activities include the following.

The Provision and Use of Work Equipment Regulations 1992[17]

These Regulations require employers to ensure that working conditions and hazards are taken into account when selecting equipment; that the equipment is suitable for its use and properly maintained; that use should be restricted to trained persons where there is a specified risk and that adequate information, instruction and training are provided. In force 1 January 1993.

The Personal Protective Equipment at Work Regulations 1992[18]

These Regulations require employers to provide personal protective equipment (PPE) where health and safety cannot be adequately controlled by other means; assess the risks and select suitable PPE; instruct, inform and train employees in the use of PPE; maintain PPE and provide accommodation for storage; and ensure proper use of PPE. The new Regulations

17 Implementing the Use of Work Equipment Directive (89/655/EEC).

18 Implementing the Use of Personal Protective Equipment Directive (89/656/EEC).

replace pre-1974 legislation and make minor amendments to modern regulations such as COSHH. No Code of Practice is proposed. In force 1 January 1993.

The Manual Handling Operations Regulations 1992[19]

Under these Regulations employers are required to avoid the need for manual handling by, so far as is reasonably practicable, removing or reducing the risk. New duties are placed upon employees to inform their employers about any health condition that might affect their ability to lift loads. In force 1 January 1993.

The Control of Substances Hazardous to Health (Amendment) Regulations 1992[20]

This amendment expands the COSHH Regulations 1988 to give greater emphasis to the prevention of exposure to carcinogens at work by means of substitution and enclosed systems of work. COSHH assessments will have to be regularly reviewed and health surveillance records maintained for 40 rather than 30 years.

Draft Construction (Design and Management) Regulations and Approved Code of Practice[21]

This consultative document was issued by the Health and Safety Commission (HSC) to implement the EC Directive on the implementation of minimum Health and Safety Requirements at Temporary or Mobile Work Sites. The draft regulations largely make explicit what is already implicit in sections 2–4 of the Health and Safety at Work Act 1974. For a more detailed discussion of the proposed regulations see below.

UK Safety Signs Regulations 1980

The requirements of these Regulations will need to be extended to comply with the Safety Signs Directive[22] which extends safety signs to other forms of communication. A consultative document in respect of amendment regulations is anticipated.

---

19 Implementing the Manual Handling of Loads Directive (90/269/EEC).

20 Implementing the Exposure to Carcinogens Directive (90/394/EEC).

21 Proposal to implement Temporary and Mobile Work Sites Directive (92/57/EEC) CD51.

22 Safety and Health Signs at the Workplace Directive (92/58/EEC).

The "six pack"

HSE has published a number of Guidance documents on the various Regulations which were brought into force earlier this year. These are referred to affectionately in the safety business as the "six pack" (because they are likely to create the biggest ever boom for safety consultants). The "six pack" is not so affectionately regarded by clients, contractors and consultants who fear that they "will crush genuine health and safety consciousness under a mound of bogus paperwork in triplicate" (Colin Harding, Chairman of George & Harding).

Proposed Construction (Design and Management) Regulations and Approved Code of Practice

The objective of the proposed regulations

The main objective of the proposed Regulations and accompanying Approved Code of Practice (ACP), is to ensure effective co-ordination of health and safety matters throughout the duration of a construction project. The proposals aim to:

- address the co-operation and co-ordination issues on construction sites *i.e.* provide a framework for site organisation in respect of health and safety matters; and
- recognise the role of clients and designers in achieving acceptable standards of health and safety on construction sites.

Traditionally, the responsibility for site health and safety has been that of the contractor. However, the proposed Regulations will bring clients and designers into the frame, placing obligations upon them as well as contractors, to ensure an integrated and planned approach to health and safety throughout the life of the project.

The Regulations build upon the existing requirements of sections 2–4 of the Health and Safety at Work Act 1974 and do not detract from the primary duty under the Act for employers, and particularly contractors, to safeguard the health and safety of their employees.

The proposed Regulations in outline

(1) The Regulations will apply to all projects which include "construction work". This is widely defined in the Regulations as the carrying out of any building, civil engineering or engineering construction work and

includes (*inter alia*) construction, fitting-out, renovation, repair, maintenance, demolition of a structure, commissioning of plant and services and cleaning. A "structure" is also widely defined, covering not only buildings but extending to (*inter alia*) tunnels, pipes, lagoons, pylons, formwork, scaffolding and manufacturing plant. (The list would seem to be comprehensive!)

(2) The Regulations involve clients to a greater degree than before whilst recognising that the client does not have day-to-day control of the site. The following duties are placed on clients:
- a duty to appoint a "Planning Supervisor" and a "Principal Contractor" to co-ordinate health and safety during the design and construction phases of a project. Those appointed must be "competent" and the appointments should be made by the client at the "appropriate time". The client is not precluded from acting as "Planning Supervisor" or as "Principal Contractor" providing the client is competent to perform the duties involved.
- a duty to notify and give certain details of sites to the enforcing authority.
- a duty, so far as is practicable, to ensure that adequate financial provision is made and enough time allowed to enable work to be done without risk to health and safety.
- a duty to ensure that the Planning Supervisor is provided with information about the state or condition of any premises or land at or on which construction work needs to be carried out.
- a duty to keep the health and safety file prepared and delivered to him by the Planning Supervisor available for inspection.

(3) The Regulations place explicit duties on designers to ensure, so far as is reasonably practicable, that:
- their designs do not expose those building, maintaining (including cleaning) or repairing a structure to risks to health and safety; and
- their designs include adequate information about any aspect of the designs e.g. materials which might affect health and safety during construction work.

(4) The role of the Planning Supervisor is to:
- oversee the design of the structure ensuring that the designer has taken account of health and safety factors in terms of construction maintenance and repair;
- advise the client on the adequacy of the financial and time provisions for construction work;
- produce the first phase of the health and safety plan for the project which will deal with the way the project is to be carried out, managed *etc.*; and

- procure the preparation of a health and safety file for each structure comprised in the project and deliver this to the client upon completion of the construction work.

(5) Once the construction phase is reached, the Principal Contractor will take over and up-date the health and safety plan and the health and safety file. In addition, the Principal Contractor is to:
- co-ordinate co-operation between contractors and make sure that they comply with relevant health and safety legislation and any rules contained in the health and safety plan;
- make sure that all contractors are appraised of risks to health and safety; and
- take the necessary steps to control access to the site.

(6) Site contractors are under a specific duty to co-operate with the Principal Contractor and inform him of possible risks to health and safety in addition to the duties they have as employers under the existing legislation.

The impact of the proposed Regulations for the construction industry

The thrust of the Regulations is to impose management responsibilities in relation to health and safety at all stages of a construction project. This means a shift in the distribution of responsibility for health and safety during a construction project from contractors to designers and clients. Health and safety issues are to be key in respect of planning (both in respect of time and cost) and this is likely to impact on procurement strategies as evidenced by the initial words of the consultative document:

> "The Regulations impose new duties upon clients, designers and contractors which require them to rethink their traditional roles in construction projects. Planning Supervisors and Principal Contractors carry out new functions, created by the Regulations, which ensure that effective direction and co-ordination of health and safety takes place throughout the Project, from conception to handover—and beyond."

Risks, liabilities and concerns

Criminal liability: The primary effect of the proposed Regulations is to increase the scope for criminal prosecution of those charged with duties. It is fair to say that the risk of criminal prosecution for clients and designers (in particular where the designer is appointed as Planning Supervisor) is increased. Given the strict nature of the duties imposed on specific individuals in circumstances where the performance of such duties may not be within the control of the person primarily charged with the duty, there is a possibility that a person may be exposed to criminal prosecution by the actions of another over whom they have no direct control. It is advocated by many in the industry that this cannot be correct in principle and that such obligations should be qualified by the familiar "so far as reasonably practicable" test.

Civil Liability: There is also an increased risk of civil claims, both in negligence and for breach of statutory duty. With regard to a claim in negligence, the proposed Regulations and ACP add to the body of knowledge in the management of health and safety matters and so, the failure to have regard to the Regulations or ACP may give rise to claims in negligence particularly where there has been a successful prosecution for breach of a health and safety regulation. In the absence of an exclusion in the proposed Regulations of a right of action for breach of statutory duty, there is also increased potential for exposure to claims for damages by persons harmed as a result of non-compliance. It is interesting here to compare the proposed Regulations with the Management of Health and Safety At Work Regulations 1992 which contain an exclusion of rights of action for breach of statutory duty.[23] The responses from the construction industry and others during the consultation period have included suggestions that a similar exclusion should be included in the proposed Regulations (seemingly with some success—see below). Increased potential exposure to damages from civil claims is a particular concern for designers and Planning Supervisors since the strict nature of their duties under the proposed Regulations may expose them to a significant increase in their professional indemnity insurance premiums if, indeed, such duties can be brought within the scope of available professional indemnity insurance cover.

Other concerns

For *clients*, the major concerns would seem to be the following:

(1) *Uncertainty as to who is the client:* The proposed Regulations define the client as "any person for whom a project is carried out". This seems to be very much a question of fact and may result in confusion, for example, between landowners, developers engaged to develop sites, an investment purchaser, a tenant requiring fitting-out and funders. It has been suggested that the definition should be clarified by the addition of the criteria that the client engages the contractor in addition to being the person for whom the project is carried out.

---

23 Regulation 14.

(2) *The requirement to appoint a Planning Supervisor for all projects:* Currently the proposals require a client to appoint a Planning Supervisor for all projects including projects of a minor nature such as cleaning, maintenance and repair notwithstanding that the role of a Planning Supervisor for these projects is likely to be limited since they are unlikely to include a design stage where the Planning Supervisor's main duties arise. This is likely to hold significant financial and time consequences for landlords undertaking a cleaning and maintenance programme for their portfolio. It has been suggested that the requirement for a Planning Supervisor and a health and safety plan should be limited to large projects and projects involving high risk activities as envisaged in the Directive.

(3) *The appointment of the Planning Supervisor and Principal Contractor:*

(i) *Who should the client appoint to fill these roles?* Should the client be permitted to appoint a project supervisor whose appointment runs from the inception of the project to its completion and who is not either a planning phase or execution phase co-ordinator or both? At present, this does not appear to be permitted by the proposed Regulations and ACP which envisage the Planning Supervisor being drawn from the design team (probably the Architect as design team leader) and the Principal Contractor as being either the main or managing contractor or a specialist contractor whose activity forms a large part of the project. Concerns have been voiced over the "self-policing" role of the Architect with preference being for the appointment of an independent Planning Supervisor.

(ii) *A "competent person"?* No guidance is given on what is to be regarded as "competent" for purposes of appointing such persons or as to how a client is to assess this. The client, particularly a lay client, can only do his best to assess whether a person he appoints has sufficient experience and knowledge to enable him to fulfil his responsibilities. More often than not he must rely on his consultants and contractors as to their experience. How is he to assess competence in health and safety issues? In the absence of recognised qualifications is he expected to investigate consultants' and contractors' track records? Will clients be prompted to seek confirmation of consultant's competence in health and safety matters in the form of a warranty from the consultant in his terms of engagement that he is experienced and competent not only in his technical discipline but in health and safety? It has been advocated that the requirement upon the client to ensure competence should be either removed or commuted to a less onerous requirement.

(iii) *When should the appointments be made?* The proposed Regulations provide that appointments should be made at the appropriate time. The ACP suggests that "appropriate time" means as early as possible during the planning of the project allowing enough time for both persons appointed to carry out their duties effectively. This is likely to vary with the procurement route followed. A client may not have the necessary understanding of the various stages of the project to enable decisions as to the timing of the appointment to be taken with confidence.

(4) *The extent of the client's duty under draft Regulation 6:* Draft Regulation 6 provides that the client is to "ensure, so far as is practicable, that tenders make adequate financial provision and that sufficient time is allowed for everyone working on the project to comply with their statutory duties". This is extremely wide and has no basis in the underlying Directive. The provision is likely to be of particular concern to lay clients. Whilst the client can check that the tender includes provision for health and safety requirements, how is he to determine that such provision is adequate without the assistance of professional advice? What action is the client supposed to take if he thinks that the tender is too low or the programme too tight? This provision is likely to impact on the way in which projects are assessed for viability as a result of increased project costs without any guarantee of improvement in contractor's health and safety procedures which are dependent ultimately on the contractor's management skills and technical competence.

(5) *The requirement on the Client to provide the Planning Supervisor with information about the site:* Although the client already has a duty to warn contractors and others about any particular dangers of the land which he either knows of or reasonably ought to have foreseen, draft Regulation 7 goes considerably further, requiring the client to provide the Planning Supervisor with all information which he needs to take account of to comply with his duty to develop the health and safety plan. In most cases, the client will be relying on its consultants' recommendations as to what investigations of the site should be undertaken, and yet under draft Regulation 7 it would not seem to be possible for the client to limit his obligation either by simply supplying such information as it would be reasonable for him to have in his possession or by imposing an express contractual duty on the Planning Supervisor or the Principal Contractor to obtain the relevant information themselves.

(6) *The financial implications:* The financial cost of implementing the proposed Regulations is likely significantly to increase project costs for clients. There could also be cost consequences if the proposed Regulations are to operate in respect of projects already underway. Currently the position in this area is unclear.

The proposed Regulations also give rise to concerns on the part of *designers*. These centre on the potential open-ended nature of the duties to be imposed on Planning Supervisors and on designers, the uncertainty of the responsibilities of Planning Supervisors and Principal Contractors when their respective roles overlap, the costs and practicability of implementing the proposals and the potential for liability to be unmanageable and possibly uninsurable. Concerns which designers have expressed include:

(1) The degree to which the proposals will require designers to consider the buildability of their designs (an area traditionally that of the contractor) and the extent to which designers will need to provide for built-in safety systems for future maintenance (*e.g.* window cleaning apparatus).
(2) Where the designer is appointed as Planning Supervisor, the likelihood of having the necessary health and safety experience to fulfil all the duties laid down in draft Regulation 11.
(3) The uncertainty as to the designer's role where he is appointed to act as Planning Supervisor for the design phase of the project and the integration of that role where there is overlap with the appointment of the Principal Contractor.
(4) The ability to insure the potential liability from the proposed Regulations and effect of the proposed Regulations on designer's insurance premiums.
(5) A fear that the obligations imposed on designers by the proposed Regulations may result in the elimination of several types of traditional construction methods on the grounds that they might be considered less safe than others and that this will impact on project costs.
(6) Whether the proposed Regulations will be retrospective so that designers will be forced to adapt designs to include provision for a health and safety plan with consequential financial implications.

Mr Building—This is your life?

Another factor to be aware of is the potential impact of the health and safety file for a project. It is intended that this will be added to and updated during the life of the project. The ACP envisages that the file should contain information on the design of the structure, the design "as-built", information provided by the client to the Planning Supervisor or gathered by the Planning Supervisor in the preparation of the health and safety plan and information which will assist persons carrying out construction work on the structure at any time after completion of the project.

Again, this is likely to impact on project costs and timing since greater emphasis will need to be placed on the preparation of "as-built" rather than "record" drawings. Preparation of "as-built" drawings will need to be focused on more closely during construction with a view to delivery of a complete package at practical completion of the project if this information is to be available within the timescale envisaged by the proposed Regulations. The existence of a health and safety file may impact also on the commercial value of a client's investment and it may well be that in the future prospective tenants and purchasers of buildings will request copies of the health and safety file in addition to the usual package of collateral warranty agreements.

The consultation period for the proposed Regulations and ACP ended on 29 January 1993 and has been followed by various discussions between the HSE and industry bodies as part of a comprehensive review of comments received from various sectors of the industry. The proposed Regulations were due to come into force on 1 January 1994 but following significant pressure from the industry it is understood that the proposed Regulations are currently being revised by the HSE. Recent indications are that revised Regulations will not be available prior to December 1993 and therefore, it would seem certain that implementation of the proposed Regulations will be delayed. Current predictions are that a six month or even a twelve month delay period is likely.

Emerging and associated trends

General

Whilst it is possible to draw upon the recent developments in statutory control of health and safety of construction sites and activities as a useful insight into the nature of the challenge facing the construction industry, a complete picture can only be gained by considering these with identified associated trends.

Emerging trends from recent developments in statutory controls

From consideration of the recent and proposed developments in statutory control in the health and safety arena, the following trends can be seen:

- European developments play a major part in influencing (and some have observed, dictating) the agenda for progress in health and safety law and standards in common with the wider area of environmental protection.
- Pro-active legislation appears to be still the order of the day although in the past pro-active provisions of a voluntary nature have not been well observed or utilised.[24]
- There is a clear shift in emphasis in the regulation of commercial activity in the health and safety context from the "work face" of the industry to the corporate management.
- Despite moves towards consolidation of legislation recently exemplified by the Clean Air Act 1993 and in the wider environmental context in the Environmental Protection Act 1990, there is no single source of legislation in either the health and safety or the wider environmental fields. This is illustrative of the *ad hoc* response of government to social concern. This is also borne out by the absence of a manual consolidating formal guidance for the industry in either area[25] which impacts on the effectiveness of training and education in the industry.
- There is an increasing focus on site organisation and management in addition to regulation of specific high risk activities increasing the potential exposure of all sectors of the construction industry to criminal and civil liability.

Associated trends

Associated trends in the health and safety arena have parallels, to greater extent, in the wider environmental context and include:

An increase in private actions for damages and private prosecutions

The increasing awareness of the public to health and safety and environmental problems has prompted the formation of a number of organisations taking an interest in and assisting members of the public in prosecuting and taking action. Further regulation in the health and safety and environmental sectors is likely to mean that private prosecutions and actions will

---

24 An example of this would be the few agreements negotiated between contractor and local authority in respect of noise from construction sites under S61 of the Control of Pollution Act 1974.

25 Identified in CIRA Special Publication 94 *Environmental Issues in Construction: A review of issues and initiatives relevant to the building, construction and related industries* Volume 2—Technical Review.

be a more regular feature. Recent examples include the Docklands litigation and action taken by Mr Philip Kremin, originally for damages in excess of £4M as a result of dust entering his flat from nearby building operations.[26]

Increase in criminal sanctions

The maximum level of fine for failure to comply with health and safety duties has recently been increased to £20,000 in the Magistrates Court. The fine is unlimited for serious offences tried in the Crown Court. Not to be forgotten is the risk of a custodial sentence with a term of imprisonment not exceeding two years. Directors may also be disqualified for health and safety mis-management under section 2(1) Company Directors Disqualification Act 1986.

It may be premature to conclude that there is a new trend towards imposing jail sentences for company directors in breach of environmental and health and safety legislation. However, it can be said that recent decisions are consistent with the trend towards tougher enforcement and stiffer penalties for environmental offences and this should not be overlooked by directors and senior managers. Until recently the number of prosecutions against individuals has been higher in the health and safety field than in the environmental field. However, there have been no prison sentences imposed on directors for health and safety offences although suspended jail sentences have been imposed. Penalties imposed on individuals under the Health and Safety at Work Act 1974 are generally lower than those imposed on companies. However, it can be seen that generally the level of fines being imposed is increasing. For companies, the average fine per conviction in proceedings taken by HSE rose from £189 in 1981 to £903 in 1990/1991.[27]

Increased emphasis on the personal liability of management

A move towards clients facing prosecution for health and safety breaches on and around construction sites was first recognised in 1989[28] where a local authority client was fined £15,000 compared with a fine levied on the main contractor of £5,000. It is submitted that the proposed Construction (Design & Management) Regulations are evidence of a continuing move against established industry ideas that main contractors are responsible for site safety.

---

26 *Kremin* v *Duke Street Investments Limited (& Others)* QBD, Official Referees Business, 14 January 1993, HHJ Bowsher QC.

27 HC written answers, November 1992.

28 *HSE* v *Derby City Council, City Plant Hire & Others* 1989.

The courts have shown increasing willingness to sanction individuals for health and safety and environmental offences by imposing custodial sentences and making disqualification orders. In 1988 a company director received a suspended prison sentence following his conviction for manslaughter as a result of a fatal accident in a factory in Lancashire. Recently, a former company director was jailed for six months in connection with the illegal disposal of waste. On the health and safety front, the first disqualification order against a director was that of Mr Rodney James Chapman who was fined £5000 and banned for 2 years following his conviction under section 37 of the Health and Safety at Work Act 1974 for his company's contravention of a prohibition notice.[29]

Increase in court intervention and enforcement

This has been highlighted in a number of recent cases. The Court of Appeal (Criminal Division) decision *R* v *Sanyo Electrical Manufacturing (UK) Limited*[30] illustrates the increased awareness of the role of the courts in securing a healthier and safer working environment by ensuring that breaches of health and safety and related legislation are effectively penalised.

Clear statements from the courts have also underlined the importance of health and safety issues by making clear that such issues are matters to which a local authority is entitled to have regard when assessing whether to invite a contractor to tender for a contract in accordance with Regulation 12 of the Public Works Contract Regulations.[31] This decision is particularly significant when considered in conjunction with the proposed Construction (Design and Management) Regulations, from which it would appear that contractors will have to submit their health and safety arrangements to whatever scrutiny the client feels appropriate to protect it from breaching the duty to appoint a "competent" Principal Contractor.

In addition, the Court of Appeal has emphasised that the primary duties on employers under health and safety legislation apply to potential risks to the public whether or not actual harm has occurred[32] thus reinforcing the preventative nature of the statutory controls. If followed in the wider environmental context, this approach holds significant implications for the interpretation of environmental legislation.

---

29 *R* v *Chapman* (1992) Unreported.

30 (1992) 156 *Justice of the Peace Reports* 863.

31 *General Building Maintenance Plc* v *Greenwich London Borough Council. The Times* 9 March 1993.

32 *R* v *Board of Trustees of the Science Museum* CA (Criminal Division) *The Times*, 9 March 1993.

A move towards greater corporate accountability

Pressure for this is becoming more extensive. Initial signs were seen in the approach taken in the Clapham disaster where British Rail were fined £1.25M. There have been several attempts to introduce UK legislation in this field namely, the Corporate Accountability Bill 1991[33] and the Corporate Safety and Environmental Information Bill 1992. Both Bills included provisions requiring the mandatory publication of information concerning health and safety performance, convictions and compensation payments in a company's annual report. On the environmental front the Right to Know Bill which requires (*inter alia*) companies to publish details on environmental offences in their annual reports, introduced by Mark Fisher (Labour, Stoke-on-Trent) received widespread support during its second reading earlier this year.[34] Pressure for implementation of such legislation is now set to increase following the Dutch Government's decision to impose environmental reporting obligations on business by requiring companies to publish detailed annual reports of their environmental impact and improvement policies. This may well prompt further developments along these lines in the UK.

Growth of health and safety (and environmental) consultants

Given the continuing pace of new legislation in the health and safety and environmental field the numbers of health and safety and environmental consultants is likely to increase.

Pressures and policies

The trends identified and considered in this paper are evidence of the increasing pressure upon the construction industry to reform its historically poor health and safety and environmental record. To date, this is being instrumented by a policy of increased regulation and to a lesser extent through encouragement of the industry to take voluntary measures. But is this set to continue?

On the one hand the pressure resulting from the raised environmental and health and safety consciousness of employees, the public and

33 This was proposed in October, 1991 and was discussed by trade unions and associations such as the CBI with a view to making representations to the Government and the European Commission for legislation.

34 This Bill was modelled directly on the CSEI Bill introduced in 1991 by Jeff Rooker (Labour, Perry Bar) but blocked by the DTI.

Europe,[35] the media and the continued activities of lobby groups suggest that calls for increased controls on the construction industry will continue at their current pace. Investors' and shareholders' attitudes are also being increasingly influenced by health and safety and environment concerns. Financial performance of a company is no longer judged simply on its balance sheet but also in terms of health and safety and environmental performance illustrated in the growing demand for corporate disclosure and accountability. Demand for such information by shareholders and investors is not altogether altruistic. The threat of potential liabilities and the spectre of more stringent regulation will impact on a company's financial performance.

Balanced against this is the need for the construction industry to retain a competitive edge in domestic and European markets. Whilst compliance with health and safety and environmental standards is increasingly a condition when tendering for business, particularly in the public sector,[36] economic pressures seek to undermine health and safety and environmental objectives. The cost implications for the construction industry of the threatened increase in regulation and improvement of health and safety and environmental goals against the background of the current severe economic recession is an overriding factor. Estimates of the cost to the construction industry of complying with the proposed Construction (Design and Management) Regulations is put at £550M a year.[37] This is exacerbated by the pressures on the construction industry flowing from the stance which insurers have indicated they are likely to take when responding to the increased risk of claims from the construction industry with limitations on the availability of cover and higher premiums and excesses.[38]

Political pressure resulting from the growing concerns of businesses including the construction industry at the cost consequences of increased regulation in the face of the current recession appears to be prompting a U-turn of the Government which in March of this year set up the much publicised De-regulation Task Force with the aim of cutting back the burden of red tape affecting British industry. However, uncertainty as to whether this can in fact be achieved remains. The Government is caught

---

35 The Fifth Action programme on the environment entitled "Towards Sustainability" has just been implemented and emphasised the need for the integration of environmental considerations and the formulation of other policies and activities so as to retain the "level playing field" of Europe and to ensure the highest level of protection for the environment.

36 *General Building and Maintenance Plc* v *Greenwich London Borough Council*, *The Times*, 9 March 1993, QBD.

37 *Financial Times* 20 October 1992 "EC Law will push up building costs" and also, see CD 51 Proposals for Construction (Design and Management) Regulations and Approved Code of Practice published by the HSE p. 13, para. 35.

38 The RICS have removed insurance cover for site investigation.

between the need not to compromise health and safety and environmental standards and the need to deliver a clear message to British industry that it is addressing the cost burden of red tape. A formidable, if not impossible, task. The controversy following the proposed amendment (as part of the de-regulatory exercise) of the recently enacted consolidating Clean Air Act 1993 indicates that uncertainty over Government intentions is likely to continue, despite the signs that the de-regulation initiative is gathering steam.[39] Confirmation of the position is unlikely before the Queen's speech this autumn when details of the De-regulation Bill which is set for the next legislative programme will be disclosed.

It seems that the Governments' de-regulatory initiatives have assisted the construction industry in making headway against the HSE during consultation on the proposed Construction (Design and Management) Regulations. Recent announcements from the HSE indicate that the revised draft Regulations will incorporate changes in a number of respects:

> "It looks as though the rules will be changed. Designers are particularly concerned about their civil liability and we will try to find a solution to this." (per Stewart Campbell of the HSE)[40]

Rumoured changes take routine maintenance work and minor refurbishment outside the scope of the proposed Regulations. The role of the Planning Supervisor is also to be subject to a re-think as is the requirement for clients to ensure that adequate finance is available for health and safety measures. A revised approach to the feared threat of increased civil actions is apparently being looked at by the HSE with a view to differentiating between breaches of administrative criteria (which it is suggested should not attract civil liability) and judgmental actions. However, the final form of the Regulations remains to be seen.

These competing pressures indicate that environment and health and safety ideals are not easily reconcilable with social and economic reality. Whether the construction industry can be convinced that protection of these ideals is commercially as well as morally worthwhile is difficult to predict and to a certain extent will be influenced by an upturn in current economic conditions.

Conclusion

Consideration of emerging trends and competing pressures indicates that the areas of health and safety and environment, particularly in relation to

39 The Government recently has launched a review of health and safety law.

40 At the Institution of Occupational Health and Safety Third European/American Construction Safety Conference held in Glasgow in May 1993.

site management, will be dynamic and will be a challenge for the construction industry in the 1990s. Despite Government moves to deregulate and the purported relaxation on the part of the HSE, there is a compelling argument for the construction industry to improve its track record in both the health and safety arena and the wider environmental context. There is much evidence to suggest that companies with effective health and safety policies and management will be better able to accommodate the wider demands of environmental legislation in view of the significant overlap in these areas. The dominance of Europe in influencing legislative activity and the clear commitment of the EC to health and safety and environmental improvement increases the likelihood of further legislative activity and with it new risks and liabilities for all sectors of the construction industry.

To date the construction industry's initiatives appear inadequate to meet this challenge. There is a need for greater awareness of, and renewed initiatives to meet, the practical and legal difficulties resulting from legislative imposition and commercial pressure. Raising the construction industry's health and safety and environment consciousness is a formidable task. Self-regulatory measures undertaken by the construction industry in the past have been singularly unsuccessful and used as evidence to support calls for legislative imposition. Perhaps now is the time for the construction industry to look again for new self-regulatory measures.

One suggestion which has arisen in this context has been prompted by an innovative contractual practice in the energy sector namely, the inclusion of a contractual provision whereby the contractor's profit and overhead element is reduced according to the incidence of accidents to the contractors' employees. A refined version of the provision could be included in construction contract conditions with the mechanism being adjusted to provide for penalty payments on the part of the employer being made in the event of accidents to employees (and possibly third parties) to a specified charity (preferably a charity assisting those who have suffered as a consequence of a construction accident).

Concluding on a lighter and less legal note, an innovative technique for combating the risk of injury for construction site workers has been suggested by Swedish health experts following site ergonomic studies. On their advice several Swedish companies have instituted "warm up" exercises for employees before commencement of works on site with the aim of combating musculoskeletal injuries. The results have been dramatic as comments from Swedish physiotherapist Tony Cedergvist show:

> "Not only have the exercises proved to be popular for team spirit and site organisation, our research shows there has been a 50 per cent reduction in musculoskeletal disorders."

One can only speculate on the reception such an exercise regime would receive from the average UK construction worker. However, it would certainly give new meaning to the term "healthy" company!

Part 3

Liabilities, Remedies and Policy

9 Risk assessment and environmental audit for contaminated land

Peter J Young

Introduction

From a purely physical standpoint, the environment has been subject to relatively constant risk from soil and water contamination over the years, but our perception of this risk has changed recently as a result of well publicised incidents both in the UK and overseas (Loscoe (UK), Lekkekerk (The Netherlands), Love Canal (USA) and more recently, Lumsden Road in Portsmouth). However, the consequences of damage to the environment are changing, particularly in financial terms, and this is making landowners and others with a financial interest in land look more closely at the magnitude of risk associated with contaminated land and groundwater.

Contaminated land can vary from the most visually obvious and intrusive derelict industrial works to apparently clean and pleasant fields supporting healthy vegetation. Appearances are often deceptive and cosmetic improvement of badly contaminated land has caused many developers to underestimate the problems that lie beneath when acquiring such land. Indeed the early practice of visual improvements to contaminated sites has too often diverted attention away from the fundamental problems of environmental damage of, for example, water resources, which remains beneath the green sward of a topsoil and re-seeding improvement. The importance of such environmental impacts, and the liability arising from environmental impairment, is changing rapidly due to the introduction of new legislation, even though there may be no change in the degree of contamination present.

This paper introduces the concept of environmental risk and describes an approach for determining whether hazards exist in a site, whether those hazards pose a risk to the environment, what the likelihood is of that risk occurring, and what the consequences may be for the landowner and regulatory authority.

Defining and identifying contaminated land

The introduction of the Environmental Protection Act in 1990 has been the principal driving force behind changes in attitude towards contaminated land. In the 1980s contamination in soil and groundwater was merely one additional factor to be costed for in the purchase of land for redevelopment, and investigation was frequently patchy or non-existent.

Occasional problems arose with such attitudes which led to major additional remedial works when difficult or extensive contamination was discovered post-purchase. One of the most extreme examples of this is described in a paper by Sury and Slingsby,[1] where low level radioactivity was found on a site purchased for housing redevelopment. It is understood that the costs of dealing with the contaminated soil was of the order of £10 million, from a site of total land area of some 12 hectares.

This example, and many others described to the House of Commons Environment Committee in 1989, led to the final Committee report[2] on Contaminated Land being published in 1990, with recommendations to establish registers of contaminated land, such that the extent of the problem could be better understood, and buyers of land would have early warning of such problems.

The Government response[3] to the report accepted that a register of land which may be contaminated should be compiled. It did not believe that it would be practical to compile a register of actual contamination, however, because of the difficulty of establishing that actual contamination exists. A policy decision on progressing some form of register is currently the subject of a wide-ranging Government review. Estimates of the amount of potentially contaminated land that exist in the UK range from 27,000 hectares[4] through to 240,000 hectares.[5] Such large discrepancies are a function of definition, as some estimates exclude operational industrial sites, or sites of less than one hectare in extent. For example, there are about 19,000 petrol filling station sites in the UK at present, and if each one is assumed to be potentially contaminated as a result of fuel leakage, then this accounts for about 7,000 hectares. It is likely that only a limited proportion of such sites are actually contaminated. There is also a blurring of meaning between derelict and contaminated land. The two have distinct definitions.

---

1 Sury M, and Slingsby. A Reclamation of the Former Laporte Chemical Works, Ilford, Essex. Proceedings of the 2nd International Conference on Construction on Polluted and Marginal Land. Brunel University, London, p 379–384. July 1992.

2 House of Commons Environment Committee. *Contaminated Land*, Volumes I, II and III. HMSO, 24 January 1990.

3 Department of the Environment. The Government's Response to the First Report from the House of Commons Select Committee on the Environment on Contaminated Land. London, HMSO, July 1990.

4 Department of the Environment. Derelict Land Survey. 1989.

5 *World in Action Report on Contaminated Land*, commissioned from Binnie and Partners. October 1992.

Contaminated land is not the same as derelict land; nor is the term contaminated land applied in the strict scientific sense of indicating the presence of an introduced substance which is harmful. If the substance is harmful, it is a "pollutant".

The Department of the Environment (DoE) defines contaminated land as "land which represents an actual or potential hazard to health or the environment as a result of current or previous use". Contrast this with derelict land which is "land so damaged by past activities that it is incapable of beneficial use without treatment". Clearly the two are independent. A worked out limestone quarry may be derelict but will not be contaminated. In contrast many established chemical factories will be contaminated but not derelict. Contaminated land poses a potential threat to the environment, but derelict land is a threat to future development, although it may be aesthetically unattractive as well.

The principal types and sources of contaminated land are listed below:

Types of contaminant

- Toxic or carcinogenic chemicals (*e.g.* cyanide, benzene);
- Toxic or phytotoxic metals (*e.g.* lead, cadmium, zinc);
- Organic contaminants (*e.g.* oils, solvents, phenols);
- Corrosive substances (*e.g.* acids, sulphates);
- Flammable, toxic or asphyxiating gases (*e.g.* methane, hydrogen sulphide, carbon dioxide);
- Combustible material;
- Asbestos; and
- Radioactive substances.

Causes of contamination

- Leaks and spillages from tanks and pipes;
- Storage and transport of raw materials or intermediate products;
- Storage and transport of waste materials;
- Disposal of waste materials on or adjacent to the site;
- Stack emissions; and
- Demolition of buildings which have contained contaminating material (*e.g.* asbestos lagging, impregnated brickwork).

Sources of contamination

- Mining and extractive industries;
- Iron and steel works;

- Metal treatment and finishing;
- Chemical industries;
- Scrap yards;
- Fragmentation plants;
- Paint and dyestuff industries;
- Sewage works and farms;
- Railway land, especially large sidings and depots;
- Application of sewage sludge to agricultural land;
- Fly-tipping;
- Cable-burning;
- Bonfires;
- Dockyards and dock basins;
- Petrol stations and refineries;
- Waste disposal sites;
- Power stations; and
- Deposition of air pollutants.

This information on the types of contamination, the pathways by which the contaminants can be spread into the environment, and an understanding of the relationship between the areas and likely concentrations of contaminants, are essential in order to be able to define the environment risks and hazards.

Guidelines and standards

The DoE, through the Interdepartmental Committee for the Redevelopment of Contaminated Land (ICRCL), has issued a series of Guidance Notes which define tentative trigger concentrations for various soil contaminants for planned site uses of differing sensitivity (allotments/domestic gardens through to buildings and hard cover).[6] Two trigger levels are defined: a threshold trigger concentration above which the risk of a hazard could be significant and some remedial action may be required prior to development; and an action trigger concentration above which some form of remedial action will be required or the form of the development changed. Trigger concentrations have been defined for the following contaminants:

- polyaromatic hydrocarbons (PAHs);
- free and complex cyanides;
- sulphate;

6 Department of the Environment. ICRCL. Guidance on the Assessment and Redevelopment of Contaminated Land. ICRCL 59/83, 2nd Ed, July 1987.

- sulphur;
- arsenic;
- chromium (total and hexavalent);
- mercury;
- boron (water-soluble);
- nickel;
- phenols;
- thiocyanate;
- sulphide;
- acidity (pH);
- cadmium;
- lead;
- selenium;
- copper; and
- zinc.

Only threshold trigger concentrations have been defined for the above metals.

The Building Research Establishment have also published guidelines for the quality of concrete required for structures in high sulphate soils in order to resist sulphate attack.[7] There are five classes of concrete in relation to sulphate concentrations in soils and in groundwater.

Guidance on soil gas concentration is also available, for example Waste Management Paper 27 (WMP 27) published by the DoE gives detailed guidance on the control of landfill gas.[8] The trigger levels set for methane and carbon dioxide in WMP 27 may also be applied to other sources of these gases, such as mine gas. The total range of guidance still remains relatively limited. Other EC countries have also produced national standards and guidelines for contaminant concentrations in soils and groundwaters, such as the A, B, C levels defined by the Dutch 1987 Soil Protection Act.[9] These guidelines remain the most detailed published by any individual country for both soil and groundwater contamination, although they are currently under review.

---

7 Building Research Establishment. "Concrete in Sulphate Bearing Soils and Groundwater". BRE Digest 363, 1991.

8 Department of the Environment. Waste Management Plan No 27: *Landfill Gas*, 2nd Ed. HMSO, 1991.

9 Van den Berg, R, 1990. "The Implementation of Risk Assessment of Soil Contamination in the Dutch Soil Clean-up Guideline." National Institute of Public Health and Environmental Protection.

The Role of the NRA

As well as catering for UK domestic needs, recent UK water legislation, including the Water Act 1989 and the Water Resources Act 1991, embodies relevant European legislation such as the EC Groundwater Directive (80/68/EC) and has provision for granting the National Rivers Authority (NRA) powers to carry out works and operations to rectify water pollution and to recover the costs. These powers, similar to those which were available under the Control of Pollution Act 1974, are contained in section 161 of the Water Resources Act.

The rate at which contaminants enter the groundwater system depends upon the nature of the geology and the hydrogeological properties of the aquifer. The NRA has statutory responsibilities for the protection of groundwater and has issued its policy and practice for the protection of groundwater[10] which set out its objectives and the way in which it seeks to proceed with aquifer protection.

An important part of the NRA's concept of aquifer protection is that of classifying groundwater vulnerability. The concept recognises that the risk of pollution from a given activity is greater in some hydrogeological, geological and soil situations than others. Using these criteria to classify vulnerability and by preventing or controlling certain activities in the most vulnerable areas, protection will be concentrated in the areas which need it most. This concept could be of particular relevance to contaminated land studies in that once the NRA has published vulnerability maps for an area, a tool is available to assist in desk-based risk assessment for contaminated land. It is understood that a start has been made in the preparation of these maps but coverage of the whole of England and Wales will not be available until some time in the future.

In their consultation document the NRA set out very clearly their intention to pursue remedial action wherever possible in respect of contaminated land.[10] They are also seeking to ensure that they are properly consulted at the planning stage of any development and to exercise all the powers available to them in cleaning up widespread contamination, "having regard to local circumstances and available funding".

UK standards for contaminant concentrations in water include the Water Supply (Water Quality) Regulations 1989.[11] These define maximum admissible concentrations (MACs) and more stringent guide levels for a wide range of contaminants in drinking water. These values may also be

10 National Rivers Authority. Policy and Practice for the Protection of Groundwater. NRA, 1992.

11 Water Supply (Water Quality) Regulations 1989, SI 1989/1147, HMSO.

applied to groundwater and surface water resources which are abstracted for potable supply.

Use of guidance

When using the guidance quoted it is worth bearing in mind that large variations exist between different guidance quoted by different organisations in the same country, and between the standards set by different European and national governments. Two examples are chosen for total lead and total sulfur to give an indication of the wide range which exists in the published guidance. For example, the New Jersey concentration used for total lead to give rise to a clean-up of a site is 100 mg/kg, and is therefore twenty times less than that set by the ICRCL of 2,000 mg/kg for contaminated land to be used for open space. Similarly the total sulfur concentration regarded as background in Holland is only 2 mg/kg although action is not recommended until 200 mg/kg. This is still considerably below the threshold levels of 5,000 and 20,000 mg/kg adopted by the UK in the ICRCL guidance. The conclusion to be drawn from these comparisons is that the actual risks and damage to the environment from specific concentrations of contaminants will vary according to the circumstances of the site and remain poorly understood. There is therefore no substitute for professional and experienced site specific risk assessment of the implications of measured contamination when making decisions about the need for clean-up and the appropriate measures to be taken.

It is essential that when evaluating contamination more consideration of the problem is given than a simple comparison against published guidelines, which may be neither appropriate nor suitable for the individual site in question. It is also worth remembering that the most relevant legislation makes specific reference to the need to assess properly contaminated land and its implications for the environment, but does not specifically require that assessment or clean-up is achieved to published guidelines.

Stage 1 assessment: desk study

Investigation should take a phased approach to understanding the history of a site and the extent of all forms of contamination. By applying a staged approach, it is likely that the most cost-effective investigations can be designed and implemented appropriate to the level of risks and hazards identified. It should be noted, however, that this approach requires a reasonable time period and cannot be compressed into a matter of days.

A thorough desk study will establish the need for further investigation, and is essential to designing the most appropriate and cost effective site investigation. Collation and interpretation of the information gathered will provide some indication of the likely nature of contamination, such as whether the soil contains heavy metals or whether gas is being generated within the site, and possibly the extent of contamination across the site. Knowledge of the nature of contaminating materials, the layout and history of the site and the local environmental conditions, including site geology, will enable the most appropriate investigation strategy to be chosen.

Site history

Much of the effort involved in investigating the history of a site is in knowing how and where to find the appropriate information. Sources of site information include:

- Maps: Ordnance Survey current and historical, geological survey maps and town plans.
- Statutory authorities: District and Regional Authorities (or Island Councils), River Purification Boards, Health and Safety Executive.
- Trade information from directories, trade associations.
- Photographic records, particularly aerial photographs.
- Technical data from published literature.
- Anecdotal information, for example from local studies, libraries, local residents, newspapers.
- Meteorological, mining and hydrogeological records.

Site geology, hydrogeology and hydrology

A study of the site geology is important in providing an assessment of the potential for migration of contaminants off the site. This includes the potential for gas migration through the surrounding strata or the migration of chemical contaminants to local groundwater, regional aquifers or surface water courses. The principal means of establishing a site's geology, hydrogeology and hydrology is through studying British Geological Survey maps and Ordnance Survey maps. The NRA have the bulk of published information on groundwater and surface water flows and quality. In mining areas, the mines abandonment plans should be consulted.

Site reconnaissance

The site reconnaissance is undertaken to examine the site with a view to designing the most appropriate site investigation. It must therefore include the following aspects:

Contamination indicators: Any further evidence of contamination should be noted. This may include evidence of underground structures and tanks, waste pits, made ground, and contamination to buildings. The risk of spreading contamination into groundwater, watercourses, or onto adjoining land by demolition or site activities should be assessed. Depending upon circumstances, it may be relevant to undertake some limited on-site monitoring or sampling at this stage generally to identify hazards.

Site safety: To identify any potential site hazards. Power cables, underground services, underground voids including mine shafts and tanks, unsafe buildings and structures, water or liquid bodies and hazardous materials on the surface such as asbestos must be noted.

Logistics of investigation: To identify the availability of any necessary on-site services (*e.g.* electricity and water) and the suitability of site access and conditions for plant and personnel.

Site neighbours: The site reconnaissance should pay particular attention to the site neighbours, including the current landowners and land uses surrounding the site of interest. This will identify whether adjacent land uses or previous land uses could have given rise to the migration of contamination onto the site being investigated, and similarly identify the sensitivity of adjacent land uses to the existence of any contamination on the site itself. Such consideration of adjacent land is particularly important when considering the implications of groundwater contamination, or the migration of gases for example from closed landfills.

Hazard ranking

Hazard ranking is an interpretive technique which can be applied to desk study information obtained from Stage 1 of the assessment process. There is an increasing need for both landowners and legislative bodies to compile initial priority lists regarding environmental risks from contaminated land. This is particularly true of urban renewal programmes where for example the Development Corporations have to consider and prioritise development plans for potentially extensive areas of contaminated land. Issues which may face such organisations range from the need correctly to assess the implications of environmental legislation on existing landholdings, through the ranking of alternative sites for land transactions, to the prioritisation of grants and remediation effort. Often it is impracticable to carry out more than a limited desk study where a large number of landholdings are involved. As a result initial hazard ranking systems based on readily accessible data are of considerable benefit in prioritising alternative sites. Obviously such simplified systems have severe limitations, but if applied rigorously and with adequate professional expertise, they can form an important part in the decision-making process for acquisition and divestiture of land, and the application of remediation funds.

One simple system which has been used with considerable effect in the ranking of 35 landholdings owned by Scottish Enterprise, is based on the concept of combining the sensitivity of a site with its contamination potential to define environmental risk. It is now being combined with economic assessment techniques to define a national remediation strategy for Scotland. Site sensitivity is defined from individual factors relating to the location and geology of the site. In addition account can be taken of adjacent landuses and the sensitivity of site neighbours. In its simplest form publicly available data from geology and Ordnance Survey maps can be used to derive a score or sensitivity analysis from surface water, geology and groundwater considerations.

Contamination potential includes consideration of the nature of the activities currently or formerly undertaken at the site, the date at which these processes took place, the nature of likely contaminants and the presence or absence of gas. Again this information can be obtained relatively easily although skill and experience in interpreting site visit and map based data are of significant benefit. The general categories used to assign priority to contamination potential are listed from which it is clear that the nature of the site use has been divided into four broad categories. The individual activities which fall into each contaminative category of use are listed in *Figure 1*. Highly contaminative industries have been assigned where a large number of different contaminants are usually present, and the nature of the industry is such that these contaminants are likely to have entered the soil environment. An example of such an industry is shipbuilding where a whole range of contamination is likely, from radioactivity and asbestos through to solvents and heavy metals.

In conjunction with the nature of the processes their age must be taken into consideration. Working practices have changed enormously on industrial sites over the past century. Until after the Second World War industrial practices were relatively unrestrained particularly during the two war-time periods. Since the Second World War planning legislation has provided some control over development at industrial sites. Since the 1970s increasing legislation has been brought into force which has put growing pressure on industries to develop housekeeping and health and safety arrangements.

The nature of contamination has simply been divided between organic and inorganic contaminants. Organic contaminants have been given a higher score as they tend to be more mobile and soluble, and therefore

Figure 1. Categorisation of Major Industrial Land Uses

CATEGORY 1

Highly Contaminative	*Contamination*
Hazardous Waste Treatment	O/I
Bulk Organic Chemicals Manufacture	O
Bulk Inorganic Chemicals Manufacture	I
Fine Chemicals Manufacture	O
Coal Gasification/Carbonisation	O/I
Landfill and Other Waste Treatment/Disposal	O/I
Steelworks	O/I
Lead Metal Ore Processing and Refining	I
Oil Refining and Petrochemical Production	O/I
Pesticides Manufacture	O
Asbestos & Asbestos Products Manufacture	I
Scrap Yards	O/I
Pharmaceuticals Manufacture	O

CATEGORY 2

Moderately Contamination	*Contamination*
Drum and Tank Cleaning/Recycling	O
Fertilizer Manufacture	I
Non-ferrous Metal Ore Mining	I
Wood Preservatives Production & Timber Treatment	O
Docks	I
Electric/Electrical Equipment Manufacture	O
Mechanical Engineering	O/I
Garages/Filling Stations	O
Minerals Processing (Bricks, Cement, Tarmac etc)	I
Power Stations	I
Sewage Works/Farms	I
Shipbuilding/Shipbreaking	O/I
Textile Production and Dyeing	O
Tyre Manufacture and Other Rubber Processing	O/I
Metal (other then iron or lead) Processing/Refining	I
Pulp and Paper Manufacture	O
Paint and Ink Manufacture	O/I
Electroplating and Other Metal Finishing	O/I
Precious Metals Recovery	I
Foundries	I
Tanneries	O/I

CATEGORY 3

Slight Contamination	*Contamination*
Timber Products Manufacture	O
Animal Processing Works	O
Glass Manufacture	I
Road Haulage Yards	O
Building Trades Products Manufacture	I
Printing Works	O

(continued over)

Research Laboratories	O
Airports & Airfields	O
Vehicle Manufacture	O
Railway Yards/Sidings	O
Toiletries, Detergents, Disinfectants etc Manufacture	O
Electricity Sub-Stations	O
Dry Cleaners	

CATEGORY 4

Low Concentration	*Contamination*
Food Preparation/Processing (inc Brewing)	I
Distilleries	I
Railway Tracks	I
Agriculture	None
Oil Shale and Coal Mining	I

Important Notes:

(1) This categorisation is for illustrative purposes. It will give a broad indication only of whether the business concerned involves a contaminative use and, if so, the degree of seriousness of that contaminative use, and nature of the contamination arising from a contaminative use.

(2) Whether a business falls within a particular category will depend on a number of further factors, such as:

- whether the previous business use of the site has given rise to contamination;
- the length of time for which the site has been used for the business purpose;
- the overall sensitivity of the site with respect to its broader environmental setting;
- assessment of the extent to which the business follows good environmental practice and management controls;
- the extent of the manufacturing or processing activity which is carried on by the business at the site; and
- assessment of the influence of the underlying geology & its hydrogeological characteristics.

(3) "O" signifies Organic contamination; "I" signifies Inorganic contamination.

more readily leached through the ground to greater depths possibly infiltrating into groundwater or nearby watercourses. Some organic contaminants are also known to be carcinogenic and the trigger and guidance values for them in both soils and groundwater tend to be much lower than for inorganic contaminants.

The presence of gas is considered separately due to the high migration potential of landfill gas and mine gas and the associated risk of explosion if the gas migrates into a confined space. Landfill gas has been given a higher score than mine gas, as landfill gas tends to be released from the soil in larger volumes and at higher pressure than mine gas, and therefore presents a greater hazard.

Stage 2 assessment: site investigation

The following aspects should be considered in planning a site investigation: soil contamination, gas migration, groundwater, and surface water contamination. The importance of each aspect will of course depend upon the nature of the proposed end use and on the contamination present. The investigation must be flexible to react to conditions encountered on site.

Soil contamination

In planning a site investigation a representative soil sampling strategy must be designed taking into account the information obtained in the desk study as well as allowing for adequate coverage of the site. Various guidance for carrying out site investigations is provided in the British Standards Institution (BSI) Codes of Practice[12,13] and by other agencies.[14] The soil sampling strategy should be designed to:

- assess areas most likely to be contaminated using historical data;
- locate the most contaminated areas (hot spots);
- adapt the planned sampling strategy as the investigation progresses depending on conditions found during the site investigation;
- apply a statistically valid sampling framework to cover the site as a whole.

Samples should be selected from areas of likely contamination from visual and olfactory evidence and to give a good indication of the contamination profiles. The skill of the site investigator is important in the selection of samples, emphasis should always be placed upon obtaining sufficient samples whilst in the field. Simple on-site monitoring techniques can assist this selection process.

Gas contamination

One of the most significant groups of gaseous contaminants derives from the degradation of the organic components of wastes in any man-made fill and is known collectively as landfill gas. Wherever degradable organic matter is present there is the potential for gas generation. Such situations may arise for example in reclaimed docks, and estuarine sites. In other circumstances, specific gaseous contaminants may be identified which will require assessment.

---

12 British Standards Institution, DD175: 1988 Code of Practice for the Identification of Potentially Contaminated Land and its Investigation.

13 British Standards Institution, BS5930: 1981 Code of Practice for Site Investigations.

14 Scottish Enterprise. Requirements for Contaminated Land Site Investigations, Revision 0, January 1993.

To assess whether or not gas will be a hazard to the development of a site, the following points will require consideration and investigation:

- existing composition and pressure of gas within the site boundary;
- extent of gas migration from the site;
- potential of organic materials for future degradation and subsequent gas production; and
- volume of gas in the soil atmosphere.

Waste Management Plan No. 27, see reference 8, provides guidance on a number of issues relating to landfill gas including survey and investigation techniques.

Surface water and groundwater

In order to assess the impact of a site on receiving watercourses, an understanding of the local hydrology is essential. The quality of surface waters may be affected by a number of factors including site topography, geology or the nature of contamination. Contamination of groundwater may arise as a result of materials leaching from the base of the site into the water table.

Information on surface water contamination may be gathered through on-site sampling and flow gauging of watercourses. An assessment of groundwater quality involves a more detailed investigation including borehole construction, water sampling and analysis. Groundwater velocity, quality and direction of flow, and also the flux and rate of contaminants leaching from the base of the site govern the impact on an underlying aquifer.

Analysis

Analysis of all samples collected on site should be undertaken by an experienced and approved laboratory. For soil and water samples a phased approach to analysis is often most suitable as this can avoid unnecessary expenditure. The results of the initial analysis give an indication of the type and degree of contamination present and allow more selective analysis of the remaining samples.

Safety on site

It is essential when carrying out site investigations that adequate and appropriate precautions are taken to ensure the safety of all those involved in the site work. Safety procedures for site workers should be exhaustive where the likely risks are poorly understood. The appropriate legislation which may apply is extensive, incorporating the general provisions of the Health and Safety at Work etc Act 1974. Safety considerations of hazards should include:

- protective clothing;
- hygiene;
- gas hazards;
- work in excavations;
- fire hazards;
- electrical hazards; and
- underground hazards.

Data interpretation and risk assessment

Once a site investigation has been carried out the significance of any contamination identified must be assessed in terms of the proposed use of the site. The DoE sets out a number of questions which should be answered following investigations. Information on "background" levels of contaminants together with the existing guidelines can be useful in assessing whether contaminants are present in sufficient concentrations to present hazards to the targets identified. However, many investigations are focused too narrowly and do not address all the risks which the contamination represents to the environment and planned land use. If the need for clean-up and potential liability is to be correctly assessed, more than the immediate health risks must be addressed. Whether on the basis of a desk study or site investigation eight separate issues must be considered. These are briefly described in the following paragraphs.

Health effects: Exposure to contaminants can give rise to health problems through ingestion (*eg* contaminated food or water), inhalation (*eg* toxic gases or dust, including asbestos), or direct skin contact with irritants or harmful chemicals.

Pollution of water: Supplied drinking water may become contaminated if water pipes pass through soils containing organic compounds such as phenol, or soluble metal compounds. Contamination of groundwater or surface waters can arise from leaching of rainwater through contaminated land. Breaches in buried tanks and pipework may release contaminated water and liquids into the ground. Several surface water pollution incidents have resulted from removal of hardstanding over contaminated ground, and subsequent leaching or washing of contaminants whilst rehabilitation work is in progress.

Phytotoxicity: Substances which are harmful to plant growth are termed phytotoxic. Phytotoxicity is particularly associated with certain metals (copper, nickel, zinc) but other substances including boron, oils, coal tars, phenols and sulphate also exhibit phytotoxic effects. Generally these effects occur at concentrations which are not toxic to humans. Carbon dioxide is directly phytotoxic and together with methane can be indirectly toxic to plants through depletion of oxygen levels in the soil.

Chemical attack: Conditions which may lead to chemical attack of building and service materials include sulphate attack on concrete and attack of plastic materials by phenolic compounds. Chloride or extremes of pH may also present structural problems, particularly with metal structures. Corrosion of underwater pipework can lead to ingress of potentially toxic fluids into water supplies, and sulphate attack on concrete can lead to structural failure in buildings.

Fires: Fires may be propagated underground if material of a suitable calorific value is present together with an ignition source and a sufficient supply of oxygen. Examples include ground containing coal or coal dust, oil shales, oils and domestic waste. Underground fires are very difficult to extinguish and the principal hazards include the emission of toxic gases and subsidence into void spaces caused by the fire.

Explosions: Flammable gases, for example methane produced by the degradation of organic material in the absence of oxygen, may form explosive mixtures if they accumulate in confined spaces under buildings, in service ducts, or other enclosed spaces. Any process which generates a spark can trigger an explosion if an explosive gas mixture is present.

Asphyxiation: Where degradation of organic materials occurs, for example at landfill sites, concentrations of carbon dioxide and other gases may exclude oxygen from confined spaces resulting in an asphyxiating atmosphere.

Odour problems: These may be associated with landfills, and may also be a problem in land contaminated with organic substances such as coal tars. Although odour problems do not necessarily represent a particularly hazardous situation, the nuisance imposed can often be difficult to control and even prevent occupation of developments on the land.

Having carried out a risk assessment according to each of the above criteria, and making use of the guidelines discussed earlier, it may be possible to agree suitable trigger levels for the site in question. Such trigger levels for clean-up must address all the risks that contamination and its treatment will represent. For example, if a remedial option involves the removal of contaminated soils to a licensed disposal site, the future presence of contamination at that site and the noise, dust and traffic associated with the transport of contaminated soil should all be considered. Such a broader approach will advantage the remedial method which destroys the contaminant rather than just moving it from place to place.

Putting risk and hazard in perspective

In many cases the interpretation and presentation of the information on contamination gained from the desk study and site investigation, will be required to meet a diverse range of interested parties. These parties will have to take regard of contamination issues as a critical input to their own decision-making. Firstly the existing liabilities of the current landowner need to be defined. The implications of the contamination identified on the value and future use of the land should be clear, and the remediation options, if required, specified in a way which allows the value of the land to be re-appraised. Liabilities may also arise with respect to responsibilities to the statutory authorities such as the planning authority, the environmental health department and the NRA. For example, the contaminated run-off from a derelict factory site can be regarded as an unconsented discharge and as such be in contravention of the relevant water legislation.

Increasingly the contamination assessment will have been carried out as part of the process of sale or redevelopment of land involving financial investment. Banks and financial institutions will have regard to contamination in assessing the security of their loans or the acceptability of the financing package proposed for the redevelopment of the site. Insurers and investors of companies involved in land transactions will also need to be satisfied with respect to the implications of contamination. It may be appropriate to seek specific site-based environmental insurance for the land, which will only be forthcoming if the work has been carried out and presented to the satisfaction of the insurer. There may be specific corporate or foreign based standards which must be met, particularly when attracting inward investment or selling the land to multi-national or foreign based companies. Under such circumstances specific legal agreements may be required and lawyers may be involved in the land transaction process. Finally, the local community has a clear right to be protected from any contamination presenting a public health hazard. It is increasingly likely that any contamination report prepared on behalf of a landowner will immediately or subsequently come into the public domain. This is a particularly important issue when discovering contamination which was not perhaps widely perceived to be present or which draws attention to liabilities or third party responsibilities with financial consequences. Given this wide range of purposes to which the report on contamination is put, it is clear that the quality and content of any contaminated land risk assessment will come under much greater scrutiny than has hitherto been the case.

Case Study 1: service station

This case study describes the development of a service station on an actively gassing, completed industrial landfill.

Investigation and impact prediction

In 1984 the Department of Transport commissioned a preliminary investigation of the site, comprising an extensive desk study and limited field works. The area previously consisted of a gently domed hill made up of natural deposits of sand and gravel which was extracted by 1974, leaving a series of water-filled lakes and random mounds of overburden. Reclamation of this area began in the 1970s with the construction of an adjacent motorway and the shaping of a recreational lake. The remaining space was used for landfilling with industrial wastes between 1978 and 1984. The final restoration profile was similar to the ground levels pertaining prior to mineral extraction at the site, and the waste covered with up to two metres of inert fill. Waste thicknesses of between 4 and 20 metres were predicted in the desk study and proved in subsequent field investigations. A detailed site investigation was undertaken to establish design parameters for foundations, gas control systems and settlement reduction techniques.

The investigation involved construction of a grid of boreholes across the site. Boreholes were completed with multi-point gas samplers to monitor gas pressure and composition at different depths in the same borehole. The results of the investigation showed slightly positive gas pressures throughout the site, although much lower than have been measured at other domestic waste landfills. Gas compositions were generally uniform across the site except in the north east corner, where some air ingress was thought to be occurring (see below). Continued gas monitoring over a nine month period indicated little change in gas composition or pressure.

Measurement of Gas Compositions (% by volume)

	Methane	Carbon Dioxide	Hydrogen	Nitrogen	Oxygen	Carbon Monoxide
Typical results	65	34	0.1	0.9	0.1	0.05
N E Corner	60	21	0.1	15	4	0.05

Trace gas analyses were carried out on samples of gas trapped in Tenax tubes, with a view to assessing corrosiveness, toxicity and odour aspects of the gas.

Fifteen halogenated and two sulphonated compounds were detected in the analysis, and the likely amounts of chlorine, fluorine and sulfur which could convert to corrosive acids were calculated (see below). The results showed that the gas at this site was markedly less corrosive than is observed at domestic waste sites.

Halogenated and Sulphonated Species in Trace Gas

	Total concentration (mg/m^3)
Chlorine compounds	4.44
Fluorine compounds	0.55
Sulfur compounds	0.29

Toxic compounds, such as benzene, were found in the analysis. However, dilution of the landfill gas to below its lower explosive limit would ensure that all toxic trace components are diluted below their thresholds of toxicity and no other air quality standards would be breached.

Odorous trace compounds detected in the gas include alkyl benzenes and terpenes. Consideration of odour thresholds indicated that a dilution of 1,500-fold would be required to reduce the concentrations of these trace gases to below the odour threshold. On this basis, it was evident that odours from the landfill gas must be controlled.

Gas protection measures

The gas control system was designed to achieve the following objectives:

(a) To eliminate the risk of explosion, flammability, toxicity, asphyxiation and odours due to the presence of landfill gas at the site.
(b) To completely exclude methane from all buildings, accessible services, ducts and enclosed spaces.

(c) To use a set of control systems which are the simplest and require the least maintenance to achieve the above two objectives.
(d) To design sufficient capacity and duplication of gas control methods to facilitate successful operation throughout the remaining gas producing lifetime of the site for all possible gas emission rates.
(e) To prevent unnecessary air ingress to minimise risks of underground combustion.

In order to achieve these objectives the following principles were applied to the detailed gas control system:

(i) Two levels of control exist; the area supporting the buildings or similar structures have more stringent controls than the remainder of the site (*i.e.* parking and landscaped areas).
(ii) Buildings have a vented void space beneath all floors and special service entries to prevent gas entry in addition to an active gas extraction system in the surrounding fill. Permanent continuous gas monitors with an alarm system are installed to demonstrate that the system is excluding gas in accordance with the design criteria.
(iii) The car parking and other hardstanding areas require a collection system which can control gas emissions over the entire surface area. In practice this means maintaining a system of active gas extraction which prevents a positive pressure of gas beneath the low permeability layer from being sustained.
(iv) The landscaped, picnic and other vegetated areas require sufficient gas control to prevent significant surface gas emissions, to keep all vegetation healthy and prevent any detectable odour from the gas.

Specific gas control measures are as follows:

Amenity building: The highest level of control was applied to this area. It comprises the use of two permeability contrasts below the structure. Pumped extraction from horizontal pipework laid in a granular blanket below the clay capping layer provides the primary protection. A ventilated sub-floor void provides secondary protection, with a membrane incorporated in the concrete floor slab. Gas monitors installed in the sub-floor void in confined areas within the amenity building provide warning of any gas ingress, although this is essentially a reassurance measure. Monitors are linked to a staged alarm system which activates a series of procedures relating to the level of gas detected.

Refuelling area: The refuelling area, consisting of petrol and diesel forecourts and payment kiosk is in an area of only approximately 8m of fill.

Consequently a philosophy of isolation was adopted. This consisted of complete removal of all refuse. The base and sides of the excavation were then lined with clay and the remaining hole infilled with a silty fine sand. Clay capping was placed over the sand fill. As a further back up a vertical well system connected to an independent ring main also surrounds the fuel area, although this is not pumped routinely.

Parking and recreation areas: A single level of control was applied to these areas, using the permeability contrast of a granular collection layer overlain by clay capping, coupled with gas extraction from horizontal pipework laid in the granular layer.

Site sealing layers: In the area of the site where refuse remained, capping material was removed and stockpiled. A 500mm clean granular layer was applied. This reduced the thickness of the granular blanket to approximately 200mm. A further 200mm granular material was overlaid to provide a transmission layer for gas. This in turn was overlain by a geotextile separator underlying 500mm of compacted clay beneath a polythene membrane. A blinding layer of sand was placed over the plastic layer, and site capping material restored to an approximate thickness of 800mm.

Gas collection from the granular transmission layer is accomplished from a network of horizontal pipes. All collected gas is burnt in a muffle flare. The site is now operational.

Case Study 2: existing housing on gassing landfill

This case study describes the successful remediation of a housing estate found to be constructed on a former domestic waste landfill which was giving rise to significant quantities of landfill gas. The interior and exterior works were carried out in order to render all of the houses safe and saleable with minimum disruption to the residents. The work is representative of a number of examples where Aspinwall has been required to investigate and remediate private housing developments constructed before such developments were prohibited due to the landfill gas hazard.

Investigation and impact prediction

An initial desk study identified residential development situated on and adjacent to a former landfill in South East England. The subsequent investigation involved the installation of gas monitoring boreholes and piezometers, the excavation of trial pits and the collection and analysis of waste samples. The boreholes and piezometers were monitored over an eight week period and gas samples collected for laboratory analysis. The results were used to fully assess the gas regime at the site and define risk to the houses.

Degradable wastes approximately 2.0m thick were identified beneath certain houses within the limits of the permitted landfill. The degradable wastes were overlain by a layer of inert clayey fill. Only 1.0m of the degradable waste was situated above the perched water table. Analysis of waste samples showed that about one third of the organic material remained for degradation and therefore the presence of flammable gas should be anticipated to persist for a considerable period of time.

Concentrations of methane and carbon dioxide were sufficiently high to represent a risk to the properties above with up to 70% methane detected, although gas pressures were negligible indicating a slow rate of gas production. Gas migration was also identified beyond the fill material and the number of houses requiring remediation were identified. Remediation works were designed on the basis of minimum disruption to occupiers, whilst ensuring a multi-barrier approach to the protection against gas ingress to each property.

Remediation

The remedial works were implemented on an individual property basis and consisted of the installation of passive venting systems and treatment of the upper surface of the groundfloor slab of properties to prevent gas ingress, together with sealing works around service entries. Within the properties a detailed house to house survey using a portable flame ionisation detector identified a variety of defects such as cracking of floor slabs, voids around service entries and gaps between vertical walls and the floor slab. These defects were sealed comprehensively and the effectiveness of the seals confirmed by subsequent house surveys for gas.

In order to intercept gas which could potentially accumulate beneath the floor slabs, a programme of installing vent trenches immediately adjacent to the sides of the houses was undertaken. According to the location the venting areas could be filled with 10mm no fines gravel and left as a gravel path or area, or covered with paviors. Alternatively a series of pipe work attached to the houses venting at roof level was used where more permanent covering of the trenches was required or beneath individual extensions such as porches.

The work was all carried out under strict supervision and using a variety of small mobile plant to minimise the contract time at each property and general disruption to the residents. Careful attention to reinstatement work, including paving, small extensions and landscaping ensured that very soon after completion no obvious signs of the work remained. This approach combined with a vigorous public relations exercise to keep all residents fully appraised of progress led to little publicity of the work and only a temporary adverse effect on property prices. To the best of our knowledge the houses are not only safe and in a better condition than before the risk from landfill gas was identified, but they are also saleable and insurable in the normal way.

Conclusions

In conclusion it is clear that the importance of applying professional experience in evaluating the consequences of contaminated land has never been more important. The implications of wrongly assessing contamination have increased rapidly and can lead to major financial decisions which must be based on a rigorous and consistent assessment of risk. In providing advice, it should always be remembered that a practical approach and intelligent appraisal should characterise the assessment, and not the dogmatic application of guidelines which are not intended to be legal and definitive standards. In many instances the environmental significance of potential contaminants is poorly understood. Practical and realistic advice given to developers, owners and occupiers will maintain confidence whilst allowing the public's interest to be protected. It is essential that the issue of contaminated land is dealt with properly and thoroughly to demonstrate that contamination need not blight the potential use and future value of land.

In this way an increased awareness of the problem of contaminated land can be used to encourage the redevelopment and regeneration of former industrial areas, in preference to the use of more and more land for urban development. It must be considered preferable to ensure that the legacy of past activities is progressively cleaned up and dealt with to leave a diminished risk and impairment of the environment to future generations. Furthermore a realistic and thorough assessment of contamination is the only way to prevent blight of land and ensure that land values are not unreasonably affected by fears arising from potential contamination. The first step to achieving these objectives must be the thorough and consistent review, investigation and assessment of contaminated land to give the right information to meet all interested parties' interests and to plan sensible, cost-effective and lasting remediation strategies.

10 Environmental management systems and construction

John Barber

Introduction

> "Fog everywhere. Fog up the river, where it flows among green aits and meadows; fog down the river, where it rolls defiled among the tiers of shipping, and the waterside pollution of a great (and dirty) city. Fog on the Essex marshes, fog on the Kentish heights . . . Fog in the eyes and throats of ancient Greenwich pensioners, wheezing by the firesides of their wards; fog in the stem and bowl of the afternoon pipe of the wrathful skipper, down in his close cabin; fog cruelly pinching the toes and fingers of his shivering little 'prentice boy on deck."

This vista of swirling fog appears in the opening paragraphs of *Bleak House*. Charles Dickens used the scene as a metaphor to convey the murkiness of the Chancery proceedings in Jarndyce v Jarndyce. Today, it would equally describe the polysyllabic impenetrability of European Community legislation on environmental matters, and of the British Standard, BS 7750, Environmental Management Systems,[1] but it also serves as a literary reminder for lawyers that pollution is not a new phenomenon, and it provides a clue to what has to be done to solve the present environmental conundrum.

The pollution which confronts us today is a different set of problems from that of Dickens' time. History tells us that the notorious fogs which then affected London, Kent and Essex were gradually defeated through a combination of legislation, action, and technology. As we embark on a fresh crusade against pollution, we may learn from the past that these three elements—legislation, action and technology—are all essential ingredients in any solution for dealing with environmental problems.

Legislation played an essential part in defeating the fogs by regulating or prohibiting certain activities, by setting standards, and by establishing statutory bodies. But law alone could have achieved little without action by

1 For example, consider the following sentence from the Introduction to BS 7750: "To be effective, they need to be conducted within a structured management system, integrated with overall management activity and addressing all aspects of desired environmental performance."

relevant statutory bodies and other organizations, and the possibilities provided by technological evolution and development.[2]

In addition to their legislative powers, Governments have the ability to apply taxpayers' money to promote appropriate action and technology, either by commissioning works or research, or by providing fiscal incentives. Governments can also, with appropriate funding, establish inspection agencies to enforce regulations but, apart from the cost, such enforcement has limited effect in motivating organizations to take positive action.[3] The urgent question for hard-pressed politicians is whether Governments and indeed the European Community (which has become a major source of law on environmental matters) can find other ways which are more effective and less costly to the taxpayer to promote positive activity and produce conformity with regulations.

The new approach, which may answer the politician's prayer, is to focus attention on the role of management within organizations by either encouraging, or imposing requirements for, formal documented management systems. The management system approach has already been widely adopted in relation to conformity with "quality" requirements and regulations, and it is now being extended to health and safety, and to environment.

Environmental management systems are concerned with the initiation and control of actions, with a view to assuring conformance with legal requirements.

Management systems

The idea of a management system is to provide a planned, documented and systematic approach towards some management function. Such an approach has long been applied to financial management and accounting functions. The 1950s and 60s saw the advent of management systems for the control of time and progress, with the development of critical path analysis and other management tools. In the late 60s and early 1970s, management systems came to be applied to the achievement of quality objectives, with a gradual change in the primary means of providing or obtaining quality assurance. The emphasis shifted from reliance on final

---

2 The law also provides means of transferring liability or obtaining indemnities in respect of environmental problems, for example, through insurance or the doctrine of *caveat emptor*. This may actually inhibit action, but that is another topic, see J N Barber, "Guide to Collateral Warranties", Association of Geotechnical Specialists, (1993).

3 Prosecuting and fining a corporation does not motivate individuals and may actually disable the organization from undertaking positive steps. Holding individual directors personally responsible may simply deter good people from taking on the job.

inspection by the purchaser, initially to systematic and documented intermediate inspections by the purchaser in the early quality assurance schemes, and more recently to management systems implemented by the supplier.

This shift involved initiatives in many different countries and international organizations, but a significant step was the publication by the British Standards Institution in 1979 of the first edition of BS 5750, Quality Systems. This was an outstanding document, tightly drafted with proper regard to matters such as authority to control. It provided an effective basis on which individual organizations could develop and operate their own quality management systems. It introduced some radical innovations, in particular, the idea of "auditability" and "auditing" as a means of checking the implementation and effectiveness of the system. It also introduced a key figure, the "management representative", responsible for the implementation of the management system, thus ensuring that controlling the achievement of required quality standards would be treated as a management function alongside controlling time and money.

The spread of quality management systems was given fresh impetus when BS 5750 was adopted (with amendments) in 1987 as a series of International (IS0 9000) and European (EN 29000)[4] Standards. This has provided a basis on which both legislation and contracts could require quality management systems, and the opportunity to do so has been taken at EC level. In 1990, an EC Council Resolution aimed at producing "a global approach to conformity assessment" adopted as a principle "generalised use of the European Standards relating to quality assurance (EN 29000)." The Resolution may be implemented either as a basic principle or as an explicit requirement. For example, it has been suggested that the procedures for Attestation of Conformity in the Construction Products Directive will be interpreted in the light of the Council Resolution.[5] The Water, Energy, Transport and Telecommunications Sector Procurement Directive makes specific reference as follows:[6]

> "Should contracting entities require the production of certificates drawn up by independent bodies for attesting conformity of the service to certain quality assurance standards, they shall refer to quality assurance systems based on the relevant EN 29000 European standards series certified by bodies conforming to the EN 45000 European standards series."

4 Council Resolution 90/C 10/01.

5 See *Knight's European Construction Documents*, pp 2–4.

6 Council Directive 93/38/EEC, Article 32. (OJ L199/100)

The introduction of quality management system requirements in regulations and procurement has become possible not only because of the publication of relevant Standards, but also because of the apparent willingness of organizations to develop and implement appropriate systems. This apparent willingness led to an intuitive feeling that if the management system approach works and is accepted in regard to product quality, it might also be applied to safety, health and environment regulations and requirements. This intuitive feeling has been quickly taken up in EC legislation. For example the Temporary or Mobile Work Sites Directive,[7] although it does not use the words "management system", requires a coordinator to produce a "safety and health plan" setting out the specific rules applicable to the site concerned, and then "to make arrangements to check that the working procedures are being implemented correctly". This is effectively a management system. It does not, however, refer to a Standard to specify the contents of the plan or the nature of the arrangements to check compliance. There is, as yet, no appropriate Standard.

The Eco-management and Audit Regulation[8] calls explicitly for adoption of an "environmental management system", which is defined to mean:

> "that part of the overall management system which includes the organizational structure, responsibilities, practices, procedures, processes and resources for determining and implementing the environmental policy."

There is a difficulty, however, that as yet there is no European Standard specifying the requirements for an environmental management system. An ISO Committee has been set up[9] to produce a Standard but it will obviously take some time. The British Standards Institution has been quick off the blocks with its new Standard, BS 7750: 1992, Environmental Management Systems, but this has not yet been adopted as a European Standard and it is premature to assume that it will be adopted.

EC Eco-Management and Audit Regulation

The early EC initiatives on the environment, prior to the Single European Act in 1987, were rather piecemeal, possibly because the original Treaty provided only a tenuous basis for legislating on environmental matters. There were, however, Environmental Action Plans published in 1973, 1977 and 1983, prior to the Act, and many legislative measures were adopted.

---

7 Council Directive 92/57/EEC (OJ L245/6).

8 Council Regulation (EEC) No 1836/93 (OJ L168/1)

9 ISO Technical Committee TC107, Environmental Management. The first meeting was scheduled to take place under a Canadian secretariat in Toronto in early June 1993.

The early emphasis was on pollution control rather than prevention. One of the early measures, however, was the Assessment Directive, adopted in 1985,[10] which requires environmental assessments for certain categories of new projects. It is still a key Directive affecting construction projects.

The current EC environmental initiatives are more soundly based on the Single European Act. This provided an explicit mandate for the EC to deal with environmental matters, and it set a number of goals, of which one is particularly relevant to environmental management systems, namely "to preserve, protect and improve the quality of the environment". It also laid down principles, of which two are particularly relevant, namely that environmental protection measures should become integrated into other EC policies and that preventive action should be taken.

The Act provided the basis of the Fourth Environmental Action Programme, also published in 1987,[11] which laid down a number of priorities, including:

"(c) prevention of industrial accidents
(d) combating noise pollution at source
(1) the development of improved waste management in relation to the reduction of quantities, treatment, recycling and reuse
(q) effective implementation of Council Directive 85/337/EEC of 27 June 1985 on the assessment of the effects of certain public and private projects on the environment and the integration of the environmental dimension in other Community policies
(r) implementation of appropriate standards in order to ensure a high level of public health and environmental protection."

More recently, a fifth Environmental Action Programme has been agreed under the title of "Towards Sustainability", and the Maastricht Treaty has added a further dimension (including the "precautionary principle"), but the Eco-management and Audit Regulation has been under discussion for a number of years. It was finally promulgated in the *Official Journal* in July 1993,[12] and, being a Regulation rather than a Directive, its provisions are of direct effect in member countries. The Regulation states that it entered into force on the third day following publication but it does not apply until 21 months after publication.

Several earlier drafts of the Regulation were also published in the *Official Journal*, and some work has been undertaken on the basis of those earlier drafts. For example, BS 7750: 1992 is based on a 1991 draft of the Regulations. Comparison reveals, however, that substantial changes were

10 Council Directive 85/333/EEC (OJ L175).
11 Council Resolution 87/C 328/01 (OJ C70/3).
12 OJ L168.

made to that draft and even to the "final" draft which was published in 1992.[13] For example, the scheme established by the Regulation became the "Eco-management and audit scheme" instead of the "Eco-audit scheme". Reference to "environmental protection systems" disappeared. Any commentaries or other documents based on drafts of the Regulations should accordingly be treated with caution.

The Regulation establishes a "Community scheme allowing voluntary participation by companies performing industrial activities". The scheme is entitled the "community eco-management and audit scheme", and is sometimes referred to by the acronym, CEMAS. The scheme is voluntary in the sense that companies are not obliged to register, but once a company has registered to participate, it is effectively locked in. If the company thereafter does not comply, the Regulation provides that the "site shall be deleted from the register". There is no provision for voluntary deregistration. A major part of the scheme is the publicity attached to registration and, therefore, also to deletion from the register. Article 16 also provides for "appropriate legal or administrative measures in case of non-compliance with the provisions of this Regulation".

The objectives of the scheme are stated to be:

> "to promote continuous improvements in the environmental performance of industrial activities by:
> (a) the establishment and implementation of environmental policies, programmes and management systems by companies, in relation to their sites;
> (b) the systematic, objective and periodic evaluation of the performance of such elements;
> (c) the provision of information on environmental performance to the public."

Boundaries

The successive drafts of the Regulation display a growing awareness of the need to define organizational and territorial boundaries under the scheme. The scheme now applies to a "site" and to "companies operating a site or sites". The intention has been made very clear in the final version of the Regulation, where a "company" is defined to mean "the organization which has overall control over activities at a given site".

"Site" is defined to mean:

> "all land on which the industrial activities under the control of a company at a given location are carried out, including any connected or associated storage of materials, by-products, intermediate products, end products and waste material, and any equipment and infrastructure involved in the activities whether or not fixed."

13 COM(91) 459(EEC) (OJ C76).

There is a tendency amongst construction professionals to link the word "site" with construction activities, given its usage in standard forms of contract to describe the land possession of which is given to a contractor. It is apparent, however, that the word is not used in this sense in the Regulation. "Industrial activity", which is the essence of a site for the purposes of the Regulation, is defined to mean:

> "any activity listed under sections C and D of the classification of economic activities in the European Community . . . as established by Council Regulation (EEC) No 3037/90 with the addition of electricity, gas, steam and hot water production and the recycling, treatment, destruction or disposal of solid or liquid waste."

Reference to the classification shows that section C comprises manufacturing industries and section D comprises mines and quarries. Construction and property development are classified in separate sections. Unless muckshifting activities come within the last part of the definition as "disposal of waste", it appears that construction companies will not generally be able to register under the scheme.[14]

On the other hand, Annex 1 para Dll of the Regulation then says:

> "Provisions shall be made to ensure that contractors working at the site on the company's behalf apply environmental standards equivalent to the company's own."

It appears that organizations involved in construction work on sites which are registered under the scheme will come within the ambit of the Regulation indirectly.

Requirements of registration

The requirements of registration under the scheme are set out in Article 3. So far as relevant, this states that the company must:

> "(a) adopt a company environmental policy in accordance with the requirements of Annex 1 . . .
> (b) conduct an environmental review of the site . . .
> (c) introduce, in the light of that review, an environmental programme for the site and an environmental management system applicable to all activities at the site. The environmental programme will be aimed at achieving the commitments contained in the company environmental policy towards continuous improvement of environmental performance. The environmental management system must comply with the requirements of Annex 1.

---

14 Article 14 allows for application by Member States, on an experimental basis, of "provisions analogous to the eco-management and audit scheme to sectors outside industry, *e.g.* the distributive trades and public service."

(d) carry out, or cause to be carried out . . . environmental audits at the sites concerned
(e) set objectives at the highest management level . . .
(f) prepare . . . an environmental statement specific to each site audited . . .
(g) have the environmental . . . management system . . . examined to verify that (it) meet(s) the relevant requirements of this Regulation.
(h) forward the validated environmental statement to the competent body of the Member State where the site is located and disseminate it as appropriate to the public in that State after registration of the site in question . . ."

Requirements for environmental management systems

Article 12 provides that companies implementing national, European or international standards for environmental management systems shall be considered as meeting the requirements of the Regulation, provided that the standards and certification procedures are recognised by the Commission and the certification is undertaken by a body whose accreditation is recognized in the Member State where the site is located.

The requirements concerning environmental management systems are set out in Annex 1, section B, under six headings:

(1) Environmental policy, objectives and programmes;
(2) Organization and personnel;
(3) Environmental effects;
(4) Operational control;
(5) Environmental management documentation records; and
(6) Environmental audits.

Most of the requirements would appear familiar to anyone accustomed to working with EN 29000 (BS 5750), but there are subtle differences. For example, B2 requires steps or procedures to ensure awareness among personnel at all levels of "the potential environmental effects of their work activities and the environmental benefits of improved performance."

The main difference, however, comes under item B3 where the environmental effects which are to be examined and assessed are listed, and item B4, where the "functions, activities and processes" which may cause these effects are to be "identified" and then "planned and controlled". Under item B3, the company is required to establish and maintain procedures to:

"record all legislative, regulatory and other policy requirements pertaining to the environmental aspects of its activities, products and services."

This brings home the point that the main objective of the scheme is to promote compliance with legislative, regulatory and other policy requirements, that is, with the requirements of European Community or national legislation or regulations. This is to be contrasted with the objective of quality management systems, which is compliance with the requirements of the purchaser who pays the money.

Past activities

The scheme is directed towards the control of present and future activities in the industrial sector. The Regulation is remarkably coy about how far there might be a need to look at past activities and particularly at contamination caused by past activities on the site. It might be expected that unearthing of the effects of past activities could arise under the process of "environmental review" of the site, but this process is only to cover the issues listed in Annex 1 Part C, which do not include the effects of past activities. On the other hand, Annex 1 Part B includes among the effects to be examined and assessed "effects arising, or likely to arise, as consequences of . . . past activities". This is particularly relevant to construction, for example, if the work involves excavation on the site.

BS 7750

BS 7750: 1992 was drawn up to meet the requirements of the eco-management and audit Regulation, based on the now superseded 1991 draft. It was not drawn up specifically for construction projects or activities. These facts raise two questions:

- whether BS 7750: 1992 is compatible with the final Regulation (irrespective of whether it was compatible with the earlier draft);
- whether it is applicable to an organization involved in construction projects and activities, either as a company with a site registered under the scheme or as an organization employed directly or indirectly by such a company.

The following attempts to answer these questions are likely soon to be overtaken by amendments. Although BS 7750: 1992 was published as a full Standard rather than a Draft for Development, its foreword explicitly stated that it was issued:

> "subject to review by the technical committee responsible for drafting no later than 1 September 1993 to facilitate pilot application. At the time of the review, changes

will be made where required in the light of the experience gained or to reflect changes to the draft European Community Eco-Audit Regulation (Version 3, December 1991) in the intervening time from publication of this standard."

In addition the Department of Trade and Industry and the Department of the Environment have issued a joint Consultation Paper on the implementation of the EC Eco-management and Audit Regulation and accreditation arrangements for certification to BS 7750. Comments on the Discussion Paper were invited by 11 September 1993.

CIRIA has identified the need for research into environmental management systems as relevant to construction[15] and is presently seeking funding for a project to develop an outline Sector Application Guide for the construction and related industries.[16]

BS 7750, BS 5750 and construction

The numbering of BS 7750: 1992 reveals a deliberate attempt by BSI to capitalise on the success and acceptance of the Quality Systems Standard, BS 5750. It should not, however, be presumed that the drafting of the new Standard matches the excellence of BS 5750. The Specification in BS 7750: 1992 does little more than recycle the eco-management and audit Regulation, and the "Guide to environmental management system requirements", which forms Annex A, would have done well to heed its own strictures in section A7 that:

> "All written procedures should be stated simply, unambiguously and understandably and should indicate methods to be used and criteria to be satisfied."

There is a further link between the Standards in that it is proposed in BS 7750: 1992 that an organization's BS 5750 quality system can and should be extended and adapted to incorporate environmental objectives or requirements. This is part of a wider campaign, which is not confined to BSI, that an integrated management system approach should be developed covering not only quality and environmental performance, but also health and safety matters. Such an integrated approach has some logic and it may produce advantages. It may also have drawbacks, as discussed below.

For those in the construction sector, there is an underlying problem (whether or not the systems are integrated) that both BS 5750 and BS 7750: 1992 were developed in the context of manufacturing industries. Manufacturing and construction differ materially in at least three areas:

---

15 CIRIA Special Publication 93, *Environmental Issues in Construction*, pp 41 and 57.

16 CIRIA Research Project Proposal: Prop 1268.

(1) Overall management control of activities on a site: Whereas manufacturing activities tend to be managed by a single organization on a single site on a long-term basis, construction activities are generally carried out on a project-by-project basis on different sites. Each construction project involves short-term activities, but leaves a long-term product. Management responsibility for each project may be divided between several organizations with none having overall management responsibility for, or control of, activities on the site. Owners or operators of sites have traditionally sought to distance themselves from control of construction activities.
(2) Planning and design: It is rare in the manufacturing sector for planning and design to be carried out by an organization which is independent of the one responsible for production, but it is quite common on construction projects. In the split reponsibility situation, the organization responsible for planning and design does not control construction activities, but it is concerned with the performance and effects of the completed works and the eventual activities to be carried out using the completed works.
(3) Existing ground conditions: Manufacturing tends to be concerned with new materials brought onto the site, whereas construction is also dependent on the ground which exists on the site.

These differences are considered below, particularly in so far as they undermine the compatibility of BS 7750: 1992 with the eco-management and audit scheme.

Integrated approach

The classification of requirements such as quality, environmental or health and safety is sometimes rather artificial. Thus the Asbestos Pollution and Noise Directives are classified as Environment, while the Exposure to Asbestos at Work and Noise at Work Directives are classified as Health and Safety. The elements to be controlled obviously coincide or overlap. This point has been taken up by the European Construction Institute, based at Loughborough University, whose Safety Health and Construction Environment Task Force has produced a useful report recommending an integrated management system for SHE (Safety, Health and Environment) aspects.[17]

---

17 European Construction Institute, *Total project management of construction safety, health and environment*, 1992, Thomas Telford Ltd.

A study of that report reveals, however, that SHE aspects are only considered to include the immediate environmental effects of construction activities, and do not include the effects of the works when constructed or their use. A different view of integration may sometimes be appropriate. For example, the IAPH "Guidelines for Environmental Planning and Management in Ports and Coastal Area Developments"[18] recommend that, in planning the design and construction of a new port, consideration should be given to the eventual management of the port activities, including emergency measures to deal with oil spills, as provision should be integrated into the design.

It may be equally important to enable aspects of the management function to be disentangled. One of the most significant innovations of management systems is the concept of auditing. Where it is intended that an organization should be accountable to an outside body for the faithful operation of a management system, that accountability is monitored though external audit. Difficulty can arise over the scope of the external audit. Is it intended to be an audit of all management systems throughout the organization, or is the scope to be limited in some way? While it may sometimes be beneficial to have an integrated approach to management systems, auditability may favour division or divisibility into discrete compartments.

It is also questionable whether the management representative appointed under a quality management system would have time to take on the burden envisaged by the Guidance Notes in BS 7750: 1992 of ensuring that "developments in environmental legislation and regulation, and in environmental issues, concerns and understanding relevant to the organization, are monitored."

Overall management control

With BS 5750, "Quality Systems", there is a sound, quasi-constitutional basis for the implementation of a quality system. The quality system applies within the confines of an "organization". It applies by the authority of the top management, who signs the quality policy. Top management has available the sanction of dismissing any employee within the organization who does not comply with the requirements of the system.

BS 5750 also has the concept of the "project quality plan", which applies to work on a specific project, but only to the part of the project undertaken

18 IAPH Guidelines for Environmental Planning and Management in Ports and Coastal Area Developments 1989, (J Barber ed.), International Association of Ports and Harbours, Tokyo.

by the individual organization and its sub-contractors. It does not embrace other organizations working on the same project. This reflects sound logic. An organization can stipulate a degree of authority over its sub-contractors, sufficient to insist on compliance with the requirements of the PQP, but it has no authority over other organizations.

This may be contrasted with the approach adopted for nuclear work, which has its own quality system Standard, BS 5882. On nuclear work, the "quality programme" starts with the promoter, and authority for an overall quality programme cascades from the promoter to cover all organizations involved. This is necessary as by statute, on nuclear work, the promoter bears primary responsibility for satisfying the regulatory body as to safety.

BS 7750: 1992 adopts a similar approach to BS 5750, in that it applies to an organization, defined as "any organized body or establishment, for example, a business, company, government department, charity or society". The definition then seeks to allow an alternative approach, stating: "For bodies or establishments with more than one site, a single site may be defined as an organization." That is confusing. The site itself cannot constitute an organization, although the part or subsidiary of the principal organization responsible for working on the site may do so.

The eco-management and audit Regulation bears more resemblance to the nuclear model than to BS 7750: 1992. The environmental management system requirements under the Regulation apply to the organization which has overall management control over activities at the site. An owner or operator of a site registered under CEMAS, contemplating construction on the site, will be required to implement an environmental management system which covers all aspects of the construction project.

The owner or operator may also be required to carry out an environmental assessment under the Environmental Assessment Directive. BS 7750: 1992 section 4.6 adds this to the environmental management system, requiring that:

> "Separate programmes shall be established in respect of the environmental management of projects relating to new developments . . . to define:
>
> (1) the environmental objectives to be attained;
> (2) the mechanisms for their achievement;
> (3) the procedures for dealing with changes and modifications as projects proceed;
> (4) the corrective mechanisms which shall be employed should the need arise, how they shall be activated and how their adequacy shall be measured in any particular situation in which they are applied."

Companies in the construction or property development sectors will not generally be eligible themselves to register under CEMAS but, as mentioned above, they may be required to show that they apply "environmental standards" equivalent to the company which is responsible for the site if it is registered under the scheme. Based on experience with quality systems, it will probably be necessary or appropriate for construction sector companies to operate their own environmental management systems as a means of satisfying this indirect requirement. BS 7750: 1992 needs to be adjusted to recognise the position of organizations in the secondary role and the relationships between the separate organizations involved on a site.

The statutory requirement for involvement of the owner or operator of the site in the environmental management system gives rise to a lack of fit with quality management systems in which there is no such requirement.

Existing ground

Construction activities commonly involve moving, exposing or disturbing the existing ground, with potential environmental effects, particularly where the ground is contaminated. This adds special significance to the requirement in the Regulation for the company to examine and assess the effects arising, or likely to arise, as consequences of past activities. This requirement is repeated in BS 7750: 1992 section 4.4.3, and it there applies to any organization implementing an environmental management system.

Where construction activities are contemplated, the requirement must be interpreted in both the Regulation and the Standard as referring to all past activities on the site, not merely past activities of the company or organization itself.

Commercial objectives

Management systems may be classified according to whether they are driven by requirements to satisfy regulatory bodies, as in the nuclear and offshore fields, or whether they are driven by enlightened self-interest—the prospect of improved long-term profitability. As management systems become more widely required through contract, there may be a tendency for them to be regarded increasingly as a burden in the first category, but the attraction of quality management systems has been that they can provide improved long-term profitability. This carrot can be the primary driving force to effective implementation of the system.

The improved long-term profitability is derived principally from savings in warranty costs and rework or rectification, and from enhanced marketability. The short-term impact is generally additional costs in setting up and operating the system (although savings may also be achieved in the short-term through more efficient working practices). There has to be an up-front investment to provide long-term profitability. The financial benefits are heralded in various British Standards, but without reference to the time lag between investment and return.

With environment, and also with health and safety, there have been suggestions that economic benefits will be achieved. For example, the ECI Report asserts that:[19]

> "As with all management and control there are up-front costs, both at a corporate and project level, associated with the introduction and implementation of SHE management. These highly visible costs are often seen as a barrier to implementation. However, it has been demonstrated that these 'costs' are more than offset by the 'hidden' benefits of planning and doing things right. The introduction of SHE management makes good business and commercial sense and is as much a part of the role of management as is the control of quality and productivity."

No source is quoted for the assertion of demonstrated offsets. Although there may be savings from environmental management, for example through energy saving, it is disingenuous and misleading to suggest that profitability is the objective or the justification. The Regulation itself makes clear that the objective is compliance with statutory or other legal requirements.

A more pragmatic appreciation appears a few pages later in the ECI Report where it highlights the resistance experienced when organizations find themselves subject to requirements which they had not allowed for in their costings:

> "Where SHE activities, and hence costs, are not explicit in the contractual arrangements, a SHE cost expectation gap is likely to arise during project execution. The SHE cost expectation gap represents the difference between the Client's SHE expectations and the SHE provisions priced by the contractor . . .
>
> In order to reflect accurately the project SHE requirements within the contract, the definition of contractual arrangements should be concurrent with the development of the project SHE plan."[20]

This advice is more difficult to follow where the requirements are imposed by legislation, but the acrimony created by the expectation gap is a matter for consideration in drafting construction contracts.

Other legal significance

There has been a tendency for the quality management movement to play down the contractual or legal significance of quality systems. Their motto

19 ECI Report, *op cit* at 39.

20 *Ibid* pp 40 and 43.

"right first time every time", if invariably fulfilled, would make the legal system redundant. All management systems do, however, have legal significance in two ways. Firstly, management systems generate documentary records which may be available as evidence in the event of a dispute. Secondly, the management system procedures may define what constitutes standards of skill and care or reasonable precautions, whether in contract or tort, or for the purpose of statutory requirements.

The legal significance of management system records generally and the need to plan their archiving with proper regard to limitation periods have been addressed elsewhere.[21] Environmental management systems are likely to have additional significance in relation to statutory requirements or arrangements.

For example, the Control of Pollution Act 1974, section 61 allows for prior consent to be granted by a local authority in regard to steps proposed to be taken to minimise noise resulting from construction works. This can avoid the risk of a prosecution under section 60, but it requires the contractor to plan his operations with regard to the environmental effect, noise, and then to control his operations in accordance with the plan.

A second example is the Environmental Protection Act 1990, section 34, which imposes a duty of care as respects waste. Section 35 allows for the grant of waste management licences subject to conditions, including the precautions to be taken.

A third example is the Building Regulations 1985, Clause D2, which requires that "Precautions shall be taken to avoid damage to health caused by substances found on or in the ground to be covered by the building."

The eco-management and audit Regulation and BS 7750: 1992 both make the point that environmental management systems are to be based on the relevant legal requirements, but the corollary is equally important. The significance of environmental management system procedures as a criterion of compliance with legal requirements and the danger of setting unnecessarily high or vague standards need to be understood when preparing the procedures, as does the significance of the records in establishing compliance or non-compliance.[22]

---

21 J Barber, *Quality Management in Construction—Contractual Aspects*, CIRIA Special Publication 84, 1992.

22 On the other hand, the defence of due skill and care may lose much of its significance if the EC Green Paper on Remedying Environmental Damage (93/C 149/08, OJ C149) is implemented, as that is based on strict liability.

11 Professional liability, risk transfer and contract documents

Michael Mendelblat

Introduction

What has gone before has largely been concerned with the impact on construction in the 1990s resulting from improved environmental protection through legislation and the application of common law. My talk fits into the section of proceedings relating to liabilities, remedies and policy, and my concern is to look at the various ways in which there will be an impact on professional liability, risk transfer, and contract documents. Obviously, these subjects are all intertwined. In basic terms, parties who may be liable for environmental damage will seek to transfer their risk to other parties to a transaction, the professionals involved, or to contractors. In any transaction, the vital element will be the commerciality of any proposed transfer of liability. Each party will also be concerned to ensure that, even where a commercial arrangement will permit transfer of liability, that liability is effectively passed on. Further, unless insurers will back the risk assumed by professionals, an obligation may be enforceable on paper only.

In many cases, the new environmental protection regime can be grafted on to current systems for allocation of risks without causing too many surprises. Indeed, the main pressure for change in this area has not been from new environmental legislation, but rather the courts' move against tortious liability which gathered pace from the mid 1980s onwards, reaching its culmination in the *Murphy* v *Brentwood*[1] and *DoE* v *Bates*[2] cases, following which parties not protecting themselves in contract were apparently without a remedy against builders for economic loss. Their only course was to seek to show reliance on another party's advice or blame professional advisers with whom they were in contract for not having protected them.

However, a trend which is likely to lead to a greater web of contractual liabilities, indemnities, etc., is the imposition of liability in novel situations. This may lead to a safety first approach. For example, the enquiry before

---

The assistance of Gordon Wood, FRICS, AMI MinE, of Messrs. Johnson Poole & Bloomer, is acknowledged by the author.

1 [1990] 3 WLR 414.

2 [1990] 3 WLR 457.

contract received by a colleague of mine, which asked whether any waste was to be kept on the premises, was met by reference to the extensive system of litter bins throughout the office! Clearly, parties must take a realistic appraisal of their potential liability, but you will have already heard enough of the *Cambridge Water* case from others to reach the conclusion that the unthinkable sometimes needs to be thought—and often well in advance of the commercial working out of a transaction.

Scope of liability

To begin with some basic principles on professional liability, I first refer to general principles, and then to some illustrations of potential new liability under recent statutory developments. I do not comment in detail on the common law actions of nuisance, negligence, *Rylands* v *Fletcher*, or trespass, as I propose to concentrate primarily on professionals' liability to their employers.

Had I prepared this paper three months ago, I would have said that a professional should have no difficulty in identifying, usually by name, those for whose loss he is or may be liable in contract. He is liable to those who employ him, or to whom he has given a collateral warranty. The latter may constitute a class; for example, purchasers of property. However, in July, the House of Lords decided the *Linden Gardens* and *St. Martin's*[3] cases. These related to contractors, but I think that their reasoning is equally applicable to professionals. In a situation where a contract of employment for works in relation to a large development prohibits assignment, a professional may be liable for breaches of contract to his employer for both his own loss and that sustained by later owners who could not themselves sue him. This was described as an exception to the general rule restricting recovery to the employer's own loss. It only applies, it seems, to breaches occurring after the sale. So, the professional has a dilemma as to whether to prohibit assignment, leading to exposure to purchasers' claims, or allow it with a view at least to knowing who will claim from him.

Specific aspects of the decision will need to be worked out in further cases, *e.g.* what is a "large development"—is it a crucial requirement and are only costs of remedial works covered as opposed to consequential losses? Must a subsequent owner be freehold? Is knowledge of the purchase by the professional a precondition?

It comes as some surprise to find that the law of contract may now be less predictable than the law of tort on this front. A professional's duty to take

---

3 [1993] 3 All ER 147.

reasonable care will arise in tort if, firstly, it is foreseeable that if his advice is negligent, the recipient will suffer damage; secondly, where there is a sufficiently proximate or close relationship between the parties; and, thirdly, where it is just and reasonable to impose liability. Foreseeability alone is not enough.

A duty of care will readily be found to exist where there has been injury to persons or to property which is not part of the structure in respect of which the professional was engaged. Otherwise, unless special circumstances apply, the professional will not owe a duty of care to avoid economic loss. Special circumstances may include those where a third party is known to an adviser to have relied on his advice in relation to a particular transaction. Further, there are other special cases where such a duty has been found which are less relevant to the present topic, such as surveyors' liability for a house purchaser's survey to the purchaser of a modest property, as in *Smith* v *Bush*[4] or liability of solicitors to beneficiaries of wills, as in *White* v *Jones*.[5] In both these types of cases, the Defendant knew or ought to have known the identity of the Plaintiff(s) and the implication of his actions in relation to the transaction affecting the Plaintiff's interests.

To illustrate these principles, the recent case of *Preston* v *Torfaen Borough Council & Others*[6] concerned a soils investigation report prepared by a surveyor for a local authority seven years before a purchase of a house from it. The purchasers never saw it, and the surveyor could not have expected them to rely on it, save as part of a general category of potential purchasers. Thus, there was no recovery for economic loss in tort, as no reliance by those Plaintiffs in respect of that transaction could be spelt out, nor was the case in any special category as in the *Smith* and *White* cases.

Further, the professional may rely on the *Greater Nottingham*[7] and *Tai Hing*[8] cases to the effect that if he has contracted with another party, he will not be liable in tort to any greater measure than that he has contracted for, save insofar as required by statute, but I comment below[9] on a "sting in the tail" on this. He is also entitled to expect that the courts will not incorporate clauses into the contract by which he is employed unless to do so is necessary.

On the other hand, he may be unwise to rely too far on exclusions within his terms of employment. Not surprisingly, if he purports to exclude all

4 *Smith* v. *Eric S. Bush, Harris & Another* v. *Wyre Forest District Council & Another* [1990] 1 AC 831, HL.

5 [1993] All ER 481.

6 (1993) 65 BLR 1.

7 [1989] QB 71.

8 [1986] AC 80.

9 See below under "Contributory Negligence".

liability to set off against fees claimed for the consequences of breaches of his duty of skill and care, then, following *Gill* v *Meyer*,[10] he can expect to have such a clause struck down under the provisions of the Unfair Contract Terms Act. This is more likely to be relevant to a sub-contractor or supplier than a professional, but is still a salutary lesson.

The professional may wish to keep his advice confidential and may well provide that it is for the use solely of the person to whom it is supplied. He might be wise to be told as little as possible about the purpose of his investigation, as the *Caparo*[11] and *Smith*[12] cases indicate that if his advice is for the purpose of being released to an identifiable person or persons and they could be expected to rely on it for a transaction of a particular kind, then he may be liable to them. So that, if he produces a site investigation report, and sees a distribution list comprising six prospective tenants, it is at least possible that all those tenants might claim that the professional knew that they were relying on his advice. Following *Smith*,[13] it may be that, to establish a duty of care, it would need to be shown that knowledge of such reliance was "in some way brought home to him". Further, his advice may reach unexpected persons taking advantage of the Environmental Information Regulations 1992. Others have summarised their impact, but I only say here that, whilst I think it most unlikely that a professional could assume liability to a class of persons who benefit under these Regulations (which is obviously unlimited both as for numbers and purposes), that does not rule out the nuisance value action in a catastrophe situation.

Guidance

In general, the professional's main routes to liability today will be through his terms of employment and/or collateral warranties he gives to funders/tenants/purchasers, *etc.* In the case of both documents of this type, he will almost certainly be obliged to exercise reasonable skill and care, and will be so obliged by statute, if not by express terms. Environmental publications in some areas giving currently authoritative guidance will clearly have an impact on the standard of skill and care, and I refer below to some examples which are material in this regard to present and future cases:

Investigations, assessments and development of contaminated land

(1) ICRCL Committee on Land Reclamation, Second Edition, July 1987.

10 31 Con LR 2.

11 [1990] 2 AC 605.

12 N 4 above.

13 N 4 above.

(2) BSI Draft for Development DD 175 for Identification of Potentially Contaminated Land and its Investigation—1988.
(3) Institution of Environmental Health Officers Guidance on Development of Contaminated Land—1989.
(4) Scottish Enterprise Handbook on Development of Contaminated Land—January 1993.
(5) Department of the Environment Waste Management Paper No. 27.

The above do not constitute a single definitive code of practice, and the BSI "Draft for Development" states that it is to be applied on a provisional basis only. Therefore, ground investigation specialists must take account of all the above and other relevant specialist publications when considering investigation and treatment of contaminated land. As an example, the ICRCL guidance does not cover either the full range of contaminants which may be encountered or all proposed uses, thus requiring the designer to consider site-specific solutions. Dutch guidelines (the "ABC" values) may appear to fill the gap in some cases, but are regarded by some experts as too onerous and/or of limited applicability to the UK in view of the different geology of that country. This would suggest that the designer should approach them with great caution and beware of unnecessary over-specification.

Groundwater protection

- NRA Policy and Practice for the Protection of Ground Water. See policy D3. and commentary on page 31.

Water disposal

- Code of Practice on Waste issued by DoE under section 34 Environmental Protection Act 1990—see especially page 4, paragraphs 16 & 17 and page 6, paragraph 30.

The professional can expect that his employer and the courts will have regard to documents such as the above when considering whether he has complied with the requisite standard of skill and care. Not all material documents are primarily aimed at the professional. What if, for example, he encourages his client to promote a planning application or appeal without having proper regard to guidance on the correct method of dealing with landfill gas? DoE Circular 21/87 makes it clear that responsibility for assessing whether land is suitable for a particular purpose rests primarily with the developer[14] and thus he will look to the professional for assistance

14 See especially paragraph 3 of the Annex.

on this. A professional failing to have due regard to current standards might expect a prospective developer to turn on him, should a planning appeal fail,[15] on the assumption that his failure was such as to indicate a departure from commonly expected standards of skill and care. Greater environmental awareness must surely mean more stringent examination of planning proposals, which in turn indicates that professionals are more likely to shoulder the blame (on the usual "deep pocket" principle), should an appeal be dismissed on purely technical grounds.

Health and safety

Another area where the professional may encounter an unwelcome additional element of liability is that of health and safety. As a general proposition, I think that professionals can increasingly expect to find themselves the subject of claims for recovery of criminal penalties. This is a difficult area. A contract to pay another's criminal penalties would, as such, be unenforceable as against public policy, but I think that if, on normal contractual principles, it could be said that at the time that a contract was entered into the parties must have contemplated that the professional would be liable for reimbursement of criminal penalties if caused by breach of his duty of skill and care, then reimbursement may be allowable if the employer did not act intentionally or was not culpably negligent (*Osman* v *J Ralph Moss)*.[16] This argument may be more firmly based where there has been an indemnity, since then there will be liability for all damage caused by the acts of a professional. As the net in health and safety areas is being more widely cast, as to which see for example the *Derby City Council* case where the client was prosecuted, then the issue of reimbursement of criminal penalties may become more relevant.

A more specific area where health and safety issues will impact is the Draft Construction (Design and Management) Regulations and Approved Code of Practice (see HSE Consultative Document 51). Their principal impact is that the responsibility for site health and safety would now be not just that of the contractor but also of the client and designer. The client's obligations are, as proposed, to be non-delegable but of course, as a matter of contract, the clients may place the obligation for their implementation on the professional, even though the client must in the first place be liable for any penalties resulting from contravention. In particular, the need to provide the planning supervisor with information about the state or condi-

15 See for example of failure on these grounds DoE decision 89/130168.

16 [1970] 1 Lloyd's Rep 313.

tion of any premises or land at or on which construction works need to be carried out, is clearly apt to be fulfilled in practice by a professional. Indeed, the planning supervisor is likely to be drawn from the design team.

Designers themselves have duties under the Regulations, in particular as follows:

(1) To ensure that their designs do not expose those building, maintaining, cleaning, or repairing the structure to risk to health and safety.
(2) To ensure that their designs include adequate information about any aspect of the designs which might affect the health and safety of any person carrying out construction work.

Each of these obligations will be directly actionable against the designer by way of criminal prosecution and endure for the duration of a project. Designers' brief within the scope of their professional responsibility (but otherwise irrespective of their terms of appointment) will therefore extend to risks they can reasonably foresee in respect of future work to the structure and the only limitation is as to work such as alteration or demolition which is too remote from the circumstances of the original design. Further, they cannot rely on an employer and/or contractor to build their design safely irrespective of cost and time. They must minimise risks as far as reasonably practicable at the design stage. If a designer is also planning supervisor, he remains responsible throughout the project for ensuring that cost and time allow all personnel working on the project to comply with relevant health and safety provisions. This may lead to a reassessment on such factors before contemplating any major variation order.

However, at the time of writing, implementation of the Regulations has been delayed to January 1995, and a revised draft will be produced.

New statutory provisions

Some of the new statutory provisions discussed by other speakers may also have an impact on professional liability, for example, section 161 of the Water Resources Act 1991. This provides for the National Rivers Authority to carry out clean-up works in a case where poisonous, noxious or polluting matter, or any solid waste matter, is either likely to enter, or to be or to have been present in controlled waters, and to be entitled to recover the expenses reasonably incurred from any person who caused or knowingly permitted the matter to be present at the place from which it was likely to enter controlled waters, or caused or knowingly permitted it to be present in any controlled waters. The definition of "caused or knowingly permitted" is of course a difficult one in law as is indicated by cases on the topic arising under the parallel criminal provisions of the Act (s85), *e.g.* *Wychavon DC* v *NRA*[17] and *NRA* v *Welsh Development Agency*.[18]

The former case decided that the definition of "cause" is such that liability will only arise from a positive or deliberate act. In the latter case the Agency having designed an industrial estate was held not to be liable for causing pollution from a tenant's factory since it was not the Agency's act which was the direct cause of pollution. The cause was a leaking seal on a pipe which it was the tenant's responsibility to maintain. Presumably, the employer—or even a professional employed by him—could be in a different position if the professional either:

(1) gave a site instruction during works which would inevitably lead to pollution ("caused") or observed and agreed to work proceeding with the same result ("knowingly permitted"); or
(2) designed a permanent (or temporary) drainage system for waste from works, which would lead to the same result and directed it to be used so as to lead to pollution ("caused"). It should, however, be noted that temporary works are usually the contractor's responsibility.

Could the agency, if found guilty, have sued the designer to recover the loss it sustained through fines? I think this is possible, as the agency would have been convicted on the basis of its own positive act, but that only consisted of approving or not objecting to its designers' acts. So, it was not itself culpably negligent nor were its acts intentional.

However, one drawback of section 161, so far as the NRA is concerned, is that it must spend the money first, and then try and reclaim it. I understand that the NRA in at least one recent case is considering going by way of civil action in nuisance or trespass, and it is worth noting that this section specifically provides that nothing in it derogates from any right or action or other remedy, whether civil or criminal, or proceedings issued otherwise under the section. Of course, there may and will be cases where clean-up cannot wait, so that the NRA will pay first and ask questions afterwards. The NRA might also seek an injunction based on repeated contravention of section 85 of the Water Resources Act, the parallel criminal provision, against future discharge.

The professional might at first sight also be wary of the reference to "duty of care" in section 34 of the Environmental Protection Act 1990.

17 *The Independent*, 9 September 1992.
18 Potts, J., unreported, 10 December 1992 (C01911/91).

However, this phrase does not connote tortious liability, as the remedy provided for by the section (subsection 6) is criminal. The duty is to take all such measures applicable to a person in certain capacities to:

(1) Prevent contravention of section 33 of the Act (unauthorised or harmful deposit, treatment or disposal of waste).
(2) Prevent escape of waste from his control or that of any other person.
(3) On transfer of the waste, to secure that it is to an authorised person and with an appropriate written description.

A person is in the relevant capacity if he imports, produces, carries, keeps, treats, disposes or has control as a broker of waste. Again, it is not inconceivable that a professional might directly be liable for contravention, although DoE guidance indicates this is doubtful.[19] A contractor almost certainly will be, as he may find himself producing, disposing of or acting as a broker for controlled waste.[20] An employer may also be liable; *e.g.* as a broker in respect of transfer between contractors. Perhaps more important to the professional is the prospect that his client may look to him to take all such measures as are reasonable in the circumstances to ensure compliance by contractors with the duty of care. These may include a greater level of site regulation and supervision, so as to prevent the contravention by any other person (*e.g.* an unlicensed manager or carrier) of section 33 of the Act. He may also need to ensure that the waste does not escape from the control of the contractor or of any other person. He may be particularly concerned where the client acts as broker for waste (for example, by letting a disposal sub-contract) to see on transfer that the transfer is only to an authorised person, and that the written description of the waste is transferred.

The client himself may escape liability if he is not directly concerned with the broking, production or the management of the waste. He will, however, expect the professional to ensure the smooth running of the site by avoiding any danger of contravention of the duty of care. No doubt, in due course, WRAs will seek to use injunctive remedies to prevent the regular contravention of the duty of care on a badly managed site. Again, this may impact on the employer, and from him to the professional.

Although the new RIBA Conditions (SFA/92) seek to exclude architects' responsibility for contractors' management and operational methods, the potential for liability of clients as brokers and disruption from WRAs

19 See para. 17, Circular 19/91.
20 See para. 17, Circular 19/91.

dissatisfied with disposal methods may lead clients to make special provisions for inspection in their terms of appointment.

Another section which may be of relevance to the professional is section 61 of the Environmental Protection Act 1990 (if and when eventually enacted). This is in some ways parallel to the NRA's powers under section 161 of the Water Resources Act 1991 in that it provides for a clean-up and then repayment approach. Effectively, the WRA has a duty in respect of land in such a condition as being likely to cause pollution to the environment or harm to human health by reason of certain factors. These are concentration or accumulation in, and emission or discharge from, the land of noxious gases or noxious liquids caused by deposits of controlled waste in the land. The WRA must do such works and take other steps as appear to the authority to be reasonable to avoid such pollution or harm. Then, they may recover the costs from the person who is for the time being the owner of the land, except such of the costs as that person shows was incurred unreasonably. They must, however, have regard to any hardship which the recovery may cause to the owner of the land.

One can envisage a situation where a professional is instructed to carry out a series of site investigations on prospective development sites. Should he consider that any site is in a condition such as to justify (in the reasonable waste regulation authority's mind) action under section 61, I suggest that it must be his duty to advise his client accordingly and to warn him of the dangers of keeping the land in the condition he finds it, even if he did not cause it to be in that state. Once the section comes into force, not to do so would, I suggest, be regarded as negligent, and the client should be advised of the scope of necessary remedial measures which he must take, unless he would prefer the WRA to take them at (for all he knows) enhanced cost.

However, at present, with section 61 not being in force, it is difficult to forecast how it may operate, and the guidance given by the Secretary of State as to the discharge of the hardship condition may need careful attention.

Finally, in this short survey of statutory provisions, I draw your attention to section 73(6) of the 1990 Act, which is a provision placing civil liability for damage caused by any person who deposits waste, or knowingly caused or knowingly permitted it to be deposited so as to commit an offence under section 33 of the Act (prohibition of non-authorised or harmful deposit, treatment or disposal of waste) or section 63(2) of the Act, which refers to other than controlled waste. It is wider than its predecessor (section 88 of the Control of Pollution Act 1974) which referred to "poisonous, noxious or polluting" waste. Again, this uses the by now over-familiar "knowingly caused" or "knowingly permitted" wording, but I think it not inconceivable that professionals might be covered by it.

Limitation of liability

Professionals may of course seek to protect themselves by limitation of liability, and I have already commented on the court's refusal to countenance a clause whereby the professional effectively exonerates himself from liability against fee claims. However, there are other less drastic ways in which the professional may seek to reduce his liability for, for example, the following:

No greater obligation or no greater liability clause

The professional may seek to limit either his scope of liability or the amount of damages he will pay, or both, when giving a warranty to a party other than his original employer. In many cases, the wording only relates to the scope of liability, rather than the quantum of damages, and a more effective approach may be to consider the type of damage for which the professional is to be liable; for example, including the cost of remedial works, but excluding consequential loss.

The "State of the Art" defence

The professional must exercise reasonable skill and care, having regard to the state of knowledge available to the general body of practitioners at the time of his acts. It may be difficult to assess responsibility in a field where no authoritative guidance is available. Take, for example, the present published documentation in relation to identification and treatment of contaminated land. I drew attention earlier[21] to a number of publications, of which one is a BSI Draft for Development. That draft, drawn up in 1988, has not been finalised. The preface states that it must be applied on a provisional basis only. So, there is no finalised Code or British Standard. If there had been, there is authority to the effect that British Standards or Codes of Practice must not be slavishly followed, but referred to the project in hand. However, due weight must be given to their contents, and failure to observe them is often regarded as indicative of failure to exercise reasonable skill and care. Where an area is developing, a designer must take into account all generally available professional knowledge at the time of the act. This is sometimes referred to as the "state of the art" defence, but is perhaps better regarded as an aspect of the duty to exercise reasonable skill and care.

---

21 See above under "Investigations, *etc.* of Contaminated Land".

Net contribution

This type of clause seeks to mitigate the effect of joint and several liability and comes in numerous forms, but each with the common intention that the professional pays no more than what would be his proper share, if all the relevant parties were before the court. Some variants require the client to sue to judgment all parties who may be liable for the consequences of a particular event. Alternatively, the warranty may not come into force unless other professionals or contractors have entered into warranties of similar effect. Other forms may require the client to take the risk of insolvency of one or more of the other parties to the extent that they may have been liable between themselves.

Such clauses find their place in the BPF forms of warranty and are, of course, commonly insisted upon by insurers, so as to avoid the "deep pocket" effect, particularly where professionals are the only party left standing after the insolvency of contractors and sub-contractors. They would certainly assist the professional in the event, for example, of liability to the client by reason of the "clean-up and recover" type of provision, or breach of the duty of care as regards treatment, etc., of waste. However, their usefulness should not be over-stated, as they are only intended to cut down recovery where liability is properly that of more than one party. In an initial investigation situation, only one party would be involved although others might eventually come on board, for example, the type of situation I mentioned earlier in relation to section 61 of the Environmental Protection Act, where the professional is carrying out a series of site investigations to be incorporated in tender documentation. In the light of this, I think that the client should be loathe to agree to the type of clause which prevents recovery altogether, unless other parties give warranties. This, surely, is an example of using a sledgehammer to crack a nut, as then the client could be left without remedy, even if his claim was solely for a design fault.

Risk transfer

I have already suggested that the likelihood of professionals to be subject to claims arising from the increasing burden of environmental legislation can be expected to lead to a more searching consideration of standard terms of employment. Clients may press for all-embracing definitions of scope of work but subject to non-exclusive lists of specific design and/or supervision obligations.

I now turn to two related questions:

(1) Other recourses of the client beyond seeking recourse from professionals.
(2) Possible liability of professionals to, and recourse from, other parties.

The first question raises a number of subsidiary issues. It is not my intention to deal with remedies arising from the property elements of a transaction, as I am considering only aspects of recovery in the construction documentation. However, in passing, I think it would be as well to remind you of the implications of the *Cambridge Water Company*[22] decision. The tort of nuisance has clearly not exhausted its usefulness where damage to adjoining property is concerned. Thus, there will be liability for pollution of an aquifer by another party, even if that pollution was not deliberate and, at the time that it took place, probably not such as to breach then applicable standards. In the light of this, it must be prudent for any purchaser to seek such indemnities as he can in respect of earlier use of the property from his vendor. In practice, save for an obviously polluting (and very recently ceased) use, such indemnities are likely to be both uninsurable and unavailable. Remedies in tort against those on the design or construction team originally responsible will almost certainly be equally unavailable, which must of course lead to the need to identify, so far as is possible, the potential of a "Brownfield" site for future pollution.

By contrast, another line of authority (see, for example, the *Stephens* v *Anglian Water Authority*[23] case) indicates that abstraction of water freely percolating under the owner's land is not actionable, even if subsidence is caused to an adjoining owner's land by such action. In both cases, the Plaintiff benefited from the exercise of a natural right. Even so, the lack of deliberate action in the defendant's actions in the *Cambridge* case seems a valid distinction from the older cases; *e.g. Ballard* v *Tomlinson*.[24] However, at present, landowners cannot regard that as a useful distinction, unless and until the House of Lords rule otherwise.

Recourse from the contractor and others

Contract documents

If, owing to an inadequate investigation, soil and ground conditions in, for example, a contaminated or former landfill site are found to be worse than

22 Court of Appeal, 19 November 1992—See also postscript.
23 [1987] 1 WLR 1381.
24 (1885) 29 Ch.D 115.

originally thought and a contract takes longer, costing more, then an employer will seek to blame the investigating professional, but at the same time he will be trying to resist claims from his contractor for delay and the cost of variations.

Whether he can do so will of course turn on the construction of the particular contract. For example, the ICE 6th Edition Conditions state that the contractor is deemed to have inspected the site and to have satisfied himself as to its form and nature, including the ground and subsoil. Without more, these words were held in the Australian case of *Dillingham* v *Downs*[25] to protect the employer where he supplied part but not all of the site information available to him. The information was misleading but not, in itself, incorrect. It was not implied that the information was complete or exhaustive. A duty to supply full information could only arise if such responsibility was accepted by the employer or the contractor relied on him to do so. Such a duty would not normally arise if tender documents were silent as to ground conditions.

However, a new sub-clause in the ICE Conditions (6th Edition) (11(1)) operates so as to correct this by providing that the employer is deemed to have made available all information on the ground and the subsoil obtained by him. The effect (perhaps not the drafting intention) appears to be to prevent the employer hiding behind non-disclosure and to allow the contractor to take the benefit of undisclosed information if he can establish that the employer had this prior to tender.

The responsibility for interpreting such information is the contractor's – which may be a limited duty if some or all of the employer's reports are interpretative.

Further, Clause 11(3) provides that the contractor is deemed to have based his tender on information made available by the Employer – presumably, this must refer to actual information, not "deemed" (but unavailable) information, as referred to in Clause 11(1).

The JCT Standard Form Contract contains no warranty on the employer's part as to feasibility of the project. However, at Clause 14, it provides that the quantity of the work is deemed to be that set out in the Contract bills. In the event of discrepancy, the contractor must therefore rely on his entitlement to variation instructions. However, in at least one case relating to the design and build form, *Bacal* v *Northampton Development Corporation,*[26] the court implied a warranty that ground conditions would correspond with those contained in tender documents.

25 13 BLR 97.
26 8 BLR 88.

Perhaps today the case would be decided in terms of reliance but it seems to me exceptional since the standard form had been amended to prevent any amendment to the contractor's design (for whatever reason) from ranking as a variation. In any event, Bills or Employers' Requirements will often contain disclaimers as to the accuracy of ground or soil information.

The ICE Conditions go on to allow the contractor, at Clause 12, a measure of recovery for conditions which an experienced contractor could not have reasonably foreseen.

The New Engineering Contract ("NEC") at Clause 60.1 (12) only allows recovery for conditions which, at the contract date, an experienced contractor would have judged to have such a small chance of occurring that it would have been unreasonable for him to have allowed for them. In judging ground conditions, the contractor is assumed under the NEC to have taken into account the site information provided to him and other information he could reasonably have been expected to have obtained.

The ICE Conditions may contain a conflict between Clauses 11(3) and 12 if the former is taken to be relevant to the extent to which a contractor should have foreseen ground conditions. However, the combined effect may be that knowledge of *actual* conditions ascertainable from information supplied to him (even if beyond a reasonable contractor's foresight) must be imported to the contractor. Both ICE Clause 12 and NEC Clause 60.1 (12) seem to me to be directed to ensure that actual conditions are taken into account, but that the contractor's foresight is seen objectively.

Guidance notes suggest that one less confrontational approach would be to adopt a boundary line between employer's and contractor's risk in terms of stated criteria; for example, as to the extent of groundwater levels to be encountered. This may only rarely be practicable; say, in the event of a site comprehensively investigated prior to tender.

Contributory negligence

I now turn to discuss the *Barclays Bank* v *Fairclough*[27] case, which is an incident of liability arising from methods of working in disposal of hazardous substances. There are two areas where the case is of interest. Firstly, on contributory negligence, which may serve to reduce contractors' liability.

The contractor had been employed to carry out cleaning works on the roof of the bank's records store which was made of corrugated asbestos

27 Unreported, 13 May 1993; Judgment reversed by Court of Appeal on 6 May 1994 holding Fairclough 100% liable on the basis that there were concurrent breaches of an absolute nature. Leave to appeal was refused by the CA but a petition to the HL is pending.

cement sheeting. The bank contracted with Fairclough, who in turn sublet the work down a chain. The work was eventually sub-sublet to a contractor located by the simple means of looking him up in the Yellow Pages. He was described as an industrial cleaner, which was of importance on another point.[28]

The court found that Fairclough were in breach of a term that they should execute the works with reasonable care and skill. They could and should have taken simple and relatively inexpensive precautions to prevent contaminated water and debris entering the building. The work resulted in contamination of the bank's documents by asbestos dust.

However, at trial the bank's claim was not pleaded in tort with a view to avoiding a finding of contributory negligence. The Law Reform (Contributory Negligence) Act 1945 only relates to tortious claims, so the result was the ungainly spectacle of Fairclough saying that they were liable in tort and the bank saying that they were not! The court found that there was liability in tort because the damage was to "other property" of the bank; namely, its files. The object of the contract was, in fact, performed as the roof was cleaned. The court held that although there were duties in contract, a duty of care in tort could exist so far as personal injury or damage to other property was concerned. Contributory negligence will therefore be applicable to claims which could be brought in both contract and tort but not if the defendant's liability arises from some contractual provision which does not depend on negligence on the part of the defendant. The defendants were to comply with all statutory provisions and had failed to comply with the Asbestos Regulations, which might at first sight appear to be breach of a contractual provision in terms of "strict liability". However, the court decided that such failures, coupled with the contractor's knowledge that he should have taken reasonable precautions, also constituted failure to exercise reasonable skill and care; hence attracting the finding of contributory negligence.

The court held that the bank was itself the architect under the contract, and could and should have secured that proper precautions were carried out by drawing the contractor's attention to dangers in their system of work. Their negligence resulted in a 40% reduction in damages. The case may leave open the issue of whether contributory negligence is available for pure economic loss cases assuming there is concurrent liability in contract and tort. In the *Fairclough* case, the point did not need to be decided. However, His Honour Judge Havery referred to a passage from the judgment of Mr. Justice Hobhouse in *Vesta* v *Butcher*:[29]

---

28 See below under "Recourse from Other Parties".

29 [1986] 2All ER 488.

"Where the Defendant's liability arises from a contractual obligation which is expressed in terms of taking care (or its equivalent) but does not correspond to a common law duty to take care which would exist in the given case independently of contract."

This is a definition of a situation where that judge held that contributory negligence may be applicable.

Such authority as there is seems to me to suggest that, where there would be no duty of care independently of any contract but the contract requires the exercise of skill and care, it is possible for there to be contributory negligence. I do not read the *Vesta* case in the Court of Appeal as having decided this point, and I suggest that if concurrent liabilities exist in contract and tort only by virtue of the existence of the contract, that is still sufficient to attract contributory negligence as being within Mr. Justice Hobhouse's definition in *Vesta*. It is true that the Court of Appeal in *Vesta*[30] approved an earlier New Zealand case to the effect that concurrent liability in contract is "immaterial", but surely this means that such liability need not be taken into account, rather than that the associated tortious liability is to be ignored. Some support for this may be found from a further passage in the *Barclays Bank* judgment:

"In my judgment, it is clear beyond argument that the expression 'act or omission which give rise to a liability in tort' [which is taken from the 1945 Act] includes acts or omissions which only in the particular circumstances, *e.g.* knowledge, give rise to a liability in tort."

Local authorities

As to other parties from whom the client might seek recourse, the scope of recovery against local authorities for failure to ensure compliance with Building Regulations has of course been drastically reduced in the light of the House of Lords' decision in *Murphy* v *Brentwood*,[31] to which I referred earlier, and is now restricted (at most) to liability for personal injury or damage to other property. However, as before, liability for negligent misstatement may yet be relevant, for example in the case of disclosure of misleading information, and might have been relevant had contaminated land registers under section 143 of the Environmental Protection Act come into force as proposed. In keeping with the trend of restricting tortious liability, claims in respect of the allegedly negligent grant of planning permission will not be allowed to proceed—see *Ryeford Homes* v *Sevenoaks District Council*.[32]

30 [1988] 3 WLR 565.
31 [1990] 3 WLR 414.
32 [1990] 6 Const LJ 170.

Possible liability of professionals to, and recourse from, other parties

In the absence of a contract, a professional's liability to or from other parties involved will be determined by the Civil Liability (Contribution) Act 1978. There may be liability for contribution as between professionals and, say, contractors, if both are liable to the employer. However, there may also be direct liability. Consider the not uncommon case where a professional's appointment is novated to a contractor. If it is to be the case that the contractor largely takes responsibility for site conditions, and the novation provides that the professional will be liable to the contractor for all breaches of duty of skill and care connected with the project, even if pre-novation, then a professional may be liable to the contractor for any failings in respect of an initial site investigation, even though at the time he was not employed by the contractor.

However, one can foresee more difficult problems for the contractor in deciding whom to proceed against if, by pursuing the professional, he has to maintain that the professional failed to spot the obvious, whereas as against the employer in terms of, say, the New Engineering Contract he may wish to maintain that he discounted a risk so small that no reasonable contractor would be concerned with it!

The operation of the Civil Liability (Contribution) Act 1978 requires an assessment of responsibility between defendants liable to the plaintiff for the same damage. In practice, the role of professionals and contractors may be easy to split in design terms but less so where overlap relates to operational matters for which a contractor may need to be carefully supervised by the professional.

This may be particularly relevant in the area of hazardous operations, such as was the case in the *Barclays Bank* v *Fairclough* case to which I previously referred, although the third party proceedings in that case were between sub-contractors who were the second and third layers in the contractual chain. Had the matter been by way of contribution, the judge's remarks are perhaps illustrative in showing a reluctance to extend "skilled knowledge" too far down that chain. The party eventually responsible for asbestos removal was a firm of industrial cleaners, who were sub-sub-contractors to a company which traded in general building maintenance, located by the simple method of looking up the category in the Yellow Pages. The actual work was done by their sub-sub-sub-contractor, also described as "industrial cleaners".

The judge said:

> "It is by no means obvious to me that the skill generally commanded by industrial cleaners includes a knowledge that high-pressured jetting may remove asbestos in

> sufficient concentrations to cause risk of injury to health . . . There is no evidence that industrial cleaners or specifically those undertaking the work of cleaning asbestos cement roofs will generally have the skill or knowledge in relation to the avoidance of health hazards generated by asbestos which I accept exist in the building industry . . . I do not understand [an expert's] reference to the building industry to be intended to extend to persons who carried out industrial cleaning on buildings."

Reversing up the contractual chain, perhaps the judge's view would have been different if even the industrial cleaners had had the benefit of a proper approach to safety policy applied by the employer.

The future

Finally, I turn to the DTI report of the Advisory Committee on Business and the Environment. The purpose of the report was to seek the views of lenders, industry and insurers on environmental liability. Two proposals may be of relevance to professionals' and contractors' liability. A "state of the art" defence was proposed to add to current defences to civil claims or prosecutions by regulatory authorities, for example as in section 85 of the Water Resources Act 1991. The effect of such a defence may not be dissimilar to that applicable to professional liability, but would, if applied, presumably cut down the scope of claims against employers, even in what is now a strict liability situation, although at present the "state of the art" issue is more commonly decided as between employer and professional.

The question of retrospective liability was also considered, in particular in the context of the position of the current owner of a polluted site which is harming third parties, even though the pollution was caused by a predecessor. He may be liable in nuisance if, knowing of its existence, he fails to take any reasonable steps to bring it to an end. Under section 61 of the Environmental Protection Act 1990, he may be liable in more limited circumstances (see above)[33] if the land is liable to cause pollution to the environment or harm to human health for the Waste Regulation Authority's costs of avoiding such pollution or harm. His right of action against a predecessor may be limited.

The Committee doubted whether current owners should be liable under statute for activities which were lawful at the time, and appeared to suggest a dilution of section 61 by distinguishing between innocent owners of polluted sites, and long-term owners whose original activities, whilst lawful at the time, resulted in pollution. Advisers to long-term owners presumably could raise a "state of the art" defence in respect of activities lawful at the

33 See above under "New Statutory Provisions".

time. However, the position would be different if they were retained to review sites on a periodic basis, as they would then need to review their advice in the light of changing statutory and advisory material becoming available.

It is worth noting that the committee was divided on strict liability with industry strongly against and lenders/insurers not fundamentally opposed but seeking a set of supporting rules, of which the above are two examples.

Conclusion

To sum up, I think that whilst the scope of professionals' liability in tort has, on the face of it, been greatly limited in recent years. There are indications from *Linden Gardens*[2] that judicial policy in this respect may have turned an unexpected contractual corner, which may once again widen the scope of potential liability. Opinion is presently divided as to whether collateral warranties remain the best method of adjusting risks; on the other hand, I think that it is still true to say that professionals should at least be able to anticipate who will sue them, but not necessarily for how much.

So far as liability of professionals in the environmental field is concerned, I have drawn attention to several areas where greater legislative and regulatory burdens may give rise to wider exposure of professionals to claims. The same may apply if the *Cambridge Water*[34] case is part of a trend to greater potential liability on the part of landowners at common law. In any event, the potential for future claims will surely be determined by the extent to which landowners and professionals' employers find themselves liable for environmental damage. The managing director of RICS Insurance Services presumably had this in mind when making his forthright comment in July 1993:

> "The underwriters of professional indemnity are determined that PI isn't going to be the vehicle which pays for the clean-up costs of this country."

However, this may suggest a separate trend for advice on, say, contaminated land issues to be confined to specialists, perhaps within a more general practice.

34 Court of Appeal, 19 November 1992—see also postscript.

12 Use of dangerous materials—the duty to warn and other problems

Philip Naughton

Dangerous materials

In this paper "dangerous materials" means substances or assemblies which are dangerous in themselves or which are capable of becoming dangerous or giving rise to a danger. And a "danger" is a risk of significant injury to a person.

In the construction industry, such materials fall into a number of categories which include:

(a) Substances which are inherently dangerous such as asbestos, mercury, phenols, radioactive materials. Generally their use is restricted and controlled by regulation—such as the Control of Asbestos Regulations 1987.
(b) Substances, or accumulations of substances which are dangerous because of their specific use or application or location, such as toughened glass windows in a skyscraper or liquid nitrogen stored in bulk.
(c) Substances or components which become dangerous or cause danger as a result of a change in conditions, for example by water penetration. High Alumina Cement is an example.

Scope of paper

The implications of using dangerous materials in construction are too widespread to be comprehensively addressed in one paper or even, perhaps, one book. Everyone connected with a building or structure may be involved—the specifier, designer, contractor, subcontractor, employer, owner, tenant, insurer. National and international regulations apply or may apply to the different parties. Obligations may arise as a result of contract, tort, nuisance or statutory duty. Issues of limitation of action and statutory restriction of attempts to exclude liability may be applicable.

The principal topic which will be covered concerns the long term obligations of the parties particularly as to the steps, if any, which might need to be taken if it is discovered that a dangerous material (as defined above) has been incorporated into a building. An obvious example is the discovery of the incorporation of a material such as crocidolite (blue asbestos) in the fabric of a public building.

The initial use and incorporation of dangerous materials is generally covered by regulation. Non-compliance with regulation and statute may give rise to a risk of prosecution as well as a risk of a civil claim. Generally, the application of the criminal law to the use of materials will not be covered. Again, the use of dangerous materials as a part of a manufacturing process is outside the scope of this paper.

The use of dangerous materials

The history of the use of asbestos in the manufacture of plant and the construction of buildings provides a good example. Asbestos was a particularly valuable building material. It was not inflammable, it was easily worked and could provide excellent insulation both on its own and in combination with other materials. It could also be employed to provide lightweight strong panels and to improve wear in floors and in the manufacture of brakes and other friction devices. Its use was widespread in the shipbuilding and railway industries, in power stations and boiler rooms, in heating and ventilation systems, in the manufacture of roofs and partitions. Those concerned in its mining, its processing and its incorporation into trains, ships, and all its many other applications were, in the early days, very badly protected. Although inhalation of dust was known to be a hazard,[1] it was not at first appreciated how deadly the inhalation of asbestos dust was. A trickle of claims gradually became an epidemic, bringing down large corporations in a welter of claims for the personal injury and death to workers. In the US, the courts are clogged with claims, many thousands more have been settled out of court.

In the world of construction, claims have arisen from workers exposed to asbestos during manufacture of components and in the incorporation into buildings and even by spouses who have breathed in dust from clothing. Many of the cases are against the Ministry of Defence, those responsible for shipyards, British Rail, power generation companies, responsible for lagging of pipework and for demolition. The claims have come, therefore, from workers, rather than members of the public, from those concerned with manufacture and construction or demolition rather than from use. Most litigation is, therefore, directed by employees against previous employers. However, the discovery of asbestos in a building may lead to very considerable expenditure if the building cannot be used or modified with-

1 The first regulations passed were the Asbestos Industry Regulations in 1931.

out removal of asbestos. The extent of such work is described, incidentally, in the *Linden Gardens*[2] case. Obligations may arise on transfer of a property. Claims alleging misrepresentation and attempts to avoid a contract may follow answers given to an environmental questionnaire in pre-contract enquiries prior to acquisition of a company or property. Other claims may arise even though no enquiry is made: see the main discussion in this paper below.

It may happen that a worker is unable to bring a claim against his employer because, for example, the employer is no longer in business and his insurer is entitled to avoid liability because of non-disclosure. He may then seek to claim against the designer of the process, perhaps an engineer, the supplier of the material, the owner of the building or plant. His chances of success will depend upon classical obligations found fully developed in the law of negligence but might also arise as a claim for breach of statutory duty,[3] a breach of the Defective Premises Act 1972, the Occupiers' Liability Act 1957, the Consumer Protection Act 1987 or the rule in *Rylands* v *Fletcher*. If a specifier wishes to avoid such liability, it must seek agreement with his employer that the latter will indemnify him against any such claim.

Dangerous materials and the duty to warn

If a manufacturer causes a dangerous substance to be provided to a consumer then, putting to one side opportunities for intermediate examination, he will be liable for injury suffered by that consumer unless he gave a warning of the danger in sufficiently clear terms. This oversimplified statement, reflecting the effect of *Donoghue* v *Stevenson* and other cases is not, perhaps, controversial. Particular cases make clear the obligations of manufacturer or supplier as to the precautions which it must take and the clarity of any warning. The greater the risk of injury, the greater the need for a clear warning.

If dangerous materials are incorporated into a building, therefore, and their presence or effect causes injury to a person then the owner, the supplier, the specifier may be liable. The extent of the duty to warn is discussed in two important decisions to which reference will now be made.

In *Wright* v *Dunlop*,[4] the Court of Appeal considered the liability of ICI for bladder cancer suffered by the employees of Dunlop, who had

2 [1993] 3 WLR 408 (HL).

3 In the recent decision of the Court of Appeal in *R* v *Trustees of the Science Museum* [1993] 3 All ER 853 the Museum was convicted of a breach of s3 of the Health & Safety at Work Act in failing to maintain its air conditioning system so as to prevent the risk of exposure of the public to legionnaire's disease. But by s47 of the Act, a breach of s3 does not give rise to civil liability.

4 (1973) 13 KIR 255 (CA).

purchased "Nonox" for use in the manufacture of tyres. Having determined that ICI became aware of the risks of using Nonox, the court held that it was under a duty to the employees of Dunlop to ensure that the material was "safe" in use. At page 272 in the judgment of the court, this obligation was broken down into a number of elements:

(a) If, when the product is first marketed, the vendor does not know that it is dangerous, he is not liable if he has done whatever it was reasonable for him to do to keep up with developments and acting with whatever promptness reflects the seriousness of possible consequences.
(b) If the manufacturer subsequently discovers that the product is unsafe he may be obliged then to withdraw it or, in some circumstances, to give proper warnings to persons supplied of the relevant facts as known or suspected as giving rise to an actual or potential risk.

In *Walton* v *British Leyland*[5] the Plaintiffs were injured when the rear nearside wheel came off their Austin Allegro. The manufacturers knew of the causative defect and had warned their dealers of it. Willis J held that, in the circumstances, they were under a duty to go further and "make a clean breast of the problem" and to recall all the cars which they could. It was relevant that the manufacturer had in fact considered recalling all cars but had made a commercial decision not to do so.

It may be concluded with some certainty that when a person has been injured as a result of his exposure to a danger which was known or should have been known to a party responsible for creating that danger then he will be able to recover damages even if the relevant risk was not known at the time when the danger was first created. Taking the factual example of the *British Museum* case, if a heating and ventilation contractor became aware of a design defect in an air conditioning system supplied by him for installation in public buildings and he knew or should have known that the defect could lead to the spread of legionnaire's disease then he is under a duty to warn those responsible for the buildings of the risk and they are under a duty to remedy it. If he fails to warn and if as a result a person dies from legionnaire's disease, he is likely to be found liable.

Although the conclusion in the preceding paragraph appears straightforward, the decision of the Court of Appeal in *Eckersley* v *Binnie & Ors*[6] demonstrates an understandable limitation. It will be recalled that in that

5 Reported in the *Product Liability Casebook* 12 July 1978.

6 (1987) (1988) 18 Con LR 1. The Court of Appeal judgment begins at page 44: the reports take up the entire volume.

case 16 people died and many were injured as a result of an explosion caused by the presence of methane in an underground pumping station. The consulting engineers were found negligent in the design of the works in that they failed to take account of the risk of the source of methane being an underground reservoir of that gas. But at page 67 Russell LJ considered the finding of the judge that the engineers were "to a slight degree negligent" in not keeping abreast with and passing on to the water company its developing knowledge about methane. Russell LJ observed *obiter* that "it would seem to place startlingly onerous responsibilities upon professional organisations . . . It would seem to involve duties relating to work completed many years before the professional organisation is actually or constructively put on notice of fresh material". In his dissenting judgment at page 146 Bingham LJ dealt with this allegation of continuing duty. He said:

> "We are told this finding had caused some concern among professional underwriters.
>
> I am not surprised. It has never, to my knowledge, been held that a professional man who advises on a tax scheme or on draft trading conditions, is thereafter bound to advise his client if, within a period of years, the statutory provisions or the relevant authorities change. Nor has it ever to my knowledge been suggested that a retired practitioner is bound, during his retirement, to keep in touch with developments in his profession in this way. These would be novel and burdensome obligations. On the other hand, counsel for the plaintiffs was able to advance persuasive examples involving dangers to life and health, where some response by a professional man may well be called for.
>
> What is plain is that if any such duty at all is to be imposed, the nature, scope and limits of such a duty require to be very carefully and cautiously defined. The development of the law on this point, if it ever occurs, will be gradual and analogical."

Thus, according to the Court of Appeal in 1988, the continuing obligations in tort of the professional to review his design or choice of materials after he has completed a project are strictly limited, if they exist at all, even in respect to dangers to life and health. A comparison of this case and the earlier unreported decision of *Walton* v *British Leyland* suggests that liability will arise if the professional actually discovers that the danger exists, even if his discovery is years later. The cases cited in paragraphs below, reinforce this view. On the other hand it is likely that he does not have a duty to review his specification in respect of completed work unless, at the very least, he is put on notice of a possible problem. It may also be very important (although the logic is not obvious) to emphasise the difference between cases concerning only commercial risk and those concerning risk to health or safety. It should also be noted that section 4(1)(e) of the Consumer Protection Act offers a specific defence to a producer able to show that at the time of supply the state of scientific or technical knowledge was not such as would permit discovery of the relevant defect.

In the two cases cited, the Plaintiff was an individual who had actually suffered personal injury. If no one is injured, can a cause of action arise? This issue can only be answered after first reconsidering the flurry of recent decisions of the House of Lords in which *Anns* v *Merton* was overruled and other cases, particularly *Junior Books* v *Veitchi* and *Pirelli* v *Oscar Faber*[7] were isolated, almost like exposed infants on Spartan hills, in the hope that they might die off from lack of attention. The attack begins with the dissenting judgment of Lord Brandon in *Junior Books*.[8] He reiterated the limit of liability of a manufacturer as being that laid down in *Donoghue* v *Stevenson*[9], that is to exercise such reasonable care as to ensure that goods can be used without causing damage to persons or their property. He went on to put this into the wider principle embodied in that case that when a person can or ought to appreciate that a careless act or omission on his part may result in physical injury to other persons or property he owes a duty to all such persons to exercise reasonable care to avoid such careless act or omission. The duty was based upon the existence of a danger of physical injury or injury to property where the relevant property was property other than the very property giving rise to the danger of physical damage. This left no room for liability for economic loss. Lord Brandon, this time giving the opinion of the House returned to the point in *Leigh and Sillavan* v *Aliakmon*.[10] As everyone knows, in *D&F Estates* v *Church Commrs*[11] the Lords stepped backwards and stated in clear terms that, in general there would be no liability in tort if as a result of a breach of duty, economic loss alone was suffered or only damage to the physical property giving rise to the risk of danger to other property or persons. *Anns* hardly survived the onslaught in *D&F* and in *Murphy* v *Brentwood DC*,[12] The Lords at last took the step of reversing *Anns* and insisting that the test as stated by Lord Brandon was correct.

The unfortunate effect of this trend in the law was made plain by the Lords in *DoE* v *Thomas Bates*.[13] When a structure was found to be weaker than necessary to support its design load and whether or not there was any present or imminent risk to the safety of the occupants, in the absence of

---

7 [1983] 2 AC 1.
8 [1983] AC 520, 549.
9 [1932] AC 562.
10 [1986] AC 784, 813.
11 [1989] 1 AC 177.
12 [1991] 1 AC 398.
13 [1991] 1 AC 499.

physical damage to other property or of injury, no cause of action in tort arose.

The Lords have not overruled *Pirelli* nor even said that it is a unique case. In *Murphy*, Lord Keith, at page 466 considered that:

> "where the tortious liability arose out of a contractual relationship with professional people, the duty extended to take reasonable care not to cause economic loss to the client by the advice given. The plaintiffs built the chimney as they did in reliance upon that advice. The case would accordingly fall within the principle of *Hedley Byrne* v *Heller & Partners*".[14]

It will be recalled that in *Pirelli* the use of the wrong material had caused a chimney to begin to crack and that eventually it would collapse, if not demolished. There are real problems in treating *Pirelli* in this way, particularly because the only reason why the action was brought in tort was because the limitation period in contract had expired and it is not clear why a *Hedley Byrne* type of liability could only arise when damage occurred. It appears to conflict with the better analysis in *Forster* v *Outred*,[15] which was distinguished. *Hedley Byrne* was not even cited in argument in *Pirelli.* And it would seem that Lord Bridge in *Murphy* (at pages 475D and 481D) was not enthusiastic about leaving in place this relic of an unfortunate and messy period of development of our law of tort.[16] But if it is good law (and it will be necessary to go to the House of Lords to show otherwise) it would seem that there is a continuing liability in tort owed by an architect or engineer to take reasonable care not to cause economic loss and this might extend to the specification of dangerous materials which the employer was obliged to take out or neutralise in order to avoid risk of injury.[17]

In the speeches in *D&F* and *Murphy*, reference is made to the decision of the Supreme Court of Canada of *Rivtow Marine* v *Washington Iron Works* ([1973] 6 WWR 692) and particularly the dissenting judgment of Laskin J which had been adopted by Lord Wilberforce in *Anns*. In *Rivtow*, the Plaintiffs were the owners of a log barge (the "Rivtow Carrier") fitted with two cranes. The Defendants discovered that cracks were appearing in the legs of the cranes. Not later than February of 1966, they knew that if not repaired they might lead to collapse of the cranes. In September of 1966 an almost identical crane owned by another logging company collapsed, killing its operator. The Rivtow Carrier was ordered back to its

---

14 [1964] AC 465.

15 [1982] 1 WLR 86.

16 See Clerk and Lindsell, 16th Ed and Supplement at paragraph 9–36 for criticism and further references.

17 See also *IBA* v *EMI* (1980) 14 BLR 1 where liability in tort of a designer or subcontractor was not challenged in the House of Lords.

base and the authorities required that the cranes be certified as structurally sound before further use. Serious structural cracking was found necessitating extensive repairs. September is the busiest month of the season for logging companies and Rivtow suffered much greater loss of profits than if they had known of the defects in January or February. They sued the Defendant manufacturers ("Washington") for loss of profits and the cost of repairs. It was alleged that Washington was under a duty to warn Rivtow of the defects and was liable for both loss of profits and the cost of repairs as a result of their negligence in the design and manufacture of the cranes. In his dissenting judgment, Laskin J followed the decision in *Dutton* v *Bognor Regis*[18] holding that Washington was responsible for the cost of repairs even though only the cranes themselves had in fact suffered damage. Lord Wilberforce followed Laskin J in *Anns*. This is no longer important as *Anns* has now been overrruled. All seven judges of the Supreme Court, however, also concluded that Washington was under a duty to warn Rivtow of defects which were likely to cause serious injury if not corrected even if no injury occurred and that the additional loss of profits resulting from having to undertake this work at an inconvenient time was recoverable.

It might have been expected that in *D&F* and in *Murphy*, the House of Lords would also have rejected the majority decision in *Rivtow*. In fact they appear to have approved it. In *D&F* at pages 206 and 215 Lord Bridge and Lord Oliver distinguished the case, Lord Oliver saying that the basis for the decision was the doctrine of reliance in *Hedley Byrne*. In *Murphy*, Lord Keith also said that the decision of the majority was founded on the *Hedley Byrne* principle and "For my part, I consider the decision of the majority to be correct" (p470A,B). It is not easy to marry this up with the decision of the majority in Rivtow. At page 1213 reference is made to *Hedley Byrne* but "solely for the purpose of showing that where liability is based on negligence, recovery is not limited to physical damage but extends also to economic loss".

We thus appear to have two quite inconsistent approaches to economic loss other than cases where a party relies upon negligent misstatement. One is epitomised by the words of Lord Bridge in *Murphy* that a dangerous defect discovered "is merely a defect in quality". The other allows that in an elusive category which might extend to the obligations of designers of structures and plant, duties of care in tort might duplicate duties owed by the same party in contract and that such duties might include an actionable duty to warn of defects or, it must be assumed, the use of materials, which

18 [1972] 1 QB 373.

are likely to cause significant injury if unremedied. This second category might be explicable upon the basis that there is a continuing actual or presumed reliance by the owners or users of structures and machinery upon those responsible for their design to disclose real inherent dangers if and when they are discovered.[19] Presumably, time will only start to run for limitation purposes when the obligation to warn arises for negligent design may not of itself give rise to a cause of action in tort if no damage results and the plaintiff cannot show reliance.

In *Hobbs (Farms)* v *Baxenden Chemicals*,[20] which is referred to in respect of liability in contract below, the deputy judge concluded his judgment by seeking an assurance from manufacturers of foam insulation which was more dangerous than hitherto believed that they would take steps to warn former customers by, for example, publishing warnings in the relevant trade newspaper, threatening them with "serious trouble" if someone was subsequently killed or injured. A question arises as to whether a cause of action in tort would arise if, on receipt of a warning, a farmer suffered loss of profits or additional costs if he was obliged to take farm buildings out of use. If *Rivtow* is good law it would seem that such a claim might be made but if a large number of claims might result the public policy "floodgates" drawn shut in such cases as *Spartan Steel* v *Martin*[21] might close again. See further *The Zinnia*, referred to below.

The obligation to warn in contract

In *Hobbs*, referred to above, the deputy judge had no difficulty in finding (at p 65) that:

> "A manufacturer's duty does not end when the goods are sold. A manufacturer who realises that omitting [*sic*] to warn past customers about something which might result in injury to them must take reasonable steps to attempt to warn them, however lacking in negligence he may have been at the time of manufacture."

Thus when the supplier of foam insulation used in farm buildings found that they had supplied foam described as "self extinguishing" which was incorrect and misleading, they owed a duty to *all* their previous customers to warn them of the risk. When their customer was sued in negligence for

---

19 However, the impression given by the speech of Lord Templeman in *Banque Keyser Ullman* v *Skandia Insurance* [1991] 2 AC 249 at 275 is of very restricted application of *Hedley Byrne*.

20 [1992] 1 Lloyd's Rep 54, Sir Michael Ogden QC.

21 A duty to warn may also arise when a contractor knows his employer is relying upon him to warn of design defects: *Brunswick Construction Ltd* v *Nowlon* (1974) 21 BLR 27 (Can).

fire damage, and they were sued for negligent misrepresentation and breach of warranty and for an indemnity, they were found liable. The learned deputy judge made a finding of 20% contributory negligence on the part of the farmer leaving the manufacturer liable for 80% contribution. It is not clear from the report whether this reflected a finding of liability in tort or the limit of damage caused by breach of contract but I have treated the case as one of breach of contract rather than an application of the *Rivtow* principle.

Hobbs is the latest in a series of English cases concerning the contractual duty to warn. Two other relevant cases were reported in 1984.[22] In *Victoria University of Manchester* v *Hugh Wilson*[23] His Honour Judge Newey held that an architect was entitled to use novel materials or techniques but that he should warn his client specifically of what he was doing. He held further that it was an implied term of the construction contract that the contractor would warn the employer of defects in the design of the works which they believed to exist. In *Stag Line* v *Tyne Shiprepair Group* ("*The Zinnia*")[24] Staughton J considered the liability of shiprepairers, *inter alia*, to warn shipowners when they discovered, after completion of repairs, that the wrong material had been used in the relining of the stern tube with a resulting risk of possible danger to life if the wrong material was not discovered. At page 218 Staughton J found this to be a "novel concept that a contractor who has broken his contract should be under a duty to inform the other party". He went on to reflect upon the self interest of the contractor:

> "At times, self interest will suggest that course, if the defect can be remedied cheaply and might otherwise cause great loss . . . The builder of a block of flats who learns that he has made a serious error in construction might be well advised to tell his employer and offer to remedy it. But at other times self interest may point in the opposite direction. In the circumstances of this case, bearing in mind the unlikelihood of the stern tube being examined . . . unless a casualty occurred . . . the possible danger to life at sea as well as very valuable property, I consider that [the Second Defendants] were under a duty to inform the owners."

Staughton J held the duty to arise from an implied term in the contract but he went on to find that in the circumstances there was also, in his view, a duty in tort to inform the owners when it was discovered that the wrong material had been used.

Although it is not easy to formulate a general proposition, it would seem that, in the absence of a contrary express term, a supplier, specifier,

---

22 [1973] 1 QB 27.

23 (1984) 2 Con LR 43, distinguished by HHJ Bowsher QC in *University of Glasgow* v *Whitfield* (1988) 42 BLR 66 at 83.

24 [1984] 2 Lloyd's Rep 211.

installer of a structure or materials which are subsequently discovered to be dangerous owes a continuing duty to the owner or occupier of premises affected to warn them of the danger. If additional loss is suffered as a result of a failure to warn (such as loss of profits if a store is obliged to close for repairs which could have been carried out before opening or at a better time) a separate cause of action may arise even if the terms of contract exclude liability for the cost of repairs themselves.

It may be of interest to compare the conclusion I have reached in the above paragraph and the terms of Clause 30.9 of JCT 80. If a final certificate is "conclusive evidence" that the quality of materials is to the reasonable satisfaction of the Architect, what duty is owed by the contractor who discovers that materials used are dangerous to life and the architect could not reasonably be satisfied as to their use? Is there a continuing duty upon the contractor to warn of the risk? I suggest that there is such an obligation.

The important difference between *Hobbs* and *Stag Lines* and the *Manchester* case is that in *Hobbs* the obligation extended to a large number of customers who might only be traceable by advertisement or otherwise by great effort and who may have purchased the dangerous product many years before. Also, in that case, the manufacturer was, or appears to have been, a contracting party. What is the position when a subcontractor supplies dangerous equipment or materials? Suppose, for example, that a manufacturer of electricity cables subsequently discovers defects in insulation materials leading him to conclude that short circuits may occur in buried cables which might lead to fires in occupied office buildings. If a fire occurs and people are injured they may have a claim against him if he knew of the risk but failed to take steps to warn those responsible for maintenance of the building. But suppose a fire does occur in one building and as a result the owners of many others are obliged to replace the electric cabling (probably at huge expense). Was the manufacturer obliged in contract to warn his purchaser? Or can he rely upon his terms of supply which may limit his liability to replacement of defective material? Further, and applying *Rivtow*, can the owners claim directly if as a result of a failure to warn they have suffered greater expense than would have resulted from more timely notice?

Strict liability and nuisance

In *Read* v *Lyons*[25] the Plaintiff was injured by an explosion at a munitions factory. She had not chosen to work there. The House of Lords held that

25 [1947] AC 156.

the principle of *Rylands* v *Fletcher*[26] did not apply because there had been no "escape" from the land of something liable to cause mischief. At page 172 Lord Macmillan accepted that there was in the case of dangerous things and operations a special responsibility to take care but that it did not amount to an absolute liability. So in England and Wales, even if a dangerous thing is brought into a building or created on premises, its inherently hazardous nature will not give rise to any absolute liability if someone is injured as a result (unless the circumstances come within the ambit of the Consumer Protection Act). The exclusion of civil liability for breach of the wider duties under the Health and Safety at Work Act gives parliamentary support for this denial of strict liability.

However, if fire, fumes, noxious substances do escape from a building and cause damage or injury to others then liability is strict if the danger results from bringing onto land or collecting something likely to cause mischief if it escapes when its use or collection amounts to a "non-natural" use of the land. In a recent case,[27] a contractor was found liable in tort for damage to office premises which resulted from high pressure jetting of an asbestos roof which resulted in contamination with asbestos slurry. It is not difficult to anticipate a similar cleaning operation resulting in escape of an injurious dust into neighbouring premises. Although an owner is not liable under *Rylands* v *Fletcher* for the acts of a stranger, he would be liable for the acts of a contractor. The escape of asbestos will be a breach of statutory regulations and so strict liability may have little relevance but employers should have in mind the possible release of dangerous substances which might result from repair or removal of substances harmless in their original form but dangerous if disturbed.

In *Cambridge Water Company* v *Eastern Counties Leather*[28], the defendant tanners had been responsible for seepage of a dangerous chemical (perchloroethylene) into the soil. Many years later the chemical had reached an impervious layer and travelled laterally some considerable distance to the site of the plaintiffs' bore hole. The plaintiffs claimed and, at first instance and in the Court of Appeal, recovered £2m in nuisance for the cost of moving the bore hole to a new uncontaminated site. In the Court of Appeal, liability was upheld on the grounds that the facts necessarily completed the ingredients of a cause of action in nuisance but this decision was reversed by the House of Lords, which determined that, whether the claim

26 (1868) LR re ML 330; [1861–73] All ER Rep 1, ML; affirming *subnom Fletcher* v *Rylands* (1866) LR 1 Exch. 265.

27 *Barclays* v *Fairclough* [1993] CILL 848. Refer to the paper of Michael Mendelblat for further details.

28 [1994] 1 All ER 53.

was properly brought within the law of nuisance or was made under the rule in *Rylands* v *Fletcher*, a necessary ingredient of the cause of action was that the type of damage suffered was foreseeable at the time when the relevant things were being collected on the defendants' land. It seems that at the time when the chemicals were being used such damage was not foreseeable and as a result although pools of neat perchloroethylene continued to lie beneath the defendants' land, they owed no duty at common law to the water company. It will be disappointing for environmentalists that ignorance of the risk of pollution will be a defence to such claims.

However, if damage had been foreseeable, the passage of years would not of itself have provided a defence. Nuisance gives rise to a continuing liability. If the use or effect of escape of a substance results in interference with the use of my neighbour's land then for so long as the nuisance continues, fresh damage is suffered and fresh claims can be made. Thus an act many years ago[29] may result in modern—and expensive—claims. It is important, therefore, to consider the long term effects on neighbouring land and property when determining the use of property or when planning its demolition.[30]

Exemplary damages

In this paper I have concentrated upon the duty of parties to warn others of things which might give rise to a risk of injury. As in the *Walton* v *British Leyland* case, a commercial decision may be taken not to attempt to warn those who might be affected.[31] It may be decided that the cost of giving a warning and subsequently undertaking remedial work will be higher, even much higher, than the value of one or two claims for serious personal injuries.

For those thinking of keeping quiet, the law relating to exemplary damages should be kept in mind. The classic example of the decision by Ford of America not to move the location of the fuel tank of the Pinto motor car provides a sobering warning.

The second of the two categories of exemplary damages set out by Lord Devlin in *Cassell* v *Broome*[32] is where the defendant's conduct has been

29 A case is recalled of an action against a local authority for flooding resulting from diversion of a river some 50 years before the claim was made.

30 Refer also to the decision of the Court of Appeal in *Leakey* v *National Trust* [1980] IQB 485 and cases there cited in respect of obligations to contain things naturally on the land.

31 This should be distinguished from a legitimate decision not to warn for fear of unnecessarily causing distress; see *Thompson* v *Johnston & Johnston* [1991] 2 VR 449.

32 [1972] AC 127 and see *AB* v *South West Water Services* [1992] 4 All ER 574 for a recent discussion of the law.

calculated by him to make a profit for himself which may well exceed the compensation payable to the plaintiff. A commercial decision, including any documents showing the basis upon which that decision was made, is very likely to have been made on the basis of financial risk. If injury does result from the undisclosed presence of dangerous materials, the defendant may find that the most careful commercial assessment of risk seriously underestimates his ultimate exposure.

Conclusion

All those concerned with the construction industry are becoming more aware of their responsibilities and potential liabilities associated with environmental matters. Although the use of recognised dangerous substances is nowadays well controlled and the degree of responsibility is known, the use of new materials may lead to new problems. The law relating to the need to give warnings is not well worked out but great care must be taken, particularly by manufacturers and specifiers when it is discovered that structures or materials thought to be safe are found to be dangerous.

13 European Commission Green Paper on remedying environmental damage

John Uff

Introduction

This Paper is an initial response addressed primarily from the viewpoint of consultants and advisers on construction projects. The question addressed is the possible impact under UK law on the liability of such professionals and their likely response in terms of protection and avoidance of liability. The principle adopted in the Green Paper is "the polluter pays". Yet many or most polluters will at some stage have taken professional advice and so the question necessarily arises, who ultimately pays? or perhaps, who is to be regarded as the polluter? A summary of the Green Paper is included as an Appendix.

Basis of liability

The Green Paper adopts the approach of individual civil liability in private law as the proposed basis for recovery of appropriate compensation. This limits recovery to property in respect of which there exists some legal interest, so that property which is not "owned" (such as the sea and the atmosphere) would have to be governed by other conventions. One of the principal objectives of the proposed Community action is to facilitate trade throughout the Community without distortion of competition, which would be the case where there existed substantial differences of liability for pollution in different Member States. Thus, the Green Paper concerns itself primarily with rights of and between individuals.

The proposed basis of individual liability may be fault-based or strict. Such distinction is well understood under UK law, but the position may be otherwise elsewhere in the community. In making the choice between fault-based or strict liability it is relevant to have regard to the difficulties of establishing fault in particular cases, *e.g.* where expensive and time-consuming testing and monitoring is required, and where the picture is complicated by past, even historical, activities on a site. Conversely, strict liability may be said to stifle innovation and industry. One advantage of a statutory approach to such liability is that its basis can be defined with these difficulties and their practical consequences in mind. The availability of insurance is also a major factor to be considered.

In many cases there will be more than one person potentially liable. Depending upon decisions as to limitation and cut-offs, there could be a number of persons attracting primary liability who in turn would seek to pass on liability to others responsible to them, and at the same time claim contribution from others against whom proceedings are, or could be, brought. Such a situation clearly militates against simple fault-based liability and in favour of some stricter well-defined system of liability. The Green Paper does not discuss the procedural mechanisms for the recovery of compensation, but the principle of subsidiarity would doubtless require this to be through national court systems. If a material volume of litigation were to result, the UK courts would become overburdened, and the parties seriously prejudiced, unless some comparatively simple and uniform basis of liability were established.

One important aspect of such liability would be to establish throughout the Community not only a common basis of liability, but common procedural rules covering, *e.g.* third party and contribution proceedings, so as to discourage "forum-shopping" where (as will often be the case) potential defendants are multi-nationally based. As with other EC legislation, such as the directive on product liability, individual national laws will remain in place, at least in the short and medium term. Thus, a polluter or other person liable to or for a polluter will also face potential liability under a battery of existing laws. In the UK, this will cover the common law of nuisance, negligence and other torts as well as substantial areas of statutory liability, principally the Public Health Acts and the Environment Protection Act. Thus, whether and how any proposed new basis of liability would succeed in eliminating distortion of trade between Member States must be open to serious question.

Problems of legal definition

The terms "damage" and "environment" invite definition. As to the former there are a wide variety of possible approaches. The hint of actual or potential "pollution" in any degree is likely to have an adverse effect on the valuation of any property, at least in areas of sensitivity, such as housing. Such damage is often ephemeral and illusory, although real enough to a vendor who receives less money on account of possible pollution. It is thought that a more robust and commercially sound definition is needed, and one that at least takes into account everyday levels of pollution which are or must be tolerated. Recent UK legislation contains some interesting examples.[1]

The definition of "environment" raises directly the issue as to what is to be protected: merely human life and artefacts or cultural heritage, plant and animal life and the wider environment including the seas and the atmosphere? The existence of other regulatory systems is relevant to the appropriate scope of any Community directive.[2]

Establishing liability will require proof of causation. There may be alternative possible causes of damage. As with the question of liability, there are potential problems of inconsistency between the laws and procedures of different Community members and further complications where several different parties are alleged to bear responsibility. Again, there is a strong case for devising a relatively direct and uniform approach to the question in order to avoid excessive reliance on scientific evidence perhaps on behalf of one or some, but not all, of the parties alleged to be responsible.

Existing environmental legislation

Any new proposals must be viewed against existing legislation and, perhaps even more important, against proposals in the pipeline. The history of environmental legislation in the UK and elsewhere over the past two decades gives a strong impression of major and far-reaching proposals being hastily assembled only to meet with delays, impediment and blockages at various stages prior to implementation; and sometimes to significant lack of support even after implementation. Furthermore, the increasing overlap between UK domestic legislation and European Community requirements poses increasing problems of duplication and even inconsistency, creating initiatives which might be seen as pulling in different directions. Given that there is a limitation upon available resources, any division of opinion as to whether efforts should be devoted *e.g.* to avoidance of pollution or towards adequate compensation after pollution, must be seen as potentially inhibiting of serious progress. The Green Paper addresses itself exclusively to the latter remedy. Other agencies address the former or both.

Examples of lack of financial or political commitment to new initiatives which have gained widespread support are numerous. In the UK, the new regime for health and safety at work commencing with the Act of 1974 is a continuing example; likewise the legislation providing for civil liability for

1 *E.g.* definition of "Dangerous to life" in the Controlled Waste Regulations 1992, Schedule 1 Pt II.

2 EPA s1(2) defines "environment" very widely.

breach of building regulations.[3] HM Inspectorate of Pollution (HMIP) is reported to have fared no better in terms of financial support than the Health and Safety Executive (HSE). Likewise the implementation of the European Environment Agency (EEA) remains blocked by lack of a decision on its site; and the far-reaching UK proposals for a new co-ordinating environment agency[4] apparently remain on hold. There are many individual provisions awaiting implementation within current environment legislation, notably sections 140[5] and 143[6] of the EPA.

Environmental protection bodies

A striking feature of environment law and technology is the vast array of institutions and organisations which have come into existence to co-ordinate and regulate activities concerning environment protection, some being set up as a direct result of legislation, some responding to new activities and others being existing organisations which have expanded their areas of operation. A reasonably up-to-date list of "key organisations" including sources of information can be found in the recent CIRIA[7] report on Environmental Issues in Construction, 1993.[8] Further research will inevitably throw up other bodies not listed: see *e.g.* the Association of Consulting Engineers Environmental Notes.[9] These two publications between them list over 100 agencies and bodies having environmental interests. A feature of most publications on environment issues or legislation is the inevitable statement that the publication itself, in view of the complexity of the subject, is not to be regarded as definitive or complete. It would be tempting to conclude that environmental issues are becoming uncontrollable or at least uncontrolled. The real difficulty, it is suggested, is that environmental issues do not presently recognise or respond to any central or unifying principles. This is perhaps a reflection on the fact that the subject is in its infancy despite having experienced massive and vigorous growth. Yet it is difficult to argue for a period of reflection and consolidation, when major environmental questions arise regularly, and must be

3 Building Act 1984, s38.

4 The subject of a discussion document "The Government's proposals for a new independent environment agency" October 1991 and extensive discussion at a conference organised by LSE in July 1992.

5 Power to prohibit injurious substances or articles.

6 Register of contaminated land.

7 Construction Industry Research & Information Association.

8 Vol. 3—Bibliography, Appendix 8.2.

9 Note 2.

seen to be under control. Until some centralised authority is established, co-ordination and awareness between the different aspects of environment protection must be a high priority. The Green Paper, by proposing yet another layer of liability contributes nothing to the solution of this problem.

The position of professional advisers

Foregoing discussion sketches the background against which professionals are liable to face censure and proceedings arising from environmental damage. While the professional adviser will ordinarily be concerned with particular activities in a particular location, the nature of pollution is such that it is readily and sometimes uncontrollably transferred from one medium to another *e.g.* terrestrial pollution readily becomes pollution of the water or the atmosphere. Such transfer renders the consequences of pollution widespread and potentially outside the ambit of the commission undertaken by the professional in the first place. This problem will not be tackled by concentrating on remedying the damage and providing compensation to persons suffering damage. Only action at the source of the pollution can prevent its spread.

To express the point in another way, environment protection is said to be a holistic concept requiring all aspects of a problem to be considered. Professional terms of engagement and practice, however, focus on particular matters upon which advice or other services are to be given. Further, in order to avoid possible consequences of the UK Unfair Contract Terms Act 1977, a person seeking to limit the area of his responsibility should be advised to do so in terms of defining (and limiting) the areas and issues for which he is responsible, rather than limiting or excluding responsibility for the consequences of his actions. This may be seen as directly inconsistent with a holistic approach to the problem of environment.

The Green Paper makes several references to channelling liability. This apparently refers to some advance designation or determination of the split of liability, presumably between the potentially polluting parties. It is said to have the advantage of directing liability to those having the means of controlling and managing the relevant risks. It is not clear whether or how the scheme would survive or supersede contribution proceedings whereby, under English law, the party sued has the right himself to claim contribution from another party who could have been sued, either in contract or tort.[10] It is clear that a great deal of work would be required before any scheme could be devised which would achieve channelling of liability under English law, let alone that of all Member States.

10 Civil Liability (Contribution) Act 1978.

The basis of professional liability

Professional liability on the basis of reasonable skill and care is firmly entrenched in English law[11] and UK insurance practices are equally firmly based on the same principles.[12] In the *Bolam* case Mr. Justice McNair (who was addressing a jury) gave what is still regarded as the classic exposition of professional negligence in the following terms:

> ". . . where you get a situation which involves the use of some special skill or competence, then the test as to whether there has been negligence or not is not the test of the man on top of the Clapham omnibus, because he has not got this special skill. The test is the standard of the ordinary skilled man exercising and professing to have that special skill. A man need not possess the highest expert skill; it is well-established law that it is sufficient if he exercises the ordinary skill of an ordinary competent man exercising that particular art."

With very few exceptions, this passage represents the law applied in cases where contractual (or, where applicable, tortious[13]) negligence is alleged against a professional person, whether that person is to be regarded as a person of ordinary professional competence or special competence. In the case of *Argyll* v *Beuselinck*[14] an attempt to render a solicitor liable in negligence on the basis of a higher standard of expertise than that of ordinary competence was unsuccessful, and *Bolam* has continued to be regarded as the classic exposition under English law.

There is, however, a further possible exception to the *Bolam* principle which might be relied upon. While the Green Paper is silent on the potential position of professional advisers, the discussion on strict liability inevitably raises the possibility of an application of the case of *Greaves* v *Baynham Meikle*.[15] This is the case in which an engineer was held liable on the basis of fitness for purpose when undertaking design work for a "package deal" contractor, who was himself liable on the same basis.[16] It is difficult to say that the *Greaves* case embodied any point of principle other than the finding that in those particular circumstances the intention of the parties was that the duty undertaken by the engineer (and therefore his liability) was to mirror that of his principal. In his judgment, however, Lord Denning raised a number of different approaches when considering whether to uphold the finding of the judge of a "higher duty". He said:

---

11 *Bolam* v *Friern Hospital Mgt Com.* [1957] 1 WLR 582.

12 But compare *Wimpey* v *Poole* (1985) 27 BLR 58.

13 See *per* Lord Keith in *Murphy* v *Brentwood DC* [1991] 1 AC 398.

14 [1972] 2 Lloyd's Rep 172.

15 [1975] 1 WLR 1095.

16 *C.f. Wimpey* v *Poole supra.*

> "The law does not usually imply a warranty that (the professional man) will achieve the desired result, but only a term that he will use reasonable care and skill. The surgeon does not warrant that he will cure the patient. Nor does the solicitor warrant that he will win the case. But when a dentist agrees to make a set of false teeth for a patient, there is an implied warranty that they will fit his gums: see *Samuels* v *Davis*."[17]

What then is the position when an architect or an engineer is employed to design a house or a bridge? Is he under an implied warranty that, if the work is carried out to his design, it will be reasonably fit for the purpose? Or is he only under a duty to use reasonable care and skill? That question may require to be answered some day as a matter of law. But in the present case I do not think we need answer it. For the evidence shows that both parties were of one mind on the matter. Their common intention was that the engineer should design a warehouse that would be fit for the purpose for which it was required. That common intention gives rise to a term implied in fact.

Later in his judgment Lord Denning quoted from *Bolam* and continued:

> "In applying that test it must be remembered that the measures to be taken by a professional man depend on the circumstances of the case. Although the judge talked about a 'higher duty', I feel sure that what he meant was that in the circumstances of this case special steps were necessary in order to fulfil the duty of care: see *Readhead* v *Midland Railway Co.*"[18]

There appear to be no reported cases since *Greaves* in which the "higher duty" has been applied. Nevertheless, it remains open to argument that similar circumstances should give rise to a degree of liability commensurate with that of the party to whom the services are being rendered. It can be argued that there are many instances where there is no such coincidence of liability, an obvious example being under the "Excepted Risks" in clause 20(2) of the ICE Conditions of Contract, where "fault defect error or omission in the design of the works" is excepted from the contractor's risk, even though the engineer is unlikely to be under the same liability. It is therefore open to argument whether in a particular case (in the absence of express provisions) a professional adviser should be taken to assume the same responsibility for damage or loss as his principal.

As already noted, ordinarily a professional indemnity insurer will not cover liability beyond reasonable skill and care. Recent experience with collateral warranties has reinforced the interest of insurers in defining their own degree of risk and in discouraging their assureds from undertaking commitments beyond their level of insurance. It is thus likely that the

17 [1943] KB 526.
18 (1869) LR 4 QB 379, 393.

combination of insurance interests and advice from professional bodies will result in professional advisers seeking to limit their liability, at least in the UK, to reasonable skill and care or other equivalent defined levels of liability, whatever definition of liability is eventually decided upon in accordance with the EC proposals. This will have a number of important consequences:

(1) It will be vital for site owners to ensure that they are adequately or effectively insured, since they are unlikely to be able simply to rely upon their professionals to maintain effective cover against any latent damage;
(2) Attempts to involve professionals in litigation will inevitably run into the problems discussed above, namely the involvement of substantial expert and scientific evidence and arguments on liability and causation.

The Green Paper does not discuss contracts as such, but there will clearly be in existence a number of contracts, some of which will contain arbitration agreements. Outside the UK, these will be enforceable as of right, under the legislation equivalent to the Arbitration Act 1975.[19] Again, if it were intended to provide a scheme of apportionment of liability, means would have to be found to supersede such private agreements.

In the light of the above, it is difficult to see how there can be created ready means of access to compensation unless through some form of project or site-based insurance, leaving the insurer to pursue any subrogated rights, if necessary through protracted litigation or arbitration. The availability of effective insurance, at least in the private market, must be open to serious doubt in the light of the present reaction of the insurance industry. The alternative may have to be a statutory fund.

Compensation funds

The Green Paper discusses existing compensation funds established in various countries including Sweden, France and Holland. One of the best publicised schemes is the US "Superfund" administered by the US Federal Environment Protection Agency, set up in 1970. The fund is provided by taxes on potentially polluting industries and is used to respond to short-term emergencies, compensation being recovered when potentially liable parties can be identified. Enforcement action is taken both at Federal and

19 Enacting provisions of the New York Convention 1958.

State level. It is said that about 70% of enforcement actions are at State level.[20] This statistic could be seen as confirming the viability of subsidiarity as one of the aims of the European initiative. Another well-established compensation system is the International Fund for Compensation for Oil Pollution Damage. This was established in 1991 through an international convention, complementing the 1969 Brussels Convention placing liability on shipowners. This fund again is established by private industry contributions. There are other existing proposals within the EC for environmental compensation funds.

Discussion

The paper does not really focus on how civil liability would interact with either the proposed environmental fund or the idea of "channelled" liability. The system would in fact operate at distinctly different points in time *e.g:*

(1) A fund would be available for immediate compensation, but there would need to be mechanisms for recovery of monies paid out from those liable, as under the US Federal scheme.
(2) A liability scheme involving channelled or predetermined liability would operate reasonably quickly if liability were strict, *e.g.* under existing civil procedure, a substantial proportion of the liability could be enforced within a reasonably short time by summary judgment.[21]
(3) If payment were dependent on claims under insurance policies, there would certainly be potentially substantial delays in a number of cases. Likewise, if liability were fault-based, litigation would inevitably be protracted.
(4) The ultimate settlement of liability through various contribution proceedings, possibly including subrogated actions, would take their usual course through the courts of member countries, probably taking in England a minimum of 2 years and a maximum of substantially more than that. In addition, civil procedure in different Member States is subject to very substantial variation *e.g.* between the English adversarial system with experts appointed by the parties, and the French inquisitorial system relying heavily on a court-appointed expert.

What are the consequences for professionals involved in commissions which might give rise to pollution and liability under the proposed new

20 Appendix 1 to paper on Environment Issues by Wilder and Plant, 1992, LSE Conference.
21 RSC Orders 14 and/or 29.

regime? The danger is that they might become involved as potential contributors to claims arising from the new basis of liability, where such claims would not have existed under present law. The new claims could arise from:

(a) redefined and wider liability, especially on the part of the person to whom liability is channelled;
(b) liability for wider ranges of damage;
(c) compensation payments giving rise to damages which would not have been suffered but for the wider basis of liability.

A crucial matter not discussed in the Green Paper is the ambit of the parties who would be covered by any new liability directive. It is implicit that the Green Paper is directed primarily at "the polluter" and the discussion indicates that this is intended to be the commercial party undertaking the hazardous or polluting operation such as the oil company or industrial plant operator. It is unclear whether there is an intention to include professionals within the wider basis of liability. There is perhaps less concern about environmental consultants and similar organisations whose principal activity is to investigate, control or remove pollution. Persons taking on such work at least do so knowing the consequences of error or failure. More concern is merited by consultants such as engineers, architects and surveyors, as well as contractors, who undertake work within their ordinary competence which might give rise to pollution, immediately or some time in the future, as a result of some act or omission done with no proper knowledge of its consequences. The imposition of liability on such persons whether strict or fault-based, will have far-reaching effects, particularly if they do not or cannot obtain insurance cover corresponding to the new level of liability proposed by the Green Paper.

Assuming that only the "client" is the party who will be subject to the newly-defined specific liability the question is then what degree of consequent contributing liability might become in effect imposed on or sought against consultants. There can be no doubt that primary liability attaching to the client could spark off attempts to claim indemnity on the basis of the *Greaves* case discussed above. In addition, there would be potential liability attaching to the giving, or failure to give, appropriate advice as to the potential liability of the client under the new European directive. There could be little doubt that enhanced liability could spark off higher levels of contribution being sought from professionals.

It is therefore appropriate to raise again the argument in favour of removing at least advisors from the whole ambit of potential liability for pollution. Such liability is inevitably based on the availability of insurance which must ultimately be paid for through enhanced fees. Few professional firms have assets which would make proceedings worthwhile without insurance being available. The expressed aim of the Green Paper of creating readily available compensation is more likely to be achieved by properly structured project-based insurance[22] which specifically excludes claims against professionals: to permit such claims simply divides the risk between policies contingent (usually) upon whether the professional can be shown to have been negligent, invariably through protracted litigation which the Green Paper would seek to avoid.

Conclusion

The Report suggests an integrated liability regime whereby compensation could be sought against individual parties, if identified, on the basis of liability as discussed in the Green Paper; while a joint compensation mechanism would be available as a fallback. What does not appear to be discussed is:

(1) Whether action would be pursued by individuals suffering damage or by an agency such as the EEA.
(2) Whether there would be a fund to provide for immediate compensation and clean-up with actions being pursued subsequently.
(3) The Green Paper discusses civil liability only, whereas the US EPA has criminal jurisdiction also.

The creation of anything other than fault-based liability will inevitably result in disparity between liability and the owner or promoter and that of professionals (and contractors) employed by him. The only viable means of recovering compensation without protracted litigation is through means of project or site-based insurance or compensation funds. Subsequent subrogated litigation would prove enormously complex and costly. It is to be doubted that the involvement of professionals at this stage, merely for the purpose of recovering through their insurers, will ever be cost-effective.

22 The same proposal is advanced by Griffiths and Taylor "Liability for Pollution and Environmental Damage" Conference on the Engineer and the Environment, July 1993.

Appendix

Summary of Green Paper

Section 1 introduces the subject and the reasons for the Community now considering action, which is essentially:

(a) perceived public demand;
(b) requests within the Commission;
(c) action by other national and international bodies; and
(d) distortion of competition through the different systems that presently exist in Member States.

The Paper addresses two questions only:

(1) the basis of civil liability (no consideration is given to criminal or other liability);
(2) remedying damage not met by the application of civil liability principles.

Section 2 discusses fault-based liability and strict liability. Multiplicity of liable parties will often be a problem. The type of damage to be protected against is considered and also whether limitation on liability should be accepted. Defining "environment" and "damage" for the purpose of any legislative proposals is discussed, together with the role of insurance.

Approaches at national and international level are discussed. A recurrent theme is the "channelling" of liability *e.g.* under the Brussels Convention whereby the owner of a ship at the moment of an incident is liable to the exclusion of others who might be sued. Under the Council of Europe Convention liability is channelled to the person having control. It is considered that such provisions should not affect subsequent civil actions under appropriate national laws to recover compensation based on such channelled liability. The Green Paper thus envisages a system under which some designated party would be primarily liable on a statutory basis (perhaps similar to the product liability regime).

Section 3 proceeds to discuss joint compensation systems which are said to be "insurance-like". The Green Paper envisages a fund similar to other national and international arrangements, which would be available in the first place for emergency action. This system is seen, however, as inconsistent with the "polluter pays" principle. It is noted that proposals already exist for the establishment of European funds for compensation for environmental damage caused by waste and landfill. Any new proposals would need to take account of existing policy.

Section 4 suggests a combination of civil liability (whether fault-based or strict) together with a compensation system or fund where civil liability cannot effect restoration or compensation.

14 The Cambridge Water Company case—a postscript

Michael Renger and Victoria Phillips

The Conference on Construction, Environment and the Law was held before the appeal to the House of Lords had been heard in the *Cambridge Water Company* case. This note updates the legal position following the House of Lords' judgment delivered on 9 December 1993.

Introduction

The House of Lords' judgment in the case of *Cambridge Water Company Limited* v *Eastern Counties Leatherwork PLC* reversed the Court of Appeal's £1 million damages award against a tannery that had polluted groundwater with solvents. This outcome should not, however, fool anyone into imagining that common law actions in the environmental field will no longer be brought. The judgment has done much to clarify the circumstances in which actions in nuisance and under the rule in *Rylands* v *Fletcher* can be a successful vehicle for the recovery of damages. Where the circumstances are right, this flashing of green lights by the highest judicial authority possible will increase the likelihood of actions being brought, although litigation will now be unlikely in circumstances where pollution damage was not foreseeable at the time when the actions leading to it occurred.

The House of Lords' response to the issues outlined in Part I

As a preliminary, the Lords, whose collective opinion was expressed by Lord Goff of Chievely, stated that, strictly speaking, Cambridge Water's appeal to the Court of Appeal should have been decided under the rule in *Rylands* v *Fletcher* since Cambridge Water had appealed on this basis. However, it said that the similarities between the two torts nuisance and *Rylands* v *Fletcher* were such that it would discuss both in its judgment.

Is there any requirement for damage to be foreseeable in a nuisance claim?

The Lords expressed the view that the Court of Appeal had wrongly interpreted the Victorian case, *Ballard* v *Tomlinson* (29 Ch.D. 115). The case should not have been taken as authority for a statement that it is not necessary to show that a defendant foresaw or could have foreseen the possibility that groundwater would be polluted at the time of the events that led to the pollution. It should only have been taken as authority for holding that a landowner has a right to abstract water percolating beneath its land and that neighbouring landowners with similar rights to abstract do not have the right to pollute that water. Although the right to abstract clean water can be protected by an injunction or action for damages, such protection can only be given if all the other elements for a successful action based on nuisance or the rule in *Rylands* v *Fletcher* are present.

Having dismissed *Ballard* v *Tomlinson*, the Lords went on to state most firmly that in a nuisance action a defendant should not be held liable for damage of a type which he could not reasonably have foreseen. It pointed out that this had been the conclusion in an authoritative case on nuisance, *The Wagon Mound (No 2)* [1967] 1 AC 617, which the Court of Appeal in the *Cambridge Water* case had omitted to consider. If foreseeability were not the rule it would be easier for a plaintiff to recover damages for interference with his property (generally an action in nuisance) than to recover damages for personal injuries suffered (generally an action under the tort of negligence where it is well established that the plaintiff must prove that the type of damage caused was foreseeable in order to succeed).

Can it be 'damage' if nobody is aware of it at the time it occurs?

The Lords did not answer this question directly. However it did hold that there could not be an actionable nuisance until damage had occurred, and, relating this principle to the present case, it decided that no damage had occurred until the regulations implementing the EC directive came into force. In this case awareness of the damage preceded the date that the regulations came into force (although awareness was apparently triggered by the Department of the Environment's advice which was based on the fact that the regulations were forthcoming).

However, the Lords went on to hold that, provided the action was not brought until after the damage had occurred, the fact that the damage did not occur until some time after the actions which led to it did not matter. Therefore an action will not be precluded by a lack of awareness that damage has been caused when it first occurs.

What is the meaning of 'non-natural user' in an action under the rule in Rylands v Fletcher

The Lords departed from the very restricted meaning that has been given to the phrase "non-natural user" in past cases, including the High Court judgment in the *Cambridge Water* case.

In the High Court Kennedy J. had stated that using solvents in a tannery in a village where the inhabitants relied on the tannery for employment could not be regarded as non-natural. The Lords disagreed stating that "the storage of substantial quantities of chemicals on industrial premises should be regarded as an almost classic case of non-natural use."

The comparable principle under nuisance was also mentioned, although it was not directly discussed in the context of this case. The Lords stated that liability is restricted by "the principle of reasonable user – the principle of give and take as between neighbouring occupiers of land". If the use to which the defendant puts his land is reasonable, he cannot be liable for harm to his neighbour's enjoyment of his own land. However if the use is not reasonable he can be liable.

Should liability under the rule in Rylands v Fletcher be limited to situations where the type of damage caused was foreseeable?

Having found that foreseeability was an element in nuisance, the Lords went on to assert that foreseeability of the type of damage is also a requirement for recovery in an action based on the rule in *Rylands* v *Fletcher*.

However the Lords were obviously aware that they were adopting a pragmatic approach rather than a strictly legalistic one. The relevant part of Lord Goff's judgment is peppered with slightly apologetic statements attempting to justify the realignment, such as "it appears to me to be appropriate now to take the view".

Foreseeability and the passage of time

It is clear that the PCE which escaped during the 1970s had gradually accumulated in large pools at the base of the chalk aquifer beneath Eastern Counties' premises and is still dissolving slowly into the groundwater.

Cambridge Water attempted to argue that, even if damage was not foreseeable at the time the PCE was spilled, Eastern Counties should be liable for damage which occurred from the date on which it subsequently foresaw or should have been able to foresee that damage. Arguably, in this case this might be from the date that the EC legislation came into effect. In other pollution cases the relevant point in time might be the point at which the detrimental effects of the relevant substances on the environment were generally known.

The Lords dismissed Cambridge Water's argument, holding that "long before the relevant legislation came into force the PCE had become irretrievably lost in the ground below." This aspect of the judgment is somewhat puzzling since it appears that it would have been possible in 1985 (and would still be possible today) to extract PCE from the groundwater by pumping it out from below ground using boreholes on Eastern Counties' premises.

However, it appears that the central point which the Lords wished to make is that foreseeability must be measured at the time when the actions leading to the pollution are carried out and cannot be reassessed at a later date when the defendant is merely continuing to harbour the conditions for causing pollution on his property.

This is somewhat difficult to reconcile with earlier cases such as *Sedleigh-Denfield* v *O'Callaghan* [1940] AC 880 which state that even if a defendant has not created the nuisance, once he knows or should reasonably know of the existence of a nuisance being caused by conditions on his property he is under a duty to take reasonable measures to bring it to an end. What is reasonable appears to depend on a number of factors, including the costs of the work and the financial resources of the parties involved.

It is likely that this point will be argued again in more detail in future pollution cases.

The implications of the judgment

The foreseeability test

The foreseeability test now appears to be firmly established for nuisance actions, although its place in actions under the rule in *Rylands* v *Fletcher* may be less secure.

Many will see the decision of the Lords to state that foreseeability of the type of damage is a requirement for success in an action under the rule as a logical way of restating that aspect of the tort which holds the defendant liable for the "natural and anticipated consequences" where he has brought onto his land material which is "likely to do harm" if it escapes. Law students, lawyers and their clients will no doubt be grateful for the simplification: it is easier to predict liability if *Rylands* v *Fletcher* is brought closer to nuisance and negligence.

However, the issue may well be reopened in the future by those suggesting, for example, that the rule in *Rylands* v *Fletcher* requires only foreseeability of some direct damage to neighbouring land in the event of an escape, rather than foreseeability of the type of damage caused.

It is interesting to note that Kennedy J., who agreed that foreseeability of the type of damage was a necessary prerequisite for nuisance and found that it had not been established on the facts in the *Cambridge Water Company* case, appears to have reached a different result when applying the *Rylands* v *Fletcher* criteria. He dismissed the action under the rule in *Rylands* v *Fletcher* only on the basis that there had been no non-natural user, stating "I would have held that some damage was foreseeable from the escape of the stored quantity of organochlorine . . . I here contemplate direct damage to neighbouring land."

The general implications of applying the foreseeability test are obvious. Knowledge about the effects of many substances on the environment has developed rapidly over the last twenty years or so. Companies whose actions during the "pre-enlightenment" period led to damage are less likely to be found liable because the type of damage which they caused was not reasonably foreseeable at that time. Companies which have caused pollution via more recent actions will not necessarily be able to argue that the type of damage which they have caused was not foreseeable at the time of the actions that led to the damage. Potential liability will have to be examined in the light of the particular substances and activities in question in each case.

In the future, plaintiffs will doubtless pay very careful attention to the evidence which they produce showing the state of knowledge at the relevant time. The decision that the damage caused by Eastern Counties was not foreseeable was a decision on the facts of the case taken by the High Court judge who considered the evidence presented to him back in 1991. His decision was not reopened by either the Court of Appeal or the House of Lords who deal only with matters of law. It is not clear exactly what evidence about the pollution of groundwater by solvents the High Court heard. It will certainly be open to future plaintiffs to argue that knowledge of the problem was much more widespread than is reflected in the *Cambridge Water Company* judgments, especially when research from the United States which was freely available is considered.

As more and more companies which carry out environmentally hazardous activities employ well-qualified specialist environmental managers and nominate directors to take control of environmental affairs the courts will also become less tolerant of defendants who plead that it was reasonable for their knowledge to fall short of state of the art. It will no longer be the site foreman or works supervisor whose foresight is assessed. This will also make it harder to argue that damage was not reasonably foreseeable.

The damage test

The use of the date regulations come into force as the point where "damage" crystallises and an action becomes sustainable, is likely to be disputed if it is used as a benchmark in future cases. Environmental science often moves well ahead of regulatory standards and plaintiffs will frequently be aggrieved at the spread of pollution onto their land or into their water supply despite the fact that there are no relevant regulations forbidding the presence of the relevant substances.

The user test

The Lords appear to have greatly widened the potential for using the rule in *Rylands* v *Fletcher* in environmental cases by departing from the restricted meaning given to the phrase "non-natural user" in previous cases. Presumably the test of reasonable user under nuisance and the test of natural user will be linked in the future and it will be difficult to plead that any industrial use involving chemicals is a "reasonable user".

The policy angle

Although the English common law is a separate system operating independently of statute, the Lords were obviously acutely aware of the wider debate concerning liability for activities which may pollute the environment. The European Commission has recommended moving towards a no-fault approach in a Green Paper on the subject[1] and the House of Lords Select Committee on the European Communities printed a report responding to this just five days after the judgment in the *Cambridge Water Company* case.[2]

Lord Goff pointed out that "as a general rule, it is more appropriate for strict liability in respect of operations of high risk to be imposed by Parliament, than by the courts. If such liability is imposed by statute, the relevant activities can be identified, and those concerned can know where they stand. Furthermore, statute can where appropriate lay down precise criteria establishing the incidence and scope of such liability".

He also expressed the view that the common law should not impose liability for damage which had occurred before legislation which classified it as damage took place, stating:

> "I wish to add that the present case may be regarded as one of what is nowadays called historic pollution, in the sense that the relevant occurrence (the seepage of PCE through the floor of [Eastern Counties'] premises) took place before the relevant legislation came into force; and it appears that, under the current philosophy, it is not envisaged that statutory liability should be imposed for historic pollution . . . If so, it would be strange if liability for such pollution were to arise under a principle of common law".

This attitude is sure to rub off on Lord Goff's judicial brethren. Future common law cases are unlikely to tighten up the liabilities imposed by the common law whilst legislation on the same subject is pending.

---

1 7099/93; COM(93)47 final – Communication from the Commission to the Council and European Parliament and the Economic and Social Committee: Green Paper on Remedying Environmental Damage.

2 Session 1993–4, 3rd Report on "Remedying Environment Damage", 14 December 1993, HMSO, ISBN 0-10-401094-0.

Conclusion

The judgment has buried one of the major concerns of industry, its insurers and bankers: being asked to pay for historic pollution which occurred in an earlier less environmentally conscious era when damage was not reasonably foreseeable.

However potential plaintiffs will be encouraged by the hefty blow dealt to the "non-natural" use line of defence and reassured by the new "cross-tort" nature of the foreseeability test. They now know that they must concentrate their efforts on proving causation and showing that defendants lacked the level of environmental awareness that should have been shown by a responsible operator in their particular industry sphere.

The "lost" pollution argument seems unlikely to survive for long in an era of rapidly improving standards of environmental management. Future EC driven legislation may also lead to the imposition of no-fault, no-foreseeability liability in any event.

Index